A YEAR IN THE COUNTRY
Wandering Through Spectral Fields

A YEAR IN THE COUNTRY
Wandering Through Spectral Fields

Journeys in Otherly Pastoralism, the Further Reaches of Folk and the Parallel Worlds of Hauntology

STEPHEN PRINCE

Published by: A Year In The Country, 2018

www.ayearinthecountry.co.uk

ISBN: 978-0-9574007-2-6

Edited by Suzy Prince
Typeset in Minion by Ian Lowey, Bopcap Book Services, Manchester.
Cover image: A Year In The Country

Contents:

Introduction 11

Notes on the Text 16

1. *Electric Eden: Unearthing Britain's Visionary Music:* Folk Vs Pop, Less Harvested Cultural Landscapes and Acts of Enclosure, Old and New 17

2. *Gather in the Mushrooms*: Early Signposts and Underground Acid Folk Explorations 24

3. **Hauntology:** Places Where Society Goes to Dream, the Defining and Deletion of Spectres and the Making of an Ungenre 27

4. **Cuckoos in the Same Nest:** Hauntological and Otherly Folk Confluences and Intertwinings 33

5. **Ghost Box Records:** Parallel Worlds, Conjuring Spectral Memories, Magic Old and New and Slipstream Trips to the Panda Pops Disco 40

6. **Folk Horror Roots:** From But a Few Seedlings Did a Great Forest Grow 49

7. **1973:** A Time of Schism and a Dybbuk's Dozen of Fractures 56

8. **Broadcast:** Recalibration, Constellation and Exploratory Pop 62

9. ***Tales From The Black Meadow, The Book of the Lost* and *The Equestrian Vortex*:** The Imagined Spaces of Imaginary Soundtracks 72

10. ***The Wicker Man***: Notes on a Cultural Behemoth 75

11. ***Robin Redbreast, The Ash Tree, Sky, The Changes, Penda's Fen, Red Shift* and *The Owl Service*:** Wanderings Through Spectral Television Landscapes 93

12. **A Bear's Ghosts:** Soviet Dreams and Lost Futures 108

13. **From "Two Tribes" to *WarGames*:** The Ascendancy of Apocalyptic Popular Culture 113

14. **Christopher Priest's *A Dream of Wessex*:** Twentieth Century Slipstream Echoes 121

15. ***Sapphire & Steel* and *Ghosts in the Machine:*** Nowhere, Forever and Lost Spaces within Cultural Circuitry 125

16. ***Kill List, Puffball, In the Dark Half* and *Butter on the Latch*:** Folk Horror Descendants by Way of the Kitchen Sink 131

17. ***The Quietened Bunker, Waiting For The End of the World,* Subterranea Britannica, *Bunker Archaeology* and *The Delaware Road*:** Ghosts, Havens and Curious Repurposings Beneath Our Feet 138

18. **From *The Unofficial Countryside* to *Soft Estate*:** Edgeland Documents, Memories and Explorations 146

19. ***The Ballad of Shirley Collins* and *Pastoral Noir*:** Tales and Intertwinings from Hidden Furrows 151

20. **"Savage Party" and *Randall & Hopkirk (Deceased)*:** Glimpses of Albion in the Overgrowth 156

21. ***Uncommonly British Days Out* and the Following of Ghosts:** File under Psychogeographic/Hauntological Stocking Fillers 162

22. ***Gone to Earth*:** Earlier Traces of an Otherly Albion 166

23. ***Queens of Evil, Tam Lin* and *The Touchables*:** High Fashion Transitional Psych Folk Horror, Pastoral Fantasy and Dream-like Isolation 170

24.	**Luke Haines:** Our Most Non-Hauntological Hauntologist	179
25.	**Tim Hart, Maddy Prior and "The Dalesman's Litany":** A Yearning for Imaginative Idylls and a Counterpart to Tales of Hellish Mills	185
26.	***Katalin Varga, Berberian Sound Studio* and *The Duke of Burgundy*:** Arthouse Evolution and Crossing the Thresholds of the Hinterland Worlds of Peter Strickland	187
27.	***General Orders No. 9* and *By Our Selves*:** Cinematic Pastoral Experimentalism	196
28.	***No Blade of Grass* and *Z.P.G.*:** A Curious Dystopian Mini-Genre	199
29.	***The Midwich Cuckoos* and *The Day of the Triffids*:** John Wyndham, Dystopian Tales, Celluloid Cuckoos and the Village as Anything But Idyll	203
30.	***Folk Archive* and *Unsophisticated Arts*:** Documenting the Overlooked and Unregulated	208
31.	**Folkloric Photography:** A Lineage of Wanderings, Documentings and Imaginings	211
32.	***Poles and Pylons* and The Telegraph Appreciation Society:** A Continuum of Accidental Art	219
33.	***Symptoms* and *Images*:** Hauntological Begetters, the Uneasy Landscape and Gothic Bucolia	222
34.	***The Spirit of Dark and Lonely Water*:** Public Information Films and Lost Municipal Paternalisms	228
35.	**Magpahi, Paper Dollhouse and The Eccentronic Research Council:** Finders Keepers/Bird Records Nestings and Considerations of Modern Day Magic	231
36.	***Vashti Bunyan: From Here to Before*:** Whispering Fairy Stories until They are Real	238

37. **The Owl Service, Anne Briggs, The Watersons, Lutine and Audrey Copard:** Folk Revisiters, Revivalists and Reinterpreters 243

38. ***The Seasons*, Jonny Trunk, the BBC Radiophonic Workshop and Howlround:** A Yearning for Library Music, Experiments in Educational Music and Tape Loop Tributes 252

39. **An Old Soul Returns:** The Worlds and Interweavings of Kate Bush 265

40. ***The Stone Tape*, *Quatermass*, *The Road* and *The Twilight Language of Nigel Kneale*:** Unearthing Tales from Buried Ancient Pasts 269

41 **Folklore Tapes and the *Wyrd Britannia* Festival:** Journeying to Hidden Corners of the Land/the Ferrous Reels and Explorations of an Arcane Research Project 278

42. ***Skeletons*:** Pastoral Preternatural Fiction and a World, Time and Place of its Own Imagining 284

43. ***Field Trip-England*:** Jean Ritchie, George Pickow and Recordings from the End of an Era 288

44. ***Noah's Castle*:** A Slightly Overlooked Artifact and Teatime Dystopias 290

45. **Jane Weaver Septième Soeur and *The Fallen by Watch Bird*:** Non-Populist Pop and Cosmic Aquatic Folklore 293

46. ***Detectorists*, *Bagpuss*, *The Wombles* and *The Good Life*:** Views from a Gentler Landscape 297

47. ***Weirdlore*, Folk Police Recordings, Sproatly Smith and *Seasons They Change*:** Notes From the Folk Underground, Legendary Lost Focal Points and Privately Pressed Folk 303

48. ***The Moon and The Sledgehammer* and *Sleep Furiously*:** Visions of Parallel and Fading Lives 310

49.	*From Gardens Where We Feel Secure, Wintersongs, Pilgrim Chants* & *Pastoral Trails*: Lullabies for the Land and Gently Darkened Undercurrents	315
50.	***Strawberry Fields* and *Wreckers***: The Countryside and Coastal Hinterland as Emotional Edgeland	320
51.	***Zardoz, Phase IV* and *Beyond the Black Rainbow***: Seeking the Future in Secret Rooms from the Past and Psychedelic Cinematic Corners	323
52.	***Winstanley, A Field in England* and *The English Civil War Part II***: Reflections on Turning Points and Moments When Anything Could Happen	331

Introduction

I BEGAN TO PUBLISH *A Year In The Country* as daily website posts in 2014, although I had been directly and indirectly carrying out related research and cultural foraging for around three years previously. Indeed, some of the roots of its inspiration stretch back a number of decades.

At its heart it is a set of cyclical yearly explorations of an interconnected set of subcultural strands; it takes in sections of culture which do not have an overarching, definitive label or genre name, but which I have come to think of in part as an otherly pastoralism.

This includes work which explores and draws from the undercurrents and flipside of the landscape, the further reaches of folk culture and points of interconnection and intermingling with what has come to be known as hauntology.

Hauntology is often considered in terms of being work which explores and utilises a misremembered past, lost progressive futures and a conjuring of parallel worlds that are haunted by spectres of the past.

With that in mind and considering A Year In The Country's explorations of hauntologically-orientated work, alongside the sense of an otherly pastoralism, I consider my related work as a wandering through spectral fields: hence the title of the book.

The project includes a website featuring writing, artwork and music which draws from that otherly pastoral/spectral hauntological intertwining, alongside a growing library of music releases, prints, badge sets, a book of my artwork and so forth.

The written aspect of A Year In The Country has taken the above areas of culture as its starting point and has resulted in considerations of a vast array of books, records, films, television series etc. as well as focussing on hundreds of different cultural artifacts.

These have included essays on the work put out into the world by the likes of Nigel Kneale, The Owl Service, Trunk Records, Broadcast, Kate Bush, Folk Police Records, Virginia Astley, Folklore Tapes, Rob Young, Ghost Box Records, Jane Weaver, Finders Keepers Records and Mark Fisher.

A Year In The Country has also taken in a considerable number of films and television programmes including *Zardoz, Phase IV, Beyond the Black Rainbow*, public information films, *Travelling for a Living, General Orders No. 9, Sleep Furiously, The Changes* and *The Wicker Man.*

This book is a distilling and revisiting of some of the major themes, recurring interests, cultural touchstones and points of inspiration that I have explored during my initial posts for the A Year In The Country website.

Alongside previously unpublished work, the book draws from the first three years of writing posted, as well as notes for the record releases, and in line with the cycle of the year it brings together their interconnected strands of cultural explorations in 52 chapters.

So why these particular cultural journeys and explorations mentioned above and within the pages of this book?

Before beginning A Year In The Country, after a lifetime living, researching and working in left field, largely city-orientated pop culture, I found myself increasingly drawn to the countryside and to rural areas.

Accompanying this shift, within me there grew an interest in work that drew from the land and what very loosely could be considered the undercurrents of folk culture, all of which inspired a curiosity about whether I could create related subcultural work.

Although there was a wealth of such work, and related work, already in existence, to me these were largely new cultural and actual landscapes and they seemed a little less well-harvested than the fields of pop culture: to have more space and even a sense of rest, repose and respite away from the hustle and bustle of urban spaces.

The resulting wanderings have taken in the beauty and escape of rural pastures, but have also been intertwined with a search for expressions of an underlying unsettledness or flipside to the bucolic countryside dream.

In parts its roots may be found during an idyllic time in a village in which I spent some of my youth; an often Blytonesque, sylvan life of bike riding, hill climbing, dam and bonfire building. However, this outwardly perfect setting had a number of flipsides.

The land around me was curiously marked and scattered with signs of the military preparedness of conflicts past and modern: unexploded arms that would be found from time to time, abandoned pillbox fortifications, air force jets flying just above roof level to practice their radar evasion techniques, a tourist information centre with a fabled map which showed the location of crashed planes and small civil defence warning sirens that literally sat on the shelves and window ledges of where we lived.

This was all set to a background of a media and world saturated with Cold War propaganda and paranoia.

At the same time, I began to devour often-dystopic science fiction via television, weekly comic deliveries to the one local shop and books that I suspect were just a touch too advanced for me.

One book in particular which stands out is John Wyndham's *The Midwich Cuckoos*, which tells of a village that is implanted and invaded by a group of (probably) extraterrestrial children with preternatural powers.

The final page of the copy that I read at the time was missing and so I never knew whether the village was saved or not.

Another point of intrigue and fascination were brief glimpses of a speculative television series called *Noah's Castle* which, although aimed at the young, had storylines which involved shortages, societal collapse and hyperinflation, reflecting and extrapolating from recent unrest and strife within Britain.

This mixture of a pastoral playground, a world on the edge and fantastic fictions proved to be a heady mix for the dreamscapes of a young mind, all of which would be some of the initial seedlings which would lead one day to the creation and ongoing themes of A Year In The Country.

To a degree A Year In The Country initially had a semi-conscious cathartic purpose connected to the above and the related "search for expressions of an underlying unsettledness"; to put away and neuter the Cold War dread-related monsters under the bed that seemed to have haunted the back of my mind since those childhood days.

That side of the journey has now been largely completed and I no longer have the urge to so expressly or underlyingly explore it within my work.

The project has come to be more an exploration of the flipside, undercurrents and subcultural areas of otherly pastoral, folk orientated and hauntological concerns.

With all the above in mind I feel that a rewriting of the brief "About" text that I have used online is appropriate.

It should now read something like:

> A Year In The Country is a set of year-long journeys through spectral fields; cyclical explorations of an otherly pastoralism, the outer reaches of folk culture and where it meets and intermingles with hauntology.
>
> It is a wandering amongst subculture that draws from the undergrowth of the land, the patterns beneath the plough, pylons and amongst the edgelands.
>
> Those wanderings take in the beauty and escape of rural pastures, intertwined with a search for expressions of the undercurrents and flipside of the bucolic countryside dream.

* * *

Thank you for taking the time to read this book. I hope that both the book itself and the cultural wanderings and explorations within it inspire you as much as the work that it considers has inspired me, and that its pathways and signposts lead you to your own precious and intriguing discoveries and explorations.

Stephen Prince (August 2017)

Notes on the Text

Following the cyclical, annual nature of *A Year In The Country*, as with weeks in the year, the book is split into 52 chapters.

It can be read in a conventional start to finish manner; however, to a degree, each chapter can be read as an individual, standalone article.

To enable that and also reflecting the recurring and interwoven exploration of particular themes and reference points in A Year In The Country, where practical, certain observations, theories, quotes, definitions and reference points recur throughout the book. This is entirely deliberate.

Where appropriate, the date of release of films, books, albums etc. is included each time they first appear in a chapter.

1

Electric Eden: Unearthing Britain's Visionary Music: Folk Vs. Pop, Less Harvested Cultural Landscapes and Acts of Enclosure Old and New

Electric Eden: Unearthing Britain's Visionary Music, the 2010 book by Rob Young, served as an ongoing reference for much of the earlier years of *A Year In The Country.*

It is an epic tome of a book which, in simple terms, is a journey through British folk and pastoral music and related culture from its roots to the modern day, but instead of serving as a straightforward documenting of such things, is more an exploration of its undercurrents, of at times semi-hidden or overlooked cultural history and its interconnected strands.

The book travels with folk revivalist collectors such as Cecil Sharp, the social idealism of William Morris and Ewan MacColl, the late 1960s/early 1970s folk rock of the likes of Fairport Convention and Pentangle, the acid or more experimental folk of Comus and Forest, *The Wicker Man* film from 1973 and related occult folklore, contemporary esoterically interconnected hauntological practitioners such as Ghost Box Records, the pastoral tinged work of pop music explorers Kate Bush, David Sylvian and Talk Talk and pastoral speculative/science fiction.

There is a sense within the book of folk and related culture seeming to point towards an otherly Britain: an imagined Albion of hidden histories and sometimes arcane knowledge, wherein there is still the space or possibility to sidestep some of the more ubiquitous, dominant and monotheistic tendencies of modern day culture and systems.

The later chapter in the book, "Towards the Unknown Region", explores the more overtly undercurrent or semi-hidden areas of pastoral-orientated work and the interconnected realms of hauntology.

In this chapter the author recalls a time when he attended a Ghost Box Records event; he relates a sense of the excitement and envelopment that stepping into a separate created world or reality via cultural forms, scenes and events can provide, even if only for the duration of a record playing, or an evening or two.

He comments that at such times the creators and participants engage in a form of consensual sensory hallucination, which is a rather succinct description of the sense of giving yourself up to otherworldly cultures and stories.

The book contains a number of phrases which deftly and briefly capture cultural activities, including "imaginative time travel".

This is used to describe a personal and cultural form of exploring and taking inspiration from different historical periods, possibly mixing them with contemporary techniques and modes to produce work that creates new forms rather than being strictly recreations of times past.[1]

For example, work within folk culture such as late 1960s/early-to-mid 1970s folk rock and acid/psych folk, where the participants at times seemed to actively attempt to will into existence musical, aesthetic and social forms that drew from the past but in a refracted and reinterpreted manner and which existed in a never-never land of their own creation.

Rob Young does not judgmentally distinguish between what could be considered authentic folk that has been handed down in an oral or traditional manner over the centuries and the latter day exoticism of contemporary folklore-influenced work such as The Wicker Man; all such strands could be seen as authentic, work has to spring from somewhere and it is the intention and effect rather than age and historical traceability that implies whether it is the "real" thing or not.

Within Electric Eden and related writing and interviews he also considers the roots of the words and concepts of folk and pop.

The phrase "folk music" can seem a little confusing initially. There is a tendency to think of folk as meaning "from the people", as in all of the folk of a land, which leads to the question, how can music that seems to have often, today at least, a relatively limited appeal therefore be called folk music?

How can it be of the people if it is not especially popular? And it is definitely not pop music.

Rob Young has put forward the case that rather than referring to a sense of all the people of the land, folk music is the music of the "volk", derived from the Germanic/Teutonic *wald* - the wild wood - whereas the word "pop" (ie. popular music) comes from the Latin *populous*, which refers more to the larger populations of cities etc.

He talks of how pop culture derives from centrally controlled, regimented urban communities (Roman urban *populi*) which were entertained, appeased and distracted by mass spectacles such as gladiatorial entertainment and comedic dramas: that pop is a culture that belongs to or springs from imperial socialisation, institutionalised religion, related consensus and commerce.

In contrast, folk is much older than pop, originating from the wild wood and a culture where peasants, vagrants and villagers bore song from those woods, the forest, the barbaric heath - societies which were sometimes savage, often ad hoc, structured in a less hierarchical manner, pre-Christian and where rituals endured and perplexed their heirs.

The Romans made efforts to clear away these potentially problematic, less governable areas but Rob Young notes that they still survive in English place names that end with "wald", "wold" or "weald".

As cultural forms and phrases therefore, one comes from the city, one from elsewhere out amongst the land.

In many ways, the story of folk music, culture and folklore is in part one that tells of the differences and separateness of culture from the city vs. the wald or the populi vs. volk or more literally folk vs. pop.

Which brings things round to to The Wombles and what happens when folk meets or tries to become pop.

What appeared to happen in the mid-1970s is that music arrived at a point where one of folk rock's more popular bands Steeleye Span have a hit single with their version of the traditional folk song "All Around My Hat", which reached number five in the UK singles charts in 1975.

The single was produced by Mike Batt, who also oversaw records for the novelty pop band The Wombles: these were a musical offshoot of an animated children's television series originally broadcast from 1973-1975 where furry, pointy-nosed creatures who live in burrows on Wimbledon Common spend their time recycling rubbish in creative ways.[2]

All Around My Hat is folk that has wandered quite a way from its roots and seems intrinsically to be nearer to pop, a kind of glam romp with folk trappings.

Which is not to dismiss this version as it is a rather catchy and full of life interpretation, with the video and the song capturing a certain point in time and period nuances of British cultural history: of pop music and culture not yet overly-styled, honed and marketed, which in its own particular way is still from a less tamed cultural landscape.

This is one of the themes of Electric Eden; a sense of a taming of the cultural and at points literal landscape, of what Rob Young presents as music and culture of a utopian or visionary nature that draws from the land and folk culture.

He has discussed the connection between such areas of work and culture and how there is a connection to historic acts of land enclosure and clearance; the way in which from around 1760 onwards common land was put into private ownership by government Inclosure Acts, forcing agricultural workers towards the newly expanding cities and factories and how this displacement could be one of the roots of the British empathy with the countryside, with relics such as songs or texts from the world before this change having come to be revered as they seem to represent or connect to a pre-industrial "Fall" golden age.

It could be said that Inclosure Acts are not a purely historical practice.

In recent years a proportion of the population have found themselves increasingly priced out of certain areas of the country; the cost of putting a roof over your head (in terms of the ever upward path of rental and property prices), of keeping the lights on and the wolves from the door seems to quietly, gradually be removing a certain less material wealth-funded or directed way of life out of the cities and in particular the city centres and the capital city of Britain.

This could be considered to be a form of enclosure: a more subtly enacted mirror image of the earlier 18th century version.

In recent times this has happened in part through decisions to not take particular actions as well as the ending of acts of Parliamentary regulation (removing or refusing to implement statutory rent control or regulation for example), as opposed to creating new legislation, with the result that the "common people" are being removed from the inner cities rather than forced into them.

Also, more physical, bricks and mortar-related acts of enclosure have been accompanied by an undercutting of the economic infrastructure for creative work, whereby large scale transnational corporations effectively gain access to a huge library of content and very low paid or unpaid workers for their delivery systems and hardware, often at miniscule cost, such as with online music streaming or even for free in the case of social media.

This has often been done under the guise of ease of distribution, expression and choice, which while it can be useful in the sense of "getting your work out there without being massively bankrolled", the end result of which is a technological or creative form of enclosure.

This often leaves the ongoing viability, in terms of keeping those aforementioned lights on and cupboards full, of such work largely in the hands once again of the few, of those selected and patronised by high-end conglomerates and/or those who are privately or institutionally funded.

Connected to this the space needed for the creation of more wayward forms of culture has become a harder path to follow.

There seems to have been an element of choice being taken away and of things reverting to older forms of wealth and class division, resulting in a form of social and economic clearing out and exclusion, a removal of access for those of lesser financial means to the clustering and critical mass of population that is sometimes required within cities for cultural forms to develop and take hold.

At the same time rural, as opposed to urban, environments do not tend to have such a publicly displayed saturation or overload of culture and input, although this can still be present in a less visible sense to a degree as many homes now contain multiple digital devices that via online access can allow or enable vast streams of cultural information and input.

Out in the country you rarely see billboards, there are fewer shop windows, generally fewer cultural events and venues, flyposters are relatively rare, the headlines and covers of newspapers and periodicals cannot catch your eye from every corner and there is also a lack of CCTV surveillance and recording out in country towns and villages compared to cities.

At times, some of the inherent character or spirit of folk music, alongside certain areas of hauntology and pastoral/subterannean ambient/electronic music, their rhythms, cadences and the stories they tell can seemingly make more sense beyond youth and out amongst the fields.

It is important to point out that all cities and compact population environments are not inherently evil, nor that the countryside and country living is all green grassed idyll, nor that pastoral and folk culture is part of some dichotomous good/bad pathway with urban/pop culture.

It is possible that we know the stories of pop and its associated alternative or fringe culture a little too well, as they have been told, retold and used too often by the mainstream and non-mainstream media, until for many people their stories no longer carry the meanings and connections they once did.

Since the advent and popularity of more urban-based pop music/

culture, what has been called folk music and culture has only periodically been popular or considered acceptable for wider marketing and consumption (at times such as the high summer of folk rock in the late 1960 to early or mid 1970s, or the interest in freak folk in the earlier-to-mid 2000s).

The direct sunlight of media and mass attention can be a potentially double-edged sword for subcultures, as at times it does not allow cultural forms the space they need to grow and develop fully and leads to culture being plucked and harvested too early.

As Jeanette Leech says in her introduction to the 2012 *Weirdlore* compilation album of underground and exploratory folk: [3]

> "...when light is not on a garden, many plants will wither. But others won't. They will grow in crazy, warped, hardy new strains. It's time to feed from the soil instead of the sunlight."

Within the undercurrents of folk and otherly pastoral culture there is a sense of it having been left alone to a degree; it is a cultural form which has been allowed to gain nourishment from the earth rather than the brighter rays of public attention. Although this is possibly less so as the years have gone by.

As is suggested by Rob Young in Electric Eden, the space around such work feels less regulated. There is still some space to move and dream around such things, which may be less so in other areas of culture; you can possibly (or hopefully) still walk these "wild woods" a little more freely.

1. This is discussed further in Chapter 14.
2. This is discussed further in Chapter 46.
3. Also discussed in Chapter 47.

2

Gather in the Mushrooms: Early Signposts and Underground Acid Folk Explorations

While wandering down the *A Year In The Country* pathways, there have been an awful lot of cultural reference points that have inspired, influenced and intrigued (the three I's as it were).

The *Gather in the Mushrooms* album is one of the first. It is a 2004 compilation curated by Bob Stanley who is a member of the band Saint Etienne, subtitled "The British Acid Folk Underground 1968-1974" and it does what it says on the can.

The period of time that the album focuses on was a point in music/culture when the likes of Fairport Convention were reinterpreting traditional folk music, combining it with the more contemporary elements of rock to produce what has come to be known as folk rock.

Acid or psych folk was an extension or offshoot of such work, which often tended to wander down more overtly exploratory or experimental avenues and at times intermingled aspects of psychedelia with folk and rock elements.

The first lines on "Morning Way", a track on Gather in the Mushrooms are "Dreaming strands of nightmare are sticking to my feet", followed closely by a somewhat angelic female voice in counterpart. It is odd and appealing.

The entire album is worth a listen, but of particular interest are:

Magnet: "Corn Riggs"; an instrumental version of the song featured in *The Wicker Man* soundtrack from 1973.

Sallyangie: "Love in Ice Crystals"; a rather young Mike Oldfield and his sister in a pre-*Tubular Bells* incarnation.

Pentangle: "Lyke Wake Dirge"; their haunting take on a traditional song.

Forest: "Graveyard"; ethereal gothic folk as a genre.

Trader Horne: "Morning Way"; as just mentioned and featuring Judy Dyble, who prior to this was a singer with Fairport Convention.

Comus: "The Herald"; this could well be called gothic folk or maybe macabre folk: epic and unsettling.

The album also features songs by Sandy Denny (also of Fairport Convention), Writing on the Wall, Bert Jansch, Heron, Spirogyra, Al Jones, Fresh Maggots, Lesley Duncan, Mr Brooks and Andy Roberts, alongside work by two of the lost women of folk: Shelagh Macdonald and Vashti Bunyan, who disappeared from public view for a number of decades.[1]

When it was released in 2004 was also around the time that there was something of a revived interest in the further reaches of folk, in part due to the popularity of folk revisitors and reinventors such as Devendra Banhart and Joanna Newsom; also the work of just mentioned one-time folk wanderer Vashti Bunyan was being rediscovered by a wider audience.

Unfortunately, the album is out of print but can still generally be obtained for purchase via an online search.

There was a follow up or sister album released in 2006: *Early Morning Hush; Notes from the UK Folk Underground 1968-1976*, which is in parts a look-see at privately pressed folk albums from that time.[2]

Both albums are well worth a wander towards and listen to begin an exploration of the flipside of British folk and its experimentations from the period in the late 1960s to mid 1970s when such things were at something of a high point, or if you should want a soundtrack for wandering through gently lysergic fields then this is a good place to start exploring.

It is curious that acid/psychedelic or psych folk grew from a mixture of sources, which at different times incorporated religious beliefs, traditional folk song (though thoroughly reinterpreted) and the late sixties counter-culture.

Subcultural/countercultural movements tend to be thought of as having sprung from the cracks beneath the city's walkways, whereas acid/psych folk seems to have been created by participants who were either physically located out in the cottages and meadows or who used a form of imaginative geographical travel to create a culture which, in contrast to urban influenced and inflected cultural movements, was hazily narcotically pastoral.

1. Discussed further in Chapter 36.
2. Discussed further in Chapter 47.

3

Hauntology: Places Where Society Goes to Dream, the Defining and Deletion of Spectres and the Making of an Ungenre

Although it is hard to precisely define what hauntology is, it has become a way of identifying particular strands of music and cultural tendencies. As a cultural form it is fluid, loose and not strictly delineated but below are some of the recurring themes and characteristics of hauntological work:

1) Music and culture that draws from and examines a sense of loss of a post war utopian, progressive, modernist future that was never quite reached.
2) A tendency to see some kind of unsettledness and hidden layers of meaning in public information films, TV idents and "a bit too scary and odd for children though that is who they were aimed at" television programmes from the late 1960s to about 1980, which include the likes of *The Owl Service* (1968), *Children of the Stones* (1977) and *The Changes* (1975).
3) Graphic design and a particular kind of often analogue synthesised music that references and reinterprets some forms of older library music, educational materials and the work of the BBC Radiophonic Workshop, often focusing on the period from around 1969 to 1979 and related culture which is generally of British origin.
4) A re-imagining and misremembering of the above and other

sources into forms of music and culture that seem familiar, comforting and also often unsettling and not a little eerie, creating a sense of work that is haunted by spectres of its and our cultural past, to loosely paraphrase philosopher Jacques Derrida.

5) The drawing together and utilising of the above elements to conjure a sense of a parallel, imagined, often strange or Midwich-ian Britain.

In this chapter, the term hauntology is largely used to refer to its British cultural and music-orientated strand which began to loosely coalesce around approximately 2003-2004, which is probably the dominant use of the phrase, although it has been used more widely to also describe American hypnagogic pop and Italian Occult Pyschedelia. The phrase itself has its roots in the theorising of Jacques Derrida, although in its more specific cultural/music sense it is thought to have been first used by the writers Mark Fisher and Simon Reynolds.

Subcultural genre labels are not problematic in themselves, as long as they are not used to enforce unmoveable, restrictive, unevolving cultural norms and regulations and at the very least they can make it easier to navigate records stores, whether of the scarcer bricks and mortar variety or the more intangible digital ones.

Those who have been identified as hauntological practitioners often had a well defined vision of their esoteric world and culture before being labelled as such and although there may be some common threads and shared sensibilities in this genre, it has retained a fair degree of cultural and aesthetic diversity.

The aesthetics and visuals of related work includes the eldritch educationalism of Ghost Box Records, the playful psychedelic whimsy and break beats of Blank Workshop and the occult, hidden history experimentalism of Demdike Stare, all of which have at one time or another been labelled hauntology.

In one of William Gibson's novels there is a discussion between two characters about how subcultures were once a place where society went to dream but they have died out because we began to pluck them too early, to shine the spotlights of media attention and mainstream cultural market forces on them too quickly before they had the time to fully develop and gestate.

Today, such things which have been able to fully bloom are rare and precious.

In light of that it can be positive to celebrate when a subculture has had the vision of its participants coupled with the space and time to gestate and so has been able to develop into what can be identified as a genre, one which has its own characteristics and world view as uniquely as the likes of Ghost Box Records and some of the cultural endeavours that have been described as being hauntological.

Because of that space, time and vision the resulting culture has often proved particularly hardy from those spotlights of attention and has not been diverted or subsumed from its path; it has been able to be a small cultural plot of land where you can go to dream or at least let your mind wander.

For a while the phrase hauntology when used to refer to a genre of music had been deleted on Wikipedia.

As author Simon Reynolds - who as just mentioned was, along with Mark Fisher, one of the first people to use the phrase hauntology in relation to such culture - points out, those doing the deleting have taken a fair few steps to make sure their own comments on Wikipedia are not deleted or modified. "Do as I say and not as I do" as it were.

Just as with deletion via consensus, a larger mass of consensus does not necessarily mean something is correct, but typing the word "hauntology" alongside "music" into a search engine at the time of writing brought up 170,000 pages to look at, while "hauntology music genre" returned over 50,000 results.

That would tend to imply that there is not a "consensus to delete" in the wider world, or at the very least there is a "consensus to discuss, explore, consider, create and debate".

So, maybe rather than deleting the whole notion, making the debate around whether hauntology exists part of its page would have been a more reasonable or culturally democratic thing to do.

RETURNING TO GENRE labels possibly being part of a process of creating and enforcing unmoveable, restrictive, unevolving cultural norms and regulations, in terms of hauntology-related music and culture something interesting happened in the world of culture since between the first year of *A Year In The Country* in 2014 and 2016 onwards.

In 2014 and in preceding years work labelled as hauntology seemed often to be something of a critical, cultural and theoretical darling: an area of culture that people and sections of the media seemed genuinely intrigued, fascinated and inspired by.

Since that time, it seems to a degree to have changed from critical darling to sometimes-cultural whipping boy and indeed become a (loose) genre of which people dare not or want to not speak its name.

It has variously been referred to as h**ntology, sometimes just the letter H, 'auntology or more generally referred to with a slightly (or more than slightly) dismissive tone.

Many cultural things which are critically revered often seem to end up being reviled, almost as part of a knee jerk, automatic cultural cycle and circle. Also, within hauntological work there has often come to be too much of a reliance on a set number of tropes and cultural reference points.

Claude Mono of *The Golden Apples of the Sun* site and radio show puts this rather well as an introduction to his "Exploration Series No.1 – Hauntology" episode:

"...by way of a brief introduction let me just say I think hauntology is a rich and rewarding musical and visual aesthetic but one that can be done really badly – you know a bus-ride of nostalgia and electronics –

full of the BBC Radiophonic Workshop, British public information films of the 1970s, eerie soundtracks, concretism, and brutalist architectural imagery – well there certainly is some of that but hopefully a little bit more such as some crucial reference points and an incredible live track from Broadcast, some drum and bass, and 80s band Japan…"

"There certainly is some of that but hopefully a little bit more…" is a particularly important point here. When a cultural movement, gathering, style or genre becomes too codified, too set in its ways (too pipe and slippers perhaps) then often apart from to its die hard followers and/or those that appreciate an endless self-referential looping, it can begin to lose its way as a vital or exploratory force.

Saying such is not a call for endless stylistic novelty, more just a note that adding a few new ingredients to a well-worn and tested recipe is often not a bad thing. Or maybe using the spirit of hauntology as a starting point rather than seeing its codified elements and references as unwaverable guidelines.

The creation of work which conjures a parallel world via a misremembered past need not necessarily draw purely from one particular period or set of cultural reference points, as has often been the case with hauntological work but rather that concept and process could be used as a general framework to also explore other eras and cultural areas.

To a certain degree this has been the case in the earlier mentioned hypnagogic pop, which draws more from the 1980s period and related culture and Italian Occult Psychedelia which focuses on non-British culture and Pye Corner Audio, who Ghost Box Records have released recordings by, appears to also extend the hauntological palette to incorporate a more 1980s VHS-esque aspect.

While a film such as *Beyond the Black Rainbow* (2010)[1] could be seen as a form of hauntological work in its creation of a parallel world that creates a "Reagan era fever dream".

Cultural forms and wellsprings are generally hardy things. They rarely disappear from the landscape completely; they may become less fashionable, wander off into niches to quietly continue their journeys, maybe to periodically be revived on a larger scale, revisited or provide inspiration at future points in time.

Once again, Jeanette Leech's thoughts and writings in her notes to the Weirdlore compilation[2] spring to mind, when she discusses the use of genre names and the brief shining of media and general cultural interest spotlights on a particular niche of exploratory folk music:

> "When light is not on a garden, many plants will wither. But others won't. They will grow in crazy, warped, hardy new strains. It's time to feed from the soil instead of the sunlight."

1. Considered in Chapter 51.
2. Also referred to in Chapter 1.

4

Cuckoos in the Same Nest: Hauntological and Otherly Folk Confluences and Intertwinings

A CURIOUS OCCURRENCE in an area or two of music and culture is the way in which folk music and folkloric-orientated work, of the underground, acid, psych, wyrd and otherly variety, has come to share common ground with synthesised work and electronica, of a leftfield and hauntological variety.

This is an area of culture where the use, appreciation and romance of often older electronic music technologies, reference points and inspirations segues and intertwines with the more bucolic wanderings and landscapes of exploratory, otherly pastoralism and folk culture, a part of the cultural landscape:

> "…planted permanently somewhere between the history of the first transistor, the paranormal, and nature-driven worlds of the folkloric…"
> (author, artist, musician and curator Kristen Gallerneaux.)

On the surface such folkloric and electronic musical and cultural forms are very disparate and yet both have come to explore and share similar landscapes. As a starting point at one time on the main *A Year In The Country* website's "About" page, the project was described as being:

*   *   *

> "A set of year-long journeys through and searching for an expression of an underlying unsettledness to the bucolic countryside dream; an exploration of an otherly pastoralism, the patterns beneath the plough, pylons and amongst the edgelands: a wandering about and through the trails of things that have influenced, inspired and intrigued me along the way, which will quite possibly take in the further flung reaches of work with its roots in folkloric concerns and what has been labelled hauntological culture."

This has taken the form of daily and weekly cultural wanderings and postings online and also the release of a number of records, which have often explored the confluence between those just mentioned "folkloric concerns" and "what has been labelled hauntological culture".

One such record would be *The Quietened Village* from 2016, which is a themed compilation that is:

> "A study of and reflection on the lost, disappeared and once were homes and hamlets that have wandered off the maps or that have become shells of their former lives and times."

It is an album which travels from quietly unsettling electronica and tape manipulation via exploratory folk tales and far distant soundscapes, featuring work by Howlround, Polypores, The Rowan Amber Mill, Sproatly Smith, Time Attendant, The Straw Bear Band, A Year In The Country, Cosmic Neigbourhood, The Soulless Party and David Colohan.

Aesthetically and sonically this is a diverse gathering and yet there is coherence to the work and its exploration of the album's themes.

Similarly, you may well find in perhaps the Ghost Box Records Guests section of their online shop (where non-Ghost Box releases are made available), an album described as "hauntological electronics" in between those with the descriptions "achingly beautiful electronic folk" and "psych folk" or not dissimilarly contrasting records reviewed in the pages of *Shindig!* magazine or on the posts of *The Active Listener* website.

Or looking back to some of the early cultural explorations that would lead to A Year In The Country, three of the first albums that provided some of the seedlings, wellsprings or inspirations were The Owl Service's *The View from a Hill* (2010), *Broadcast and the Focus Group Investigate Witchcults of the Radio Age* (2009) and the compilation *Gather in the Mushrooms* (2004).

These wander respectively from a subtly experimental revisiting and reinterpreting of folk rock that has taken the name of a seminal otherly pastoral book and television series (Alan Garner's book and Granada Television's TV adaptation of *The Owl Service* from 1967 and 1969 respectively), to an overtly experimental sample and synthesiser-created phantasmagorical vocal and dreamlike cut-up exploration of hidden cultural layers and transmissions via a delving and unearthing of late 1960s and early 1970s underground British acid folk.

Somehow, it all made sense that these things fitted together.

So, where did this confluence, interweaving and intermingling all start? How are such things linked and connected? Some explanation, definition and description of recurring characteristics could well be in order here.

To precis a definition in Chapter 3: "Hauntology: Places Where Society Goes to Dream...", hauntology could be loosely described as music and culture which yearns for a lost post-war utopian future, that often tends to see some kind of unsettledness and hidden layers of meaning in public information films, TV idents and television series from the late 1960s to around 1980 and which draws from the graphic design and often analogue synthesised music of older library music, educational materials and the work of the BBC Radiophonic Workshop.

This is accompanied by a reimagining and misremembering of the above and other sources into forms of music and culture that seem familiar, comforting, unsettling and not a little eerie: ones which are haunted by spectres of its and our cultural past, alongside a drawing together and utilising of these elements above to conjure a sense of a parallel, imagined, Midwich-ian Britain.

Underground, acid, psych, wyrd, otherly folk and folkloric music and culture is not an easy thing to provide an encompassing description of as it covers a wide, differing range of work and approaches, and indeed there has not necessarily come to be one overriding genre title (hence the use of a multi-worded one here).

At heart it is often folk-orientated work that is experimental and explorative; sometimes in an audiological sense and/or sometimes in spirit.

This difference to non-underground or mainstream folk can at times be quite subtle, at least via a passing glance but is nonetheless most definitely present; it is something that may well at times be found more in intention or that just-mentioned spirit rather than distinct musical differences.

This is music that, while often drawing from the tropes and traditions of folk/folkloric culture, wanders elsewhere. From that multi-worded genre title, "otherly" is a word that may be used in relation to this, or more specifically "otherly pastoralism".

"Quietly transgressive", "unsettling", "eerie" or "eldritch" may well also at times be suitable descriptions.

One point of origin would be the late 1960s and early 1970s when folk music began to co-mingle with acid/psychedelic culture, often wandering far from but still maintaining a connection to its traditional roots and leading to the genre titles acid folk and psych folk (often used together as acid/psych folk).

As the years have passed, such work could be seen to be the forebear of the above-mentioned underground, acid, psych, wyrd, otherly folk: work that in part has been inspired by those traditional folk forms alongside its acid/psych antecedents.

What may be one of the underlying linking points with both otherly folk and hauntology is that earlier-mentioned yearning for lost utopias.

To that trio of A Year In The Country wellspring albums, add in Rob Young's *Electric Eden* book from 2010 (subtitled "Unearthing Britain's Visionary Music", in part as a reference to a utopian spirit), that was an early reference point and inspiration for A Year In The Country, alongside his related writing and interviews.

In particular this observation on the connection between folk culture and utopian impulses and desires resonated:

> "...I think the industrial revolution has much to do with it - beginning around 1760, when a Parliamentary act called 'Inclosure', forcibly removed common lands from the folk and scooped them into private ownership. That pushed many agricultural workers towards the new cities and factories where the only remaining employment opportunities lay. This displacement is at the bottom of so much of the British empathy with the countryside, I believe, as so much utopian thought and music here seems to desire to tap into folk memories of an unsullied rural state of mind which now appears like a golden age. Surviving relics from the world before that industrial 'Fall' are revered: old buildings, texts, songs, etc., are like talismans to be treasured, as a connective chain to the past."

With hauntology there is also a sense of a Fall but in this case it is more a reference to a "loss of some kind of utopian, progressive, modern(ist?) future that was never quite reached":[1] a point in time probably more specifically located towards the end of 1970s and the rise of neo-conservatism in politics, the economy and wider society.

Hauntology also has its talismans in the form of old buildings, texts and songs etc. but these are more likely to be found amongst an interest in the progressive intentions of some socially/municipally focused brutalist architecture and explorations of the BBC Radiophonic Workshop.

As with "surviving relics from the world before that industrial Fall" and related Arcadian rural dreams, there is a sense of such things being spectrally imprinted with some form of loss, of lost progressive futures.

The hauntological talismans would also include items from the loose definition of earlier: TV idents, public information films and television series from the late 1960s to late 1970s which have gained "unsettledness and hidden layers of meaning" with the passing of time.

SUCH TELEVISION SERIES and public information films provide a point of confluence for these areas of otherly folk music and hauntology. To semi-quote the A Year In The Country website and referring back to cultural folklore:

> "In contrast to the often oral telling of tales from the wald/wild wood in times gone by, today the stories that have become our cultural folklore we discover, treasure, pass down, are informed and inspired by, are often those that are transmitted into the world via the airwaves, the (once) cathode ray machine in the corner of the room, the carrying of tales via the zeros and ones of technology that flitter around the world and the flickers of (once) celluloid tales."

This cultural folklore would probably take in the likes of television programmes *The Changes* (1975), The Owl Service (1969), *Children of the Stones* (1977), *The Stone Tape* (1972) and the film *The Wicker Man* (1973), and a touch or two of the odder side of *Doctor Who* from way back when.

While often being set rurally, in contrast to much of popular culture which concerns itself with towns and cities, they have come to be touchstones or lodestones that seem to invoke a hidden, layered history of the land but which also encompass and intertwine with a wider hauntological, parallel, alternative version of Britain.

Some of their musical accompaniments could well be said to form an early part or antecedent of the meeting of the strands of otherly folk and hauntology.

In the above list the "patterns beneath the plough" are soundtracked by imagined and re-imagined folk music (The Wicker Man), synthesised elsewhere explorations by the BBC Radiophonic Workshop (The Changes, Doctor Who and The Stone Tape), spectral yet beautiful choral nightmares (Children of the Stones) and quite frankly still unnerving and experimental collaging (The Owl Service).

All quite different musically/aesthetically and yet all conjuring both (to again quote the A Year In The Country website) "an underlying unsettledness to the bucolic countryside dream" and a Midwich-ian take on the landscape.

If you should consider the descriptions of the above soundtracks, you may well find that a line could be drawn between them, the earlier description of three early A Year In The Country wellspring albums and much of more recent work that could be called hauntological and/ or which explores the outer reaches and undercurrents of folk music.

These two strands of otherly folkloric and hauntological work and culture may appear at first to be cultural cuckoos in the same nest but have come to be fellow travellers in an alternative landscape, informing and accompanying one another's journeys; this is a sharing of ground founded in similar exploratory and sometimes visionary or utopian spirit rather than divided by aesthetics.

1. To quote from chapter 3.

5

Ghost Box Records: Parallel Worlds, Conjuring Spectral Memories, Magic Old and New and Slipstream Trips to the Panda Pops Disco

The description on Ghost Box Records website describes it as:

> "...a record label for a group of artists exploring the misremembered musical history of a parallel world. A world of TV soundtracks, vintage electronics, folk song, psychedelia, ghostly pop, supernatural stories and folklore."

The label was founded in 2004 by Jim Jupp and Julian House, who respectively also release music via the label under the names Belbury Poly and The Focus Group.

Via its record releases, events, videos and artwork Ghost Box conjures its own particular parallel world: one that harks back to some previous age, though not necessarily a time or place that strictly ever existed but which could be said to loosely take place approximately from around the early 1960s to the late 1970s and which also looks towards some form of a related lost utopian, modernist and progressive future.

Within the Ghost Box parallel world there is a sense of the creation of and signposting to hidden away and not fully revealed or explained fragments of culture, events and even myths.

There is a hazy familiarity to the work of Ghost Box due to the way it references cultural forms and work such as the BBC Radiophonic

Worshop, public information films, library music and educational literature from earlier eras, but the resulting aesthetic and parallel world is not a retreading, rather an often quietly unsettling reimagining or as they put it themselves, a misremembering.

Connected to such aspects, although not a label that Jim Jupp and Julian House have overly applied themselves or used in relation to their work, they have come to be one of the record labels most closely connected to, and intertwined with, the loose musical genre known as hauntology, some of the defining aspects of which are work which, as with Ghost Box, often looks towards and draws from a sense of lost progressive futures, spectral histories and parallel worlds.[1]

In the Ghost Box world, previous era's television station idents, social planning and education policies, alongside the chocolate box bucolia of the English village all come to have an eerie, uncanny aspect; occult could be an appropriate phrase to use, though in the sense of hidden rather than the more overtly supernatural usage.

The ghosts or spectres in the Ghost Box parallel world are more likely to be conjured via that misremembering of television and other media than wraith like creatures brought forth via rituals in the woods.

In work such as Ghost Box's where, as just mentioned, for example television station idents can be seen to have become or contain occult messages and symbolism, media transmissions may have come to serve a not dissimilar purpose to that which past era's magic and/or folkloric rituals at times did.

Certain pieces and areas of culture could be seen to possess a form of magic or cast a spell but not in a way that these terms were used previously. It is more that they have a transportative element to them; they can create a world to step into or that draws you in.

"Magic", "spells" etc. are phrases and ideas from a previous era's belief systems but that does not mean that they cannot still be of use or have an evocative effect.

They have gained a certain exotic, otherly, touch of the forbidden currency as the years have gone by and while they have largely been marginalised by new techniques, ways of conjuring worlds and weaving tales, there could also be seen to be an overlap between the old and the new.

This is an area which Ghost Box explores or to quote Julian House when being interviewed by Rob Young in Wire magazine, it is "a strange interzone between pop culture and what is nudging the idea of the occult".

An expression of this can be found in the Ghost Box-related album *Broadcast and the Focus Group Investigate Witchcults of the Radio Age* from 2009, which was a collaboration between Julian House and Broadcast.

At points this features samples from soundtracks of previous decade's exploitation-esque witchcraft focused documentaries and creates a collaged, woozy, hallucinogenic atmosphere via music which Joseph Stannard described in Wire magazine as being "occult pop laden with pagan psychedelia".[2]

The above themes and interweaving of the old and new are also referred to at the Ghost Box website where The Advisory Circle album *From Out Here* released in 2014 is referred to as being "darkly melodic electronic magic".

While a poster that accompanied the Ghost Box-released Belbury Poly's *Belbury Tales* album from 2012 talks of the record taking in:

> "...medievalism, the supernatural, childhood, the re-invention of the past, initiation and pilgrimage (both spiritual and physical)."

One of the defining aspects of Ghost Box Record's work and releases is the creation and keeping of some areas of mystery: a sense that not everything is or is going to be fully known or explained, that the work is part of a creation of its own, not completely explained or explainable myths.

As is often the way with Ghost Box, there is a whole otherly world presented and created on Belbury Tales; in this case it is the re-imagined pastoral but quietly discomforting bucolic village pleasures of a parallel plot of England from who knows quite where and when.

There is something not quite so in this parish but whatever it is that is occurring is happening just out of sight, flickering away in the corners of your eyes.

Midwich-ian could be an apposite phrase to use in reference to such atmospheres that Ghost Box at times conjure, in the sense of it referring to the preternatural occurrences within a bucolic English village that can be found in John Wyndham's *The Midwich Cuckoos* novel from 1957 and its film adaptation as *Village of the* Damned in 1960.[3]

That subtle sense of unease is something that can also be found on The Advisory Circle's "And The Cuckoo Comes" from the early Ghost Box-released album *Mind How You Go* (2005).

It uses a vocal sample of nature-related studies, observations or prose that I do not know where it came from, although it conjures a sense of being an artifact from the 1960s or 1970s.

A brief half-listen of the words imply that it should be all pastoral delight as it describes the changes of the seasons. However, it is anything but an idyllic journeying through such things:

> "In the summer, well, it's usually cold and sometimes it snows.
> The winds blow.
> In the autumn the flowers are out and the sun shines.
> In the winter, the leaves grow again on the trees.
> And in the spring the winds blow and the leaves fall from the trees.
> And the sun shines and the leaves grow again on the trees.
> And sometimes it snows... and the cuckoo comes."

The dislocation in the words seems hidden as their delivery flows quite naturally, causing initial association with its fractured quality more with the song's multi-layered, swirling, repetition.

Some of the above points can make Ghost Box-related work seem heavy, darker and serious but it often has a very playful element which intertwines with the more parallel world or occult side of things. This is particularly present on the Belbury Poly album *New Ways Out* from 2016, which *Electric Sound* magazine described as:

> "...transporting you to those especially daft places only Belbury Poly can – Tizer-fuelled 70s youth club discos with side-rooms for Ouija boards..."

That quote creates anticipation of a sense of fun or playfulness from the album and indeed New Ways Out has that via a set of rather catchy pop hooks, but with that playfulness being quietly filtered through a Ghost Box parallel world filter.

As mentioned in Chapter 13: "...The Ascendancy of Apocalyptic Popular Culture" and Chapter 15: "...Nowhere, Forever and Lost Spaces within Cultural Circuitry", Mark Fisher spoke of how the circuit between the avant-garde and the mainstream was broken and how exploratory culture now has its own niches and audiences separate to and no longer crossing over with that of the mainstream.

In another cultural landscape, where that circuit is not broken, on a Thursday evening at some loosely defined point in the Ghost Box parallel world timeline you might expect to hear the words:

> "And now, on *Top of the Pops* with a track taken from their album New Ways Out, here's Belbury Poly with 'The New Harmony'."

While seven-inch singles of "Playground Gateway", also taken from the album, would be piled up in Woolworths.

In part, the album conjures and refers to an imagined, indefinable golden age of synthesised exploration, one where such things were intertwined with the pop/mainstream music world and charts.

This is experimental and explorative music but it is such things not as a moody teenager in its bedroom with the curtains drawn, more a form of such work that has got itself down the Panda Pops disco and is having "a bit of a boogie".[4]

In the mind's eye, on that just mentioned episode of Top of the Pops, "The New Harmony" would have shared a set of stages on a show that featured Kraftwerk, Donna Summer collaborating with Giorgio Moroder, Lieutenant Pigeon, a band playing a Chin and Chapman glam rock classic, The Wombles and possibly a folk band having their pop moment in the charts in between moonlighting for the *Bagpuss* soundtrack.

Possibly, if it was a particularly good week and just to show that the avant-garde/mainstream circuit was alive and functioning well it might also include some early-ish work by Kate Bush.

Ah, we can but dream.

A particular highlight of the album is that parallel world Top of the Pops performance of The New Harmony, which seems to channel the aforementioned Kraftwerk, Donna Summers at her Moroder peak and who knows quite what?

Which is one of the defining characteristics of this album and indeed much of Ghost Box's output, such as the woozy cut-up sampling of The Focus Group; often it is reminiscent of something just on the edge of memory.

Also, as with much of work created and released by the label there is a sense of reference points and lines drawn from the past but without it being overly or overtly retro: more that it exists in a separate slipstream of its own.

Returning to The New Harmony, on first hearing there is a temptation to check that somehow it is not playing on a seamless loop. It has an endless, almost Kafka-esque quality, filtered via a warm, synthesised Ghost Box viewpoint, a sense of never leaving and it seems to make time lose traction.

"Playground Gateway" ends the album and in that other slipstream-world it begins as though it would be the second single taken off the album, starting with a knockabout schoolyard glam chant air before it wanders off to possibly soundtrack science fiction tales that may well have featured gleaming golden crystal floating cities that our hero approaches via a winged white horse.

"Starhazy" from the album is the slightly more challenging third single that was played on late night radio.

The devoted fans loved it, the audience on Top of the Tops did their "not quite sure if I like this/if I should dance to this" shuffle that they often did for such not quite so commercially mainstream things and there were headlines after the recording of the show along the lines of "Police called to break up pitched battle between Polyites and Numanoids".

It would not necessarily have been quite as big in the charts but would still have had gents at EMI Records and the like popping champagne corks to a backdrop of one those upward travelling sticky taped sales charts.

"Hey Now Here He Comes" is the album's other glam-stomp (with a mild pastoral air) that the record company wanted as an A-side in the UK, but which due to scheduling and contractual problems in the Ghost Box parallel world only came out as a small quantity of 7-inch singles in Belgium, and many years later was rediscovered and featured on a compilation of lost glam rock along the lines of the 2003 album *Velvet Tinmine* which collected such records.

As always with the Ghost Box releases the packaging and design adds an extra layer of complimentary, constellatory elements to consider and peruse, including an illustration by Jim Jupp.

This depicts a pastoral landscape and has a gentle bucolic air while also somehow managing to convey an atmosphere of off-centredness and seems to be both contemporary but also to have tumbled from a never-was but is out there somewhere children's television show from an indefinable time back when.

Ghost Box co-founder Julian House is generally responsible for much of the design work for the label, and the resulting visual work plays an important part in creating the overall Ghost Box world, myths and aesthetic and the hazy familiarity referred to earlier.

It often plays with or conjures a sense of being parallel world governmental departmental or educational literature, the utilitarian nature of which seems to have quietly stepped to a place elsewhere.

At times the work contains Op art mandalas and geometric shapes, and while they may share an hallucinogenic quality with it they do not put me in mind so much of 1960s-esque psychedelia but rather they often contain a more subtly unsettled, darker aspect and atmosphere.

The Ghost Box design work is often created in part or whole via collage and found images but this is not always perfectly polished and may be presented nearer to a form of raw visual jump cutting where components are cut out inexactly, often leaving parts of their original background still present.

This is not dissimilar to the way in which Julian House's Ghost Box musical output under the name The Focus Group, abruptly and irregularly cuts and splices samples and other elements, a technique that is also present in his collaborative musical and video work with Broadcast.[5]

Rather than jarring you out of the created world, such techniques seem to draw you in, to create and spin a form of modern day magic or spell.

In this design work one of the intentions could be seen to be a fracturing of time, a recalling of the past in the present and looking ahead to futures that never were and there is a blurring, indistincting and reimagining of now, then, reality and memory.

This blends with similar elements of misremembering that can be found in the music output of Ghost Box and combines with it in the production of the label's very particular parallel world of space and time.

1. Hauntology is discussed and defined more extensively in Chapter 3.
2. The album is discussed further in Chapter 8.
3. Discussed in Chapter 29.
4. I tend to think of youth club discos from back when as being more Panda Pops rather than Tizer fuelled - perhaps this is the result of different geographic fizzy pop distribution areas in the days before the universal brand ubiquity and organisation of such things.
5. Discussed in Chapter 8.

6

Folk Horror Roots: From But a Few Seedlings Did a Great Forest Grow

FOLK HORROR IS A LOOSELY defined genre of fictional works which create an alternative, flipside view of the landscape and pastoralism; these works draw from and/or are frequently set in the landscape, creating unsettled and unsettling tales, in contrast to more bucolic representations of the countryside as a place of calm and restful escape.

They may tell stories of the patterns underneath the plough, may include elements of a more hauntological nature rather than being purely rurally based and can take in the hidden, layered histories and atmospheres within places.

There is often a sense of their inhabitants living in, or becoming isolated from, the wider world, allowing moral beliefs to become untethered from the dominant norms and allowing the space for ritualistic, occult, supernatural or preternatural events, actions and consequences to occur.[1]

As a phrase, "folk horror" conjures images of a trio of British films released between 1968 and 1973; *Witchfinder General* (1968), *The Blood on Satan's Claw* (1971) and *The Wicker Man* (1973).

Looking back today such films could be seen as a result or offshoot of there being, at the time of their production, a growing interest in folk music and culture, which was accompanied by a romantic sense of wishing to return to and embrace simpler and more natural or rural ways of living.[2]

However rather than being an expression of such inclinations and idyllic bucolia, folk horror's often bleak nihilistic nature and stories seem to be more an expression of the souring of related dreams and yearnings: a rural/folk reflected curdling of 1960s utopian optimism as it entered the 1970s.

These are not always easy films to watch and particularly the first two could be seen as sharing ground with exploitation cinema.

Along which lines, both Witchfinder General and The Blood on Satan's Claw featured Tony Tenser as their executive producer.

Tony Tenser had a cinematic background as a producer in the more lurid side of the film industry - more Soho backstreet than high-end Cannes - producing titillating and/or exploitation semi-documentaries such as *Naked as Nature Intended* (1961), *Primitive London* and *London in the Raw* (both 1965), which provided often prurient views of naturism and events in the capital as their prime exploitation selling points.

Witchfinder General and The Blood on Satan's Claw are films which could be seen to have their roots and onscreen expression in both the more art inclinations of their directors (Michael Reeves and Piers Haggard respectively) and the exploitation aspects of their producer Tony Tenser.

Although over time critical appreciation has tended to tip more towards the art side of things, without both sides of this coin one could debate whether these films would have existed or have come to be such resonant cultural artifacts.

Their visceral, more shocking exploitation-esque moments may be part of what has helped to create their cult appeal and have become confluent with consideration of them as films which also explore such themes in a more layered, explorative manner than that which may be found in more strictly straightforward exploitation work or some areas of mainstream cinema.

Tony Tenser, with his exploitation sensibilities, seems to have been partly responsible for a considerable portion of the late 1960s/early 1970s arrival of folk horror as he was also executive producer on *Curse of the Crimson Altar* (1968), which deals with some of the themes of folk horror (a rural setting, connections to the old beliefs and magic).

This film is particularly memorable in its conjuring up of phantasmagorical occult scenes, which are made all the more striking by a film-stealing Barbara Steele as Lavina Morley, Black Witch of Greymarsh, who is dressed in striking, opulent and almost surreal folkloric garb, including a behorned headdress.

She serves as mistress of the film's woozily transgressive dreamlike ritual ceremonies, helping create almost a film within a film: one which seems quite separate to the more mainstream, potboiler-like story and presentation of the film as a whole.

(And which, as with The Blood on Satan's Claw and Witchfinder General, also borrow from the more sensational aspects of exploitation cinema while intertwining such elements with something of a more layered, exploratory cinematic aspect.)

The late 1960s to around the mid 1970s was the main era for the production of the initial, classic examples of film and television that have come to be known as folk horror.

However, in terms of cinematic forebears, around 1960 there was a small grouping of horror and/or supernatural films which could be seen as being part of a lineage that would one day become or bring about what is known as folk horror.

These include Mario Bava's *Black Sunday* from 1960, also starring Barbara Steele, Jack Clayton's *The Innocents* from 1961 and Roger Vadim's *Et Mourir De Plaisir* (or *Blood and Roses* to use its American title) from 1960.

Their tone and expression varies from the classic black and white gothic and grotesque horror of Black Sunday to the almost decadent aristocratic Technicolor sensuality of Et Mourir de Plaisir via the repressed supernatural hauntings amongst the reeds and willows of the British countryside in The Innocents.

All of these films are set rurally, but it is not this which causes them to be gathered together in this way (and what has come to be known as folk horror does not *have* to be exclusively set rurally); it is something more subtle and underlying, possibly something in their atmosphere, their spirit and a sense that they are telling the stories of unsettled landscapes.

As with the later films that are mentioned above, these early 1960s films variously contain a curious and intriguing mixture of mainstream, transgressive, almost exploitation and arthouse cinema, the themes and tropes of which are used and explored to create rather classy, exploratory and nuanced work.

On British television a number of series and plays were produced around a roughly similar period to The Wicker Man, The Blood on Satan's Claw and Witchfinder General, which could to varying degrees be connected to the phrase folk horror.

Such programmes could include the work of Nigel Kneale such as the pre-hauntological investigations of *The Stone Tape* (1972) and the nature terrors and conflicts of *The Beasts* (1976) and other notable series including the made-for-children but curiously disquieting likes of *The Owl Service* (1968) and *Children of the Stones* (1977).

Alongside which the BBC's *Ghost Stories for Christmas*, which often adapted M.R. James fiction, such as *Whistle and I'll Come to You* (1968), *The Ash Tree* (1975) and *Play for Today* broadcasts including *Robin Redbreast* (1970) and *Penda's Fen* (1974),[3] contain many of the themes of folk horror; landscape-set tales of the supernatural, the persecution of those who practice the old ways, the flipside and undercurrents of the land/history, rural isolation and sacrifice.

You could also cast the net wider and include the Czech New Wave fantasia of *Valerie and her Week of Wonders* (1970)[4] and the high-fashion fairytale-gone-rotten in the woods of Italian-made *Queens of Evil* (1970).[5]

However, despite this breadth of work those earlier mentioned three British films The Wicker Man, Witchfinder General and The Blood on

Satan's Claw still remain the core wellspring and root system of all things folk horror.

They have become a canonic trio: towering behemoths within this area of culture, which over time have to varying degrees, along with folk horror as a genre/phrase, stepped out of their cult landscapes and into a more mainstream cultural conversation.

It seems like not all that long ago that folk horror and related work was still a relatively esoteric, hidden area of interest.

When *A Year In The Country* began in 2014, now-disappeared websites such as *Folk Horror Review*, which intermittently posted about such films and television as those mentioned above, felt like still fairly off the beaten track places: a wandering through the briars and undergrowth of a not overly harvested eldritch rural cultural landscape. This has changed somewhat in recent years.

While not quite yet an overtly mainstream genre name, as an example of how embedded folk horror has become as a descriptive phrase and cultural strand, if you should type it into a search engine then many millions of results will be returned.

Alongside which, a focal point of interest such as the website and social media group *Folk Horror Revival* has an online following which at the point of writing numbered in five figures, and in 2016 hosted its *Otherworldly* event at The British Museum.

Folk horror has also become a legitimate area of academic research as shown by conferences/events such as *The Alchemical Landscape* and A *Fiend in the Furrows*, which have concentrated on associated areas of study, accompanied by screenings of related film and television.

Meanwhile, probably the most well known folk horror cultural artifact, The Wicker Man,[6] seems to have passed from cult to mainstream acceptance and become part of the canon of respected British cinema, with almost endless reissues of its soundtrack, DVDs and Blu-rays and regular inclusion in Top British Film lists.

In wider culture elements and influences of folk horror can be found in a number of areas and projects.

This is particularly so within music, including the sometimes Midwich -ian or Nigel Kneale-esque parallel worlds of Ghost Box Records and projects such as *The Book of the Lost* (2014) and *Tales from the Black Meadow* (2013),[7] which alongside other elements featured music intended to accompany imagined, layered backstories which draw from the tropes of folk horror.

A song such as She Rocola's "Burn The Witch" (released in 2014 by A Year In The Country) and its glacial, haunting tale of love and persecution could well be a soundtrack to a lost classic British folk horror film: one which may have accompanied the canonic trio of such things back when.

In a wider cultural sense, lines could be drawn from the reinterpreting of traditional folkloric, sometimes non-Christian pagan interests and music that Paul Giovanni and Magnet created for the soundtrack of The Wicker Man and more recent explorations of acid, psych, leftfield, wyrd, exploratory or underground folk such as Sproatly Smith, The Hare And The Moon and The Owl Service.

While the Marshlight Software computer game *Edgelands* (2017) takes folk horror themes into interactive realms and is described as a psychogeographical folk tale:

> "Magic and folklore… entangle the modern world… in an uncanny rustic adventure… Tapping into the sense of overwhelming feelings that being in a particular landscape can give you and exploring the idea that these feelings are related to some intangible forces that are deeply rooted in that landscape… you soon find yourself exploring an uncanny rustic twilight landscape in which familiar rural landmarks overlap with otherworldly occurrences, creating a dream-like blurring of the ordinary and the supernatural."

Over the years from but a few seedlings, folk horror as a cultural strand has created ever growing reverberations that are still being felt throughout culture and indeed which may now only be truly flowering and finding fully fertile ground.

1. These themes are also discussed in Chapter 16.
2. Such inclinations are also referred to in Chapter 7.
3. Discussed in Chapter 11.
4. Discussed in Chaper 45.
5. Discussed in Chapter 23.
6. Discussed in Chapter 10.
7. Discussed in Chapter 9.

7

1973: A Time of Schism and a Dybbuk's Dozen of Fractures

A *Year In The Country* has often meandered over to the year 1973 and the culture that was produced around that time, and this has been reflected and explored, both in posts at the main website and a related album release.

When perusing culture later than this particular year it is often the case that something in its spirit or atmosphere represents a move towards a sea change in society and the associated political, social and economic realignment.

With earlier work, particularly from around 1970, there still tends to be a 1960s psych/mod sharpness to it; culture from that time did not yet seem to have become a reflection of the end of a period of optimism and could be regarded as being from a society that was not yet fully struggling with the changes and aftermath from the resulting hangover or comedown.

In 2016 as part of A Year In The Country, the themed conceptual compilation album *Fractures* was released, which took as its inspiration 1973 as a particular cultural and historical juncture and explored related themes. Below is a section of the sleeve notes for the album:

> "Fractures is a gathering of studies and explorations that take as their starting point the year 1973: a time when there appeared to

be a schism in the fabric of things, a period of political, social, economic and industrial turmoil, when 1960s utopian ideals seemed to corrupt and turn inwards.

As a reaction to such, this was a possible high water mark of the experimentations of psych/acid folk, expressions of eldritch undertones in the land via what has become known in part as folk horror and an accompanying yearning to return to an imagined pastoral idyll.

Looking back, culture, television broadcasts and film from this time often seem imbued with a strange, otherly grittiness; to capture a sense of dissolution in relation to what was to become post-industrial Western culture and ways of living.

When viewed now, such transmissions and signals can seem to belong to a time far removed and distant from our own; the past not just as a foreign country but almost as a parallel universe that is difficult to imagine as once being our own lands and world.

Fractures is a reflection on reverberations from those disquieted times, taking as its initial reference points a selected number of conspicuous junctures and signifiers."

In the album sleeve notes, some notable events and cultural productions were then listed, which are gathered below, together with other appropriate points of interest from 1973 which were originally included in a related post on the A Year In The Country website.

Together they form a dybbuk's or devil's dozen (ie. 13) of those junctures and signifiers and provide a glimpse into part of the character of that point in time which was undoubtedly an era of schism.

1) Electronic music innovator and pioneer Delia Derbyshire left The BBC and the BBC Radiophonic Workshop: she deliberated later that around then "the world went out of time with itself".
2) Electricity blackouts in the UK: these were due to industrial

conflicts and the resulting restrictions on power production, with a state of emergency and the three day working week being declared by the then-government in order to attempt to conserve energy supplies.

3) *The Wicker Man* film was released: quite possibly *the* touchstone for all things interconnected to A Year In The Country, explorations of an otherly Albion and the flipside or undercurrents of folkloric culture. It is also possibly in part an ambiguous reflection of 1960s countercultural urges and explorations gone wayward or bad in its depiction of the pagan, permissive attitudes and transgressive activities of the islanders in the film.

4) *The Changes* children's television series was recorded but remained unreleased: its plot concerns a world that has undergone a form of induced psychosis, resulting in the rejecting and destroying of all modern technology and a return to an almost medieval or feudal way of life, one in which the sound of the combustion engine has become the mark of the devil and overhead power or communication lines are known as "the bad wires".

The suspicion is that it was considered a little too close to home in the year it was produced to be considered appropriate broadcast material for a nation huddled around candles due to electricity shortages and a three-day working week.

5) Richard Mabey's *The Unofficial Countryside* book was published: an early and influential study of transitional/liminal edgeland spaces and where the city meets nature.

6) *The Spirit of Dark and Lonely Water* was released: probably the definitive hauntological public information film - all scattered debris, a ghostly black-clad figure and the distinctively chilling voice of Donald Pleasance in a film intended to warn children of the dangers of careless or foolhardy behaviour near water but which had the effect of traumatising considerable swathes of its viewers.

Public information films were short government sponsored/produced films for television broadcasting which were intended to give advice, information and warnings to the general public. Their sometimes odd or unsettling atmosphere has meant that they have gained a cult interest.

These films, along with a number of other items in this dybbuk's dozen, have become particular touchstones or ongoing points of interest, inspiration and fascination for what has come to be known as hauntology and in particular a connected sense of an eerie, unsettled or even at times macabre atmosphere.

7) *Psychomania* film was released: Nicky Henson stars as the leader of a gang of returned from the grave zombie motorcyclers who terrorise the locals in rural and small town 1970s Britain.

This is a curiously British, low key and understated take on biker and other myths that seems far removed from say the often glamorous cinematic presentations of American biker culture; it includes portrayals of dabbling in the black arts but the overall effect seems more to represent a society where even such occult activities have an air of not so much an attempt at empowering dissoluteness but rather an enfeebled dissolution.

8) Sometime Fairport Convention and Trader Horne member Judy Dyble stepped back from making music; her departure from music could well be filed alongside that of Delia Derbyshire's and for a number of years she would become one of the lost voices of British exploratory folk music from the later 1960s and earlier 1970s, alongside the likes of Vashti Bunyan and Shelagh Macdonald.

9) The Michael Fassbinder-directed German television series *World on a Wire* was released; this was a rather prescient representation of virtual reality and also in the world it created went curiously against the grain of more gritty, murky atmospheres which were often prevalent in films and television of the time.

10) The film *Soylent Green* was released: this was part of a film

mini-genre of ecology and resources having gone to heck in a handbasket which was prevalent in the 1970s. Spoiler alert: "Soylent Green is people". Make room, make room.

11) *The Final Programme* film was released: it is mentioned previously about films released prior to 1973 often seeming as though they still contained elements of 1960s psych/mod sharpness: however, this is something of a cuckoo in the nest.

Based on Michael Moorcock's 1968 novel, which was written in 1965 as that decade's underground culture began to more noticeably gain form and later prominence, the film shows decadence having tipped over into darkness as was often the way with culture from around 1973.

However it also seems to connect more directly with 1960s culture, particularly in terms of its dandified, frilly shirted, counter-cultural anti-hero and pop-art-esque giant-sized pinball table set.

12) *Blue Blood* film was released: the plot involves a debauched young aristocrat who entrusts the running of his estate to his butler, played by a glowering Oliver Reed, who begins to control and dominate his master and appears to possibly have demonic intent.

The film shares some similar territory to the corrupt, insular decadence of the 1970 film *Performance* (and maybe a touch of 1963's *The Servant* in the way that power balances blur and tip between master and servant) but with a background of truth: the book it was based on was written by an actual British lord whose stately home the film was shot at, who kept multiple "wifelets" and had a tendency for redecorating the manor house with self-created erotic, provocative murals.

Who knows if this particular celluloid story would be made today? "Unsettling" and "troubling" are words that come to mind.

13) The initial deadline for Nigel Kneale to deliver the script for the final *Quatermass* series: looking back, this series and its depiction

of a society which was in a state of collapse seems in part to be a reflection of a continuum of real world societal strife throughout the 1970s.

8

Broadcast: Recalibration, Constellation and Exploratory Pop

The band, Broadcast, formed in Birmingham, England in 1995 and have featured a number of different members and collaborators, including Roj Stevens, Steve Perkins and Tim Felton, with the core of the band being James Cargill and Trish Keenan.

They are an odd, intriguing cuckoo in pop's nest; they have been described as avant-pop, which is probably heading along the right lines. Their recordings feature a mixture of electronic and acoustic elements, melodic pop and more experimental audio techniques.

While their work as a whole connects with, signposts, layers, explores and takes inspiration from a wide variety of cultural reference points, including psychedelia and Czech New Wave film, although this is more in a reinterpreted rather than recreated manner.

Their album *Broadcast and the Focus Group Investigate Witchcults of the Radio Age* from 2009 was something of an early research and reference point for *A Year In The Country.* It explores a number of pathways that have come to be a part of or an influence on the project; from half-remembered (or misremembered), half-seen television of my youth to the undercurrents and flipside of pastoral concerns.

The album is a collaboration between Broadcast, the members of which at this point were James Cargill and Trish Keenan and their longstanding visual collaborator/designer Julian House (of Ghost Box

Records) working under the name of his musical project The Focus Group; it is a music box collage of the "classic" dream-like exploratory pop sound of Broadcast and the jump-cut, woozy, disorientating loops and sampling techniques of The Focus Group.

Exploring connections to the album led to an interview with James Cargill of Broadcast by website *XLR8R* in November 2009 around the time of the Witch Cults release, wherein he talks of drawing from witchcraft references but not taking it too seriously, more as a pulp cultural reference point by way of older horror films such as 1968's *Curse of the Crimson Altar.*

(Related to which some of the audio sources that form Witch Cults appear to be in part previous era's exploitation-esque witchcraft orientated pseudo-documentaries.)

Cargill also discusses how British children's television of the late 1960s and 1970s such as *Children of the Stones* (1976), *Sky* (1975) and *The Owl Service* (1969) and their odd, sometimes unsettling, "why were they like that when they were intended to be viewed by children?" atmospheres were also a reference point for the album.

He comments that he only half remembers the programmes, that they are just fragments of memory and that is part of the attraction of them, he does not want to know everything about them and how having watched them on breaking up television receptions or an old faded video recording added something to the aspects which made the memory of them interesting.

That half-remembered sense of programmes from youth was an early ongoing theme of A Year In The Country; there are television programmes which I only saw in snatches at the time, but which intrigued me for years and partially led to the creation of the project.

One example of children's television which dealt with unsettling, challenging themes and which I just glimpsed at the time is the speculative fiction series *Noah's Castle* from 1979.[1] This reflected and extrapolated from then-national worries and conflicts, taking as its core the surprisingly serious and adult subjects of hyper inflation, societal collapse and food shortages in contemporary Britain.

Partly through only knowing about or remembering them in a fragmentary manner, over the years some of such programmes existed for this author merely as loosely defined themes and concepts; that not fully knowing meant that they had space to gain layers of interest and mystique.

Watching them now that could sometimes be dispelled, or the experience was closer to viewing a completely different programme to my hazy or misremembered cultural memory of them.

This may in part be a result of an aspect of the programmes that James Cargill comments on in the above XLR8R interview, where he says that in order to watch these shows you need to recalibrate yourself, as these previous era's broadcasts had a different, slower pace; the modern mind and viewer is not necessarily always geared towards their rhythms.

Alongside which it is also possible that related misremembered cultural memories have already been effectively subconsciously recalibrated, which may heighten the sense of disjuncture when rewatching the actual programmes and their use of different rhythms and pacing.

The introduction sequences to such series can seem to capture and conjure that misremembered spirit in a condensed form without the need for a form of recalibration.

Along which lines, an interesting starting point for exploring such things if you are new to them is the introduction to The Owl Service television series.[2]

This layers a gently tinkling melody, dissonant noise, pastoral scenes, a flickering solitary candle against a blackened background, pulsing geometric shapes, hand shadow games and a mirrored illustration where the same elements can be seen as both owls and flowers.

Viewed today it feels like an almost otherworldly flipside of folklore and the landscape communique from another time.

Interconnecting Broadcast and their interests and inspirations with such things, in 2007 when Trish Keenan and James Cargill appeared as guest record selectors on Jonny Trunk's *OST* radio show,[3] amongst their selections they included the music from the introduction sequences for both The Owl Service and Children of the Stones.

Trish Keenan of Broadcast has been quoted as saying that the avant-garde without the popular can be rubbish, the popular without the avant-garde can be rubbish, which could almost be seen as a manifesto for the group and their work: their exploration and blurring of the boundaries between the two.

Witch Cults more overtly steps towards the avant-garde than pop or popular music but if you should want to hear a melding of those two sides then a visit to their *Mother is the Milky Way* release from 2009 may well be the thing to do.

It is not the easiest of records to obtain as it was released and sold only during a selection of live dates, has never had a full widely commercially available release and is probably one of the rarest of their artifacts.

It is in fact one of those relatively occasional items that are genuinely rare in these days of general second hand ubiquity via online sales or the further corners of online digital music.

Despite its EP or mini-album running time, it is more of an album, possibly because by the record's end it appears to have explored, created or conjured a world, themes and atmosphere that the space within a longer playing record would allow.

Mother is the Milky Way could be seen as the summation of a particular set of peaks and aims of Broadcasts work: a collection that gathers both their more pop and avant-garde influences, mixing, matching and balancing both sides of such things in a way that somehow makes its mixture of quite off centre jump cuts, lo-fidelity nuances, a certain dreamy surreality, dissonance, scattering and gathering of pop melodies and the use of reversed and found sounds all seem very accessible.

It also seems at times to be a very personal, intimate record and possibly some kind of insight into the actual lives of its makers (whether real and/or imagined), with the song "Elegant Elephant" in particular serving as a fond homage to a mantelpiece ornament and the memories it keeps.

Albeit it is homage to a mantelpiece ornament that in a melodically woozy way connects to James Cargill's comments and other points of reference for the band, as it variously recalls a forgotten previous era's children television series and possibly a soundtrack to a fantasia like Czech New Wave film.[4]

Czech New Wave film has been referenced and mentioned as a point of inspiration by Broadcast a number of times over the years, in particular the unsettling fairytale-like *Valerie and her Week of Wonders* (1970). On their 2003 album *Haha Sound* the song "Valerie" was inspired by the film and its soundtrack album which was released in 2006 by Finders Keepers Records featured sleeve notes by Trish Keenan, in which she wrote:

> "Not since *The Wicker Man* has a soundtrack occupied my mind like Valerie and her Week of Wonders. It was like a door had been opened in my subconscious and fragments of memories and dreams rejoiced right there in my living room."

In its use of the sounds of nature and in particular the gentle ambling of "Milling Around The Village", the Mother is the Milky Way album may also be a pointer towards the post-Broadcast undercurrents of folklore and at points pagan-influenced work of Children Of Alice.

This music project features Broadcast members and collaborators past and present James Cargill, Julian House and Roj Stevens and their music initially appeared on various Folklore Tapes releases between 2013 and 2016, which were collected on a Warp Records-released album in 2016. (Apart from a couple of early singles most of the Broadcast releases have also been on Warp Records.)

The visual elements of Broadcast's work, including the packaging of their albums, videos and live projections have been an inherent part of their exploratory avant-pop nature.

Generally this aspect has been instigated and/or created by Julian House, at points to varying degrees in collaboration with the band and for Witch Cults they produced the *#1: Witch Cults* and *#2: I See, So I See So* videos, which feature two of the more conventional songs on the album.

Julian House's video work for Ghost Box Records, of which he is the co-founder, often features a signature style that includes mandalas, Op art graphics, rapidly changing layered and dissolving images and psychedelic lights and patterns, all of which make an appearance in these two videos.

These bring together many of the above and other strands that can be found in Broadcast's work, being layered, occult (in the sense of hidden) collages of the land, bucolia as imagined through a lysergic glass darkly and pop filtered through the avant-garde.

They may also act as signposts towards the more pastoral concerns of Mother is the Milky Way and then once again onto Children Of Alice in their phantasmagorical representation of rural settings.

Of the two #1: Witch Cults is the more overtly surreal, with the normal world and its colours very rarely making an appearance and the video containing imagery which seems to invoke a sense of an otherworldly rural summoning.

The video features (presumably) Trish Keenan's silhouette flickering and strobing in the landscape in ritualistic stances, as the natural world melds and dissolves into an unsettling almost psychedelic set of images before the more conventional melody of the song also dissolves to become a gently unsettling set of tinkling noises accompanied by what may be roaring wind.

The final section of the video promises a return to the ease and calm of an almost natural world and sunset with the reappearance of the lone silhouetted figure in a windswept landscape but it is only the promise as once again the imagery melds and layers to become some kind of ritualistic summoning.

#2: I See, So I See So is more obviously set in a recognisable real, realist or natural world, but it is still very much a view through the looking glass.

Connecting back again to James Cargill's comments about children's television broadcasts from earlier eras and their unsettled atmospheres, the video and its layering of geometric shapes, objects and the natural world brings to mind the introduction sequences of the likes of *The Tomorrow People* (1973-1979) and possibly The Owl Service or maybe some flipside *Camberwick Green*-esque (1966) animation series and seems to shadow, layer and reflect such things but without being a replication.

At one point a crudely rendered orb flies across the screen, from a room to outside a building, out into the countryside and almost to a child's hand, which calls to mind an effect from a 1960s or 1970s Children's Film Foundation release of some flying creature, spirit or visiting alien.

Elsewhere in the video a box is filled with objects, shapes and a staring disembodied eye, which also seem to connect back to a previous era's children's television, although it is a view of such things through an avant-garde, experimental film co-op filter.

As mentioned previously the songs which accompany these videos are two of the more conventional songs on Witch Cults. However, they still contain elements of the collaging and jump cuts that characterise the album as a whole, of which and in reference to Broadcast's collaborative work with Julian House on the Witch Cults album the following has been said:

> "(Julian) House is a fan of the inadvertent avant-gardness of 'bad' or 'clunky' design, as seen in Polish movie posters or library music sleeves. He intentionally achieves similar effects through 'bad looping, looped samples that change their start and end points'. With visual collage there's a way in which images that are cut out 'badly', maybe with bits of their background or surrounding image, make it difficult to discern where one part of the collage begins and another ends. This *trompe l'oeil* effect (a visual illusion)

brings you deeper into the collage, confuses your ability to discern images as surface."[5]

"...assembled using a sampling method which makes a virtue of its imperfection. (Julian) House evidently delights in the inexact fit, the abrupt cut, and for the most part, the rhythms on Witch Cults are irregular, giddily tripping over themselves and each other. In drawing attention to the awkwardness of each edit, House does not demystify the art of sampling so much as emphasise its position at the intersection of magic and science..."[6]

It is difficult to fully describe or categorise Broadcast's work on the likes of Witch Cults and Mother is the Milky Way but in the above article Joseph Stannard describes it as "occult pop laden with pagan psychedelia", which along with the earlier mentioned avant-pop description, is again probably heading in the right direction.

Psychedelia and 1960s influences are often mentioned in reference to Broadcast, in particular the influence of the group The United States of America, whose solo eponymous album released in 1968 melded elements of melodic pop music, psychedelia, the avant-garde and art rock in a manner not dissimilar at points to Broadcast.

However, as with the references to older television series, the psychedelic elements to be found in Broadcast's work are not a slavish recreating of times gone by, rather such things are seen at an oblique angle, reimagined rather than revisited.

The music they have released is both contemporary and also seems to belong to some separate time and place all of its own, with psychedelia incorporated in a manner nearer to an explorative portal then rosy-eyed nostalgia:

"I'm not interested in the bubble poster trip, 'remember Woodstock' idea of the sixties. What carries over for me is the idea of

> psychedelia as a door through to another way of thinking about sound and song. Not a world only reachable by hallucinogens but obtainable by questioning what we think is real and right, by challenging the conventions of form and temper."[7]

The sense of culture as a doorway or portal has been a theme which has recurred around Broadcast's work; as mentioned earlier Trish Keenan used not dissimilar language when discussing Valerie and her Week of Wonders.

Connected to the earlier-mentioned sense of misremembering, in the above interview Joseph Stannard describes Broadcast's songs as often resembling memories, of being similar to distant, fuzzy impressions of an emotion, time or place while Trish Keenan describes such things as being formed from imaginary time travel: a way of creating music where time and space dissolve to create shadowy, faint impressions through clouded lenses.

It is the underpinning of their work by such faint, clouded impressions that is part of what is so intriguing about Broadcast; associated interviews, videos and imagery do not seem to be purely merely another aspect of standard promotional exercises but rather to belong to an overall process of multi-layered cultural exploration and inquiring, a tumbling and delving through the looking glass and sometimes hidden sides of things.

Mark Fisher in his 2014 book *Ghost of my Life* talks about how it is the culture that surrounds and constellates around music that has been as important as the music itself in conjuring seductively unfamiliar worlds, that during the 20th century these gatherings of culture acted as a probe for such explorations and alternatives to existing ways of living and thinking.

Broadcast are a fine, brightly shining example of such constellations and constellators and to this day continue to act as a guide to such explorations and alternative pathways of culture.

1. Discussed in Chapter 44.
2. Discussed in Chapter 11.
3. Discussed further in Chapter 38.
4. An area of cinema discussed further in Chapter 45.
5. From the article "Haunted Audio", written by Simon Reynolds and published in *Wire* magazine issue 273, November 2006.
6. Written by Joseph Stannard, in an article on/interview with Broadcast in Wire magazine, issue 308, October 2009.
7. Trish Keenan, also from the above-mentioned Wire magazine article written by Joseph Stannard.

9

Tales from the Black Meadow, The Book of the Lost and *The Equestrian Vortex*: The Imagined Spaces of Imaginary Soundtracks

OVER THE YEARS, the notion of soundtracks for imaginary films, or even visual work which creates imagery from imaginary films has often appealed. An example of such is the album *Tales from the Black Meadow* (2013).

This is part of a multi-faceted project which has taken the form of, amongst other things, books, album and video work, taking as its core story the imagined story of Professor R. Mullins who went missing in 1972 in an area known as the Black Meadow atop the North Yorkshire Moors.

The accompanying story tells of how he left behind an extensive body of work regarding his investigations of the folklore and oral history of the Black Meadow, in particular with regard to the phenomena of a local disappearing village.

As part of this fictional history within the world of the Black Meadow it is said that in 1978 Radio 4 produced a rare documentary about the folklore, mystery and tales surrounding the Black Meadow area and commissioned music for the show, which has been unearthed and released to the public.

The resulting soundtrack is available on CD as *Tales from the Black Meadow* by The Soulless Party.

Even though it is widely known that it is a created history, revisiting the project leaves some lingering doubt.

It plays with a hauntological sense of misremembered and faded cultural memories through the documentary backstory and the use of created archival material.

The soundtrack could also belong to a period television programme, the name of which cannot quite be remembered, but which is possibly a forgotten, somewhat unsettling series, something that may belong in similar territory as *Tales of the Unexpected* (1979-1988), but as if it was created by Nigel Kneale.

A further example of such imagined soundtracks is *The Book of the Lost* (2014): a collaboration between Emily Jones and The Rowan Amber Mill. As a project it draws from the folk horror likes of *The Wicker Man* (1973), *Witchfinder General* (1968), *Blood on Satan's Claw* (1971) and *Psychomania* (1973) and creates a world and backstory for the resulting music.

Instead of an imagined documentary as is the case with Tales from the Black Meadow, The Book of the Lost creates the soundtrack to episodes from an imagined period television series, which are called to life via the project and accompanied by details of their casts, synopsis, crew, production companies etc.

The backstory says that these films would have been broadcast as part of a late night television series called The Book of the Lost, from which the album took its name.

The setting is reminiscent of early 1970s British portmanteau horror: the type that often featured Joan Collins. In particular, *Tales from the Crypt* (1972) or *Tales That Witness Madness* (1973), films which have a certain period charm, entertainment value and cultural interest but which also reflected a time when British cinema was tumbling and hurtling towards its own demise via its focus on cheap exploitation fare, sex comedies or schlock and horror.

Along loosely similar lines is *The Equestrian Vortex*: a film-within-a-film that appears in Peter Strickland's cinematically released 2012 film *Berberian Sound Studio*; this is set in and around 1970s Italian giallo[1] film culture, creating the phantasmagorical closed world of a recording studio which is being used to produce the sound effects for that film.

As with The Book of the Lost, it draws from many of the classic tropes of folk horror and lists credits for an imagined cast, director, soundtrack and so forth.

Created by Julian House of Ghost Box Records/Intro design agency and soundtracked by Broadcast, The Equestrian Vortex appears purely as an introductory sequence created using found imagery and via sound effects in Berberian Sound Studio but without ever showing the actual film. It offers a brief window into the complete film; when watching it, there is a wish to see the full-length version, to seek out something that logically does not exist.

This is a reflection of the strength of such work as the above-imagined soundtracks and films; they present only glimpses and fragments of the imagined worlds, tales and histories that they are said to come from, drawing on shared and sometimes faded cultural memories, leaving the viewer/listener space to weave, create and imagine the fully finished programmes and films.

It may not be merely budgetary or resource constraints that stop practitioners from creating whole new films or programmes, as work along these lines can be more part of a process of interacting with, distilling and capturing the spirit of the original programmes and films.

They could be seen as expressions of an urge to remember, misremember, reinterpret, rehabilitate, create and recreate connected themes, sounds and imagery: a way in which to summon or revisit the thoughts, visions and journeys that they have inspired rather than creating or attempting picture perfect simulacra of fully-realised episodes of television programmes and finished feature films.

1. Giallo refers to an Italian thriller genre which peaked in popularity during the 1970s, sometimes containing elements of supernatural horror and in which often transgressive and violent actions were often accompanied by distinctive aesthetics and cinematic stylishness.

10

The Wicker Man: Notes on a Cultural Behemoth

OVER THE YEARS, since initial small box office returns and relatively low level distribution, the 1973 film *The Wicker Man*, directed by Robin Hardy, from a screenplay by Anthony Shaffer, has become something of a towering cult celluloid behemoth. This is particularly the case amongst all things on the flipside of folkloric, as well as within areas of culture that have come to be known as folk horror.

As a brief precis (please note, the following text contains spoilers), the film tells of an insular, isolated island which is visited by a devoutly Christian police sergeant who is investigating the report of a missing child. He is lead on a merry chase by the island's inhabitants and their aristocratic leader Lord Summerisle, being variously frustrated, tempted and incensed by the islands uninhibited pagan belief system, before being sacrificed by the islanders who believe that doing so will ensure the return of good harvests.

The casting of the film includes Edward Woodward, who plays Sergeant Howie and was known for playing "Callan" on British television, iconic Hammer Horror actor/Dracula portrayer Christopher Lee who plays Lord Summerisle and a varied casting for the other islanders.

These include Ingrid Pitt, who was also known for Hammer Horror roles, other well known actresses such as Diane Cilento and future Bond Girl Britt Ekland, alongside dancer, actor, teacher, mime artist and choreographer Lindsay Kemp.

Local people from the area where filming took place were also cast as islanders, and uncredited roles were played by the director and screenwriter. The film also includes appearances by Paul Giovanni and Gary Carpenter, who were involved in the creation of the soundtrack.

At its heart, The Wicker Man could be viewed as a mystery thriller, although in actuality it is a film which defies categorisation, mixing elements of fantasy, horror and musical.

Within its enclosed rural setting it intertwines folkloric practices, pagan rituals, reimagined and reinterpreted traditional and folk music, unfettered sexuality and an older religious faith in conflict with a more contemporary Christian belief system.

These elements, along with a background of its at-times troubled production and distribution, have come to create a heady mixture, which includes imagery and a soundtrack that have gained iconic status and the creation of an almost myth-like set of stories and reference points which surround it and that have reverberated throughout wider culture.

Cultural tales such as those told in The Wicker Man and other cinema, television and media via technological means could now be considered to form our modern-day folklore, folktales and myth.

Such tales can at times become our totems and the physical media that contain them our contemporary secular sacraments and none more so than The Wicker Man.

Due to the ease of digital recording, reproduction, backup and copying we are living in an age where there is a loss of loss (to semi-quote writer and lecturer Mark Fisher) with most forms of media being able to be preserved intact for posterity in one form or another.

However The Wicker Man is from a previous era, where recordings were stored on potentially fragile and more easily disposed of or damageable physical media.

This is one of the aspects of the film that continues to fascinate; the stories around how a complete, high quality version of the film no longer seems to exist, owing in part to the film being re-edited at the original time of its release by the production company and allegedly footage being discarded.

The film has developed its own inner mythology, part of which tells of film canisters used as filler below motorways, of versions of the film being sent abroad and then disappearing and so on.

The background to this is that The Wicker Man had a convoluted production and was produced during an unsettled time in the British film industry.

British Lion Films who produced the film were in financial trouble at that time and the company was bought by wealthy businessman John Bentley who, in order to convince the unions that he was not planning on asset stripping the company, quickly put the film into production.

This meant that, although set in spring, filming began in October 1972, meaning that artificial leaves and blossoms had to be glued to trees in some scenes and extras had to suck ice cubes in order that their breath could not be seen in the cold air.

By the time of the film's distribution, British Lion had been bought by EMI and was managed by Michael Deeley; it has been alleged by Christopher Lee amongst others that Deeley hated the film, was not interested in its success and it is thought that the company could not figure on how to sell this genre-straddling film to audiences.

The producers of the film enacted creative control over the finished version, removing director Robin Hardy from his duties and editor Eric Boyd-Perkins was tasked with making cuts to the film, which resulted in extensive sections being removed from its 99 minute running time and a much shorter 87 minute version ultimately being cinematically released.[1]

Over time, various versions of the film have been seen by audiences at the cinema, on television and via DVD/Blu-ray, including a 96 minute Middle Version that was theatrically released in 1979 after having been reassembled by Robin Hardy from a version that had been sent to US film producer, director and actor Roger Corman in the early 1970s.

In 2002 a Director's Cut (or Long Version) was released on DVD, assembled by Eric Boyd-Perkins and Robin Hardy and running at 95 minutes, but which still had a number of sequences missing and with some of the reinserted footage being of lower quality due to the original source material no longer being available.

In 2013 a "40th Anniversary" - possibly misleadingly named - Final Cut of the film, running at 91 minutes, was released cinematically as well as on DVD and Blu-ray.

This was not a complete, cinematic quality version of the film but rather an intermediate director-approved version which, as with earlier restored versions, featured segments which had varying levels of reproduction due to original source materials not being available.

In one sense, the sections where the quality varies are appealing; the shift in quality can give these scenes a slightly surreal, almost parallel plains of 3D or cutout look, similar to the effect that viewing a faded set of images through a Viewmaster children's toy might do.

It would be interesting to see the entire film represented in this manner, to step away from the ongoing quest for a picture perfect representation of the tales of The Wicker Man and to embrace its otherworldliness more overtly with regards to its visual presentation.

While waiting for an actual final complete version there have been an ever-proliferating number of re-releases of the film and its soundtrack that have been released on video tape, DVD, Blu-ray, CD and vinyl, along-side period and modern associated posters, trading cards, books, zines, magazine articles and so forth.

The resulting releases have become part of a whole not-so-mini industry that could keep industrious collectors busy but there are a few related items of particular interest.

One is *Willow's Songs*: an album released in 2009 by unearthers of rare and sometimes previously lost recordings Finders Keepers Records and which aims to showcase the British folk songs that inspired the soundtrack to The Wicker Man.

Traditional song "Highland Lament", a different version of which accompanies the opening scenes of the film, is the standout track. A case where one song is worth the price of entry on its own.

Its lyrics tell a tale of agricultural dispossession and intriguingly it is not credited to a performer on the album, which in these times of instant knowledge about almost everything via online searches adds a certain appealing mystique that this author is loath to puncture.

As is often the way with Finders Keepers' releases, the album is rather nicely packaged, and includes hauntingly ethereal photographs of folk dancers, which once upon a time were probably just ordinary snapshots, but as can be the way sometimes the passing of time has added layers and patinas of intrigue to the photographs.

The soundtrack to The Wicker Man was variously composed, arranged and recorded by Paul Giovanni and the band Magnet (which was assembled by the film's Associate Musical Director Gary Carpenter), with some sections also being performed by members of the cast and it mixes traditional songs, original compositions by Paul Giovanni and nursery rhymes.

One of the curious things with The Wicker Man soundtrack (and indeed the film itself) is that this is a case of where something authentic has been created from an inauthentic or commercially-orientated premise.

The soundtrack has come to feel as though it features songs which have belonged to these isles for centuries: ones which are deeply rooted in the land, its folklore and history, when in fact a number of them were written and all were recorded especially for the film.

This could be looked upon askance as not being historically authentic but such communal cultural tales all must have a beginning and maybe in the past were conjured literally from the air and mind in a similar manner, differing only in their technological recording and dissemination.[2]

As referred to at the start of this chapter, in culturally mediated times the stories contained within celluloid, vinyl, digital data etc. may have become our communal or folk culture: one which is passed from person to person in a similar way that oral and folk culture once would have been, with The Wicker Man being an expression and reflection of such processes.

Finders Keepers Records also reissued *Ritual* in 2011, which is the 1967 book by David Pinner, the basic idea and structure of which was in part the inspiration for what became The Wicker Man after David Pinner sold the film rights of the book to future Wicker Man cast member Christopher Lee in 1971.

In both, a police officer attempts to investigate reports of a missing child in an enclosed rural area and has to deal with psychological trickery, seduction, ancient religious and ritualistic practices.

The Finders Keepers reissue contains an introduction by writer and musician Bob Stanley called "A Note On Ritual", which serves as an overview of and background to this very particular slice of literature which deals with pastoral otherlyness, the flipside and undercurrents of bucolia and folklore:

> "...be warned, like The Wicker Man, it is quite likely to test your dreams of leaving the city for a shady nook by a babbling brook." (Bob Stanley on Ritual from the introduction.)

It opens with a sense of how nature can come to almost dwarf you and of how our layers of urban and modern security can easily be dismissed by the ways and whiles of nature.

His introduction captures and conjure the stories and atmosphere of the novel, summoning a sense of the potential wildness of rural life and ways and in its expression of this seems to almost exist as a thing unto itself, separate from the following pages.

Over a number of years Bob Stanley has been collecting and writing about particular niche and at times overlooked areas of music and culture and has curated a number of related compilation albums.

One of these is his *Gather in the Mushrooms* compilation of 1968 to

1974 acid, psych or underground folk[3] and which in terms of dealing with the flipside of the landscape and folk culture could well be considered a companion piece to his Ritual introduction.

It also links more directly to The Wicker Man in that its opening track is an instrumental version of the song "Corn Riggs" by Magnet, the vocal version of which is included in the film's soundtracks.

The Wicker Man has been extensively written about over the years, both online and in print, including Allan Brown's entertaining and extensive unearthing and researching of the background and myths that surround the film in his book *Inside The Wicker Man: How Not to Make a Cult Classic* (originally published in 2000 and revised in 2010 post the 2006 Hollywood remake).

A concise and revealing look at the film is also included in the 2002 book *Your Face Here* by Ali Catterall and Simon Wells. This was published just after the turn of the millennium and takes a wander through British cult films since the 1960s, dedicating a chapter to each and alongside The Wicker Man it includes chapters on amongst others *Blow Up* (1966), *If...* (1968), *Performance* (1970), *Get Carter* (1971), *Clockwork Orange* (1971), *Quadrophenia* (1979) and *Withnail & I* (1987).

There is a rigour to the research in the book without it stepping into the sometimes drier grounds of academia and the text reflects a genuine love for and appreciation of these films.

The list of films the book features may seem like a fairly obvious selection of cult films, a canon of such things that have been written about and discussed extensively elsewhere but this is not a book which is written by rote or which only reproduces previously well visited stories.

The authors have put in a considerable amount of footwork: visiting locations, interviewing a wide variety of associated participants and bringing forth something of a wealth of new information and connections and it acts as an in-depth precis of the story of the themes, production, loss and part-refinding of the film.

Your Face Here was published after Trunk Records made the soundtrack of The Wicker Man available for the first time in 1998, around the same time that the longer Director's Cut version of the film was released on DVD in 2002 but before the more recent Final Cut version was reissued on DVD/Blu-ray, the Hollywood remake or its semi-sequel *The Wicker Tree* (2011) were released.

This timescale has given the chapter in the book an extra level of historical interest as it was written at a point when the film's long march towards cultural rehabilitation, inspiration and seemingly ever-increasing popularity had just started to gather pace.

In that sense, the chapter now reflects a sense of the ongoing and growing story of this now quite well harvested in one form or another film, albeit one which through its ongoing appreciation and cultural inspirations/reverberations still occupies apparently quite fertile and not yet completely unearthed or unburied ground.[4]

Of the reams of writing on The Wicker Man, Vic Pratt's article "Long Arm of the Lore" from the October 2013 issue of the BFI's *Sight & Sound* magazine is well worth seeking out (the printed magazine is now hard to find but the article is available to read at the BFI's website).

Sight & Sound magazine featured it as the lead cover article alongside an associated image from the finale of The Wicker Man and the strapline "Still burning after forty years" (it was published at the time when the earlier mentioned 40th Anniversary Final Cut edition was released).

The article intertwines the cultural and historical context of the film, the romance of analogue recording techniques and the inner and wider myth and folkloric aspects of it, while the section below connects with my earlier comments regarding wanting to see a version of the film "reinterpreted" in the manner of the aesthetics of the degraded sections, rather than seeking a perfect, complete and final release.

> "The archivists among us surely long to see a fully restored version of the film derived from 35mm elements and the new Final Cut should almost provide that, bar a few mainland minutes. Yet

folklorists must surely enjoy the flawed long version; that old variation in quality, the sudden grainy sequences, are textural scars that remind us of a chequered past. The multigenerational flaws of decades-old transfer technologies are embedded in the images. Forever incomplete, with something added, something removed, like an old folk ditty with lyrics honed and melodies reshaped by time, The Wicker Man remains splendidly imperfect, the perfect folk film artifact."

The article is a refreshingly calm, considered and reflective piece of writing. In it Vic Pratt places The Wicker Man in its period cultural context of changing times and mores, considering how the children of the 1960s had grown up and taken their place in respectable society and sometimes the media, bringing or infiltrating their countercultural interests with them, possibly having lost some of their political fervour while also looking for the more authentic or spiritually fulfilling but not via traditional avenues.

The article describes how accompanying this was a sense of folk custom, witchcraft and the occult no longer being quite such marginalised or extreme interests; they had become the stuff of relatively mainstream film, television, music and publishing and a reflection of this can be seen in the themes of The Wicker Man.

Alongside which it tells of how while the early 1970s became a time of increasing permissiveness and easing of censorship, the likes of campaigner Mary Whitehouse's Nationwide Petition For Public Decency could still have a powerful effect on what could be shown in the media.

It positions The Wicker Man amongst such changes, interests, battles and debate around censorship, saying how its tales of an openly libidinous pagan isle were not able to hide behind the period settings of say *Witchfinder General* (1968); rather it contained the folk devils of the permissive society writ large on the screen in a very worryingly contemporary manner.

In many ways, both this and the issue of the magazine could be seen as a companion to the August 2010 Sight & Sound issue, which has as its cover strapline "The Films of Old, Weird Britain", accompanied by a Wicker Man-like, landscape myths and folk horror-esque illustration and features "The Pattern Under the Plough" article by Rob Young as its main feature.[5]

That article delves beneath the topsoil of British cinema to find a rich seam of films and television which take the landscape, rural ways, folklore (of the traditional and reimagined varieties) or "the matter of Britain" as their starting point.

These are productions that often wander off through a celluloid and cathode landscape which the article describes as one where an older, weirder Albion peeps through the cracks or that have a "sense of the past lying just behind the present" and which is a description that could be applied to The Wicker Man and the folkloric practices and rituals of its pagan islanders.

Alongside Vic Pratt's article, it further contextualises The Wicker Man, placing it alongside other such folk horror films as *Witchfinder General.*

It then goes on to consider an interrelated loose grouping of films and television which in part explore those flipside Albionic cracks in the landscape.

These include *Winstanley* (1975) and its dramatising of historical English Civil War era searching for an earthly paradise, the journey through a rural year of *Akenfield* (1974), the almost straight documentary that also seems to quietly explore the undercurrents of the land *Sleep Furiously* (2008) and the likes of what has become part of pastoral hauntological television such as *The Changes* (1975), *The Owl Service* (1969) and *Children of the Stones* (1977).[6]

It also includes considerations of and connects the above with the art film experiments and psychogeography (a form of explorative wandering) of Derek Jarman's *Journey to Avesbury* (1971), Patrick Keiller's *Robinson in Space* (1997) and Chris Petit's *London Orbital* (2002), the atavistic memories of *Quatermass and the Pit* (1967) and the layered spectral rural history tales of *Penda's Fen* (1974).

Alongside being a companion piece to Vic Pratt's article, it could also be considered a companion to or lost chapter from Rob Young's own *Electric Eden* book from 2011 and its explorations of the intertwined connections of the undercurrents and at times flipside or further reaches of folkloric, pastoral and related music and culture.[7]

Such undercurrents and layers of folk tales, customs and histories, related explorations of an otherly Albion and their reflections within film, television, music and other culture seem to have found something of a nodal point and ongoing central repository within The Wicker Man.

It has also come to form part of a trio of films, alongside 1968's Witchfinder General and 1971's *The Blood on Satan's Claw*, which are seen as the root source or initial canon of a genre of film and other culture that is now known as folk horor; work which often mixes pastoral or rural settings, folklore, the uncanny and horror.[8]

Part of that nodal or touchstone aspect can be notably seen in areas of folk which have come to be known loosely and variously as for example wyrd, exploratory, neo or underground folk: the influences, aesthetics, tropes and roots of which can often be connected back to the film's themes and the folkloric re-imaginings of its soundtrack.

The Wicker Man has also acted as a wider source of musical inspiration and influence, branching out into more mainstream and even chart music.

The band Sneaker Pimps recorded a song called "How Do", which is a version of "Willow's Song" from The Wicker Man soundtrack and includes samples from the film.

The song is the last track on their 1996 album *Becoming X* and it was also a b-side on one of the editions of the 1997 re-release of their single "Spin Spin Sugar".

Sneaker Pimps' music was a form of left-of-centre electronic pop that was linked to the trip hop genre at the time and had a fair degree of commercial success with the album selling over a million copies and a number of Top 40 and Top 10 singles were released from it.

(Trip hop originated in Britain during the early 1990s and was a generally downbeat, atmospheric loose genre of music that often used hip hop beats, fusing them with electronica and sometimes also mixed elements of dance, soul, dub etc. The performers and bands who are well known in connection to it include Tricky, Massive Attack and Portishead.)

How Do is something of a melding of styles and elements; it opens with samples from The Wicker Man and is in part a gentle, lulling atmospheric pop song with a touch of triphop and as it progresses it increasingly incorporates swirling, almost helicopter-like electronic sounds.

It was a curious thing for a quite pop orientated band, even if a more left-of-centre one, back then to include a song from The Wicker Man soundtrack.[9] At the time of How Do's release The Wicker Man was a known film but its extended and ever growing cultdom had not really started to gather pace yet and Trunk Records' release of the soundtrack was still a couple of years away, so information about the film was probably still relatively thin on the ground.

In an interview at the time, when asked what would be his perfect film to create a soundtrack for, Chris Cornell of Sneaker Pimps said this:

> "The whole band is into a film called The Wicker Man, it's a sort of obscure 70s English film and the last track on our album, How Do, is a cover-version of a track from that film, which is originally a traditional folk tune. So, that music and filmwise is everybody's sort of favorite film and I think I would have liked to have written for that. In the future – well, I can't speak for everyone else here, but something along those lines."

In connection to information about The Wicker Man being thin on the ground at the time of How Do, is the above mention of Willow's Song being a traditional folk tune; without more information, in the setting of the film and the way in which it and the soundtrack seem to conjure in part a sense of being documents of actual folklore, it would be easy to think of it as being traditional rather than having been written specifically for the film by Paul Giovanni.

In a possible further example of the ongoing influence of the film, in 2008 Kelli Ali, who was the singer with Sneaker Pimps at the time of Becoming X, released a pastoral folk inflected album called *Rocking Horse* on record label One Little Indian, which was produced by Max Richter.[10]

Although not expecting performers to purely explore one set genre, Rocking Horse's folk direction is possibly surprising, as Kelli Ali is known more for her electronic pop work with Sneaker Pimps.

However, looking back at the above comments by Chris Cornell and on rediscovering Sneaker Pimps' cover of Willow's Song, it is less surprising and it would be possible to draw a line from them to some of the possible roots and inspirations of Rocking Horse.

After Rocking Horse Kelli Ali self-released an album called *Butterfly* in 2009, which is a more intimate, acoustic extension of Rocking Horse and in part features new versions of songs from that album.

On Butterfly there is also another version of Willow's Song, which takes it back nearer to its purely imagined folkloric roots and although being her own interpretation it is closer to how the song was performed for The Wicker Man's soundtrack than the Sneaker Pimps version and indeed would not seem all that out of place if heard amongst the other music in the film.

In a further Wicker Man connection with one time chartbound bands, Pulp included a song called "Wickerman" on their 2001 album, *We Love Life.*

Pulp were connected to the Britpop and indie genres/scenes and in the 1990s they released a number of records that reached the top or higher reaches of the British charts. Their songs often featured evocative snapshots or vignettes of every day life in an at times almost kitchen sink like manner, while also incorporating a certain offbeat take on glamour.

Russell Senior in *Freak Out the Squares*, his autobiographical book released in 2015 which focuses on his time with the band, talks about how in their pre-fame era he and other former members of Pulp went on an expedition through tunnels beneath Sheffield that were used for sluicing industrial run off, how that journey became increasingly dangerous-feeling and that it inspired the Pulp song Wickerman (which was recorded after he left).

The song is a multi-layered piece of culture, one that interweaves samples from the original The Wicker Man film soundtrack recording and hence otherly folkloric concerns, alongside a sense of urban exploration, the true life history of the band, spoken word, a certain grandiosity in its production (possibly courtesy of producer Scott Walker), the social history of Sheffield and surrounding areas and a yearning, wistful love story.

Lead singer Jarvis Cocker, who presumably wrote the lyrics, said that he used to live on The Wicker which is a street in Sheffield and so one assumes that is where the title in part comes from.

In a further connection with otherly folklore, what the real life story of the band wandering through those tunnels also brings to mind is the underground tunnel sequence in Ben Wheatley's 2011 film *Kill List*,[11] and its related occult vision of folkloric machinations; lines from which could be connected backwards to The Wicker Man and its flipside views, expressions and interpretations of folklore and an unsettled take on pastoralism.

The We Love Life album is a mixture of classic Pulp-like kitchen sink-esque observation and an interest or attempt to connect with the basics of a more natural life, particularly so in related artwork and on songs such as "The Trees" and "Sunrise".

The band also played a series of concerts in forests to support its release, with these more nature-inspired elements connecting to and fitting with the inclusion of Wicker Man-related work on the album.

Along with the above books, articles and records which explore and/or draw inspiration from The Wicker Man there are an extensive number of websites and documentaries which focus on the film.

One of the most in depth of such websites is *The Wicker Man (1973) Wikia* site which on a recent visit had 138 different pages related to the film.

Many of these have literally dozens of photographs, hundreds of pieces of information etc.: maps, autographs, scripts, newspaper articles, behind the scenes photographs, location photographs then and now, scripts, production notes, floor plans, reunion photographs, memoirs from cast and crew, images from missing scenes, fanzines, construction plans etc.

Of particular note are the images of the construction of The Wicker Man structure used in the film and also the numbered on-set and press photographs taken from contact sheets.

Even though they are on a public site these seem to offer a semi-hidden view or a glance behind the curtain of the film.

However, despite this they do not diminish the mystique or myths of the film, which can sometimes be the case with such photographs or "How We Made the Film" documentaries and DVD extras.

This is possibly because The Wicker Man has such a multi-layered set of myths around it, some of which are intrinsically connected and interwoven with the production of the film itself and related backstories, all of which have become part and parcel of its intriguing nature.

Further behind the scenes views and discussion can be found in a now quite considerable number of The Wicker Man documentaries, including those on the various DVD/Blu-ray releases of the film and also in documentaries which were originally broadcast on television.

These include:

1) *The Wicker Man/BBC Scotland on Screen* (2009), in which actor Alan Cumming wanders around the film's locations, with how they are today segueing into scenes from the film.

This features him meeting with the likes of the film's director Robin Hardy, as well as Britt Ekland's body double, one of the public house musicians who played in the film and the woman who runs the gallery where the sweet shop scene was filmed (who says something along the lines of some visiting tourists thinking that those who live in the area actually are pagans).

Alongside which Allan Brown, the aforementioned author of Inside the Wicker Man, film critic and broadcaster Andrew Collins, novelist Christopher Brookmyre and cast member Edward Woodward all appear and comment on the film and its surrounding myths and intrigues.

2) The Wicker Man episode of the BBC 4 series *Cast and Crew* (2005), which hosts a round table discussion of the film.

This features cast members Christopher Lee, Ingrid Pitt being her delightfully eccentric and expressive self (slightly embarrassing/awkward for more reserved British sensibilities to know how to cope with this), art director Seamus Flannery, associate music director Gary Carpenter and as with the *BBC Scotland on Screen* broadcast also features director Robin Hardy and Edward Woodward (who was filmed separately from the other participants).

One of the pieces of information that sticks in the mind from this documentary was Seamus Flannery saying how the actual wicker man sculpture in the film was built from pre-woven panels that were designed to be used as wind baffles in fields for sheep to shelter behind and which they bought very cheaply wholesale for just a few pounds each.

Robin Hardy also briefly mentions the successor to The Wicker Man that he was planning at the time called *May Day* (which Christopher Lee was set to appear in and who in this programme is at baritone, strident pains to make clear that it was not a sequel) and which presumably eventually became The Wicker Tree which was released in 2011.

3) *Sing Cuckoo: The Story and Influence of The Wicker Man Soundtrack*, which is available to watch online via the BFI Player and was

> recorded around the time of and connected to the BFI season *Gothic: The Dark Heart of Film* in 2014. As the title suggests this focuses on the soundtrack of the film and its reverberations throughout culture.

As WITH THE PREVIOUS two documentaries it once again features Robin Hardy and Gary Carpenter, alongside the musicians Stephen Cracknell of The Memory Band and Mike Lindsay of Tuung (who have both created and released The Wicker Man-related work) and Jonny Trunk who is variously an archival record researcher, collector, writer and was responsible for the release of the first commercial edition of The Wicker Man's soundtrack via his label Trunk Records.[12]

There is something very evocative and moving about this particular documentary and it has a certain classiness to it, a sense of a deep respect for the film both by those shown in it and from behind the camera.

Part of that is the way it is divided into titled chapters that connect with the themes of the film and its influence; Creation, Isolation, Resurrection, Inspiration and Resolution.

Who knows if it was a deliberate choice but those directly involved in the film – Robin Hardy and Gary Carpenter – are filmed against a featureless black background, whereas Jonny Trunk, Stephen Cracknell and Mike Lindsay are filmed set against tools of their trades (shelves of vinyl records and banks of modular synthesisers).

There is a touching moment when Jonny Trunk talks about how it is a shame that the soundtrack's author Paul Giovanni passed away before he could see how it had gone on to gain such an extensive following: he could have possibly even played it live.

Connected to that, there is a poignancy to all these documentaries; as the years have passed few of the principal participants featured are still alive, with Christopher Lee, Ingrid Pitt, Robin Hardy and Edward Woodward all since having passed away.

In terms of some of the reasons for the ongoing and expanding appeal of the film and its soundtrack, Stephen Cracknell makes an incisive point about how the songs have become like folk standards for young indie-folk musicians and says:

> "I think it will go on influencing people by giving them this idea of 'Wow, you can be playful and sexy and daring and scary, not just reverential with old music and make it new and vibrant'. It stands like a beacon for that really."

Which seems like a rather apt point on which to leave this chapter.

1. Edward Woodward recalls this editing being done in order that the film could be screened as the second feature as part of a double bill, with Nicolas Roeg's *Don't Look Now* also from 1973 as the top billed film.
2. Also discussed in Chapter 1.
3. Discussed in Chapter 2.
4. A topic discussed further in Chapter 6.
5. At the time of writing the article is not available at the BFI's website and the printed magazine is fairly scarce but it is well worth seeking out.
6. Discussed in Chapter 48.
7. That book is discussed further in Chapter 1.
8. Discussed further in Chapter 16.
9. Although this was not without precedent as in 1989 The Mock Turtles, who would go on to have a top 20 hit with their song "Can You Dig It?" in 1991, released the EP Wicker Man which included a version of Willow's Song titled "The Willow Song".
10. Max Richter is the producer of the once "lost-lady-of-folk" Vashti Bunyan's *Lookaftering* album from 2005, whose work is discussed in the chapter 32
11. Discussed in Chapter 16.
12. His work is discussed further in Chapter 38.

11

Robin Redbreast, The Ash Tree, Sky, The Changes, Penda's Fen, Red Shift and *The Owl Service*: Wanderings Through Spectral Television Landscapes

Robin Redbreast is a 1970 television programme, which although it was originally made and broadcast in colour, now only a black and white version is known to exist. It contains a plot and atmosphere that draw you in, grip and unsettle you.

The story involves a London-based television script editor who decides to stay in the country house that her and her partner owned after they separated. She and her friends are outsiders, visitors to the countryside; city sophisticates, all cocktails and slightly groovy clothing, who consider themselves slightly above the local rural folk.

The main female character becomes pregnant via a local man, after a one night stand.

She is slowly cut off from the outside world by the local people (who cut the phone lines, the bus drivers refuses to stop for her etc.) and she begins to worry that they plan to sacrifice her and take her child; the local's actions seem to have a ritualistic nature which may be connected to the fertility of the land.

If any of that plot sounds slightly familiar, it may be because in terms of its themes it is not dissimilar to *The Wicker Man* (1973). It is easy to assume that Robin Redbreast may have influenced The Wicker Man but I have not seen it referenced by that film's makers.

It does tread similar pathways but that may have been coincidence or it may be part of the way that similar themes can appear in different work around a particular time in culture, even though they are not directly connected with one another.

Sometimes it is as though something is in the air and in that sense Robin Redbreast could be seen to be part of a cultural arc that took in folk horror films such as The Wicker Man, the esoteric wanderings of folk music at the time and an interrelated interest in the otherly side of the landscape which was expressed in television series that explored such things from the late 1960s to mid 1970s, for example *Penda's Fen* (1974), *The Changes* (1975) and *The Owl Service* (1969).

ROBIN REDBREAST IS NOT an as-overtly visual representation of folkloric rites as say The Wicker Man is (apart from one brief moment where the locals gather, clad in folkloric attire, which could almost be a photograph by late 19th/early 20th century documenter of folk customs Benjamin Stone or a modern day re-enactment of his photographs); it does not have the broad cinematic sweep or cult musical accompaniment of that film but this is a different creature.

It is a more intimate, enclosed story, a television play with I expect a relatively small budget, a small cast and a quite limited number of locations but none the worse for it.

Talking of visual representations of such things, some of the most intriguing pieces of work leading up to and during the creation of *A Year In The Country* have been the introduction and end title sequences to some of those television series and plays from the late 1960s to mid 1970s; this probably extends to around 1980 to take in *Children of the Stones* (1977), *Sky* (1975), *The Tomorrow People* (1973-1979), *Noah's Castle* (1979), *The Omega Factor* (1979) and the final series of *Quatermass* (1979).[1]

They often seem to represent a very concise, at points quite surreal capturing of the otherly spirit of the various series, related flipside and undercurrents of bucolia, hauntological concerns and a particular era.

The intro sequence for The Tomorrow People is a collage of images that include geometric science fiction-esque shapes, a single eyeball, cosmological swirls, a hand opening and closing, a shadowy figure in a doorway etc.

It could be a mixture of the stark, darkly pastoral covers of The Modern Poets series of book covers from the 1960s and 1970s and Julian House of Ghost Box Records' design work tumbling backwards and forwards through time, filtered somehow through an almost Woolworths-esque take on such things but still having a particularly unsettling air.

The Owl Service's intro sequence mixes and layers imagery that includes tinted largely monochromatic images of the forest, pulsating geometric circles, a candle flame flickering against a black background, hands making bird silhouettes and a mirrored illustration where the same elements can be seen as both owls and flowers.

The images are soundtracked by a medieval sounding harp-like melody that recalls a gently tumbling waterfall and which is periodically interrupted by the sound of running water and what could be either a revving motorbike or possibly a chainsaw.

This conjures and creates an atmosphere which seems to hint at the land as a place layered and imbued with some unknown and possibly unknowable magic, while at the same time it has an avant-garde air to it, being nearer to say a short artist's film than something you would expect to find as the introductory section to a children's television series.

Children of the Stones' intro is presented in a more realist, visually conventional manner, though it still more than hints at flipside tales of the land.

To a soundtrack of a memorable, spectral, eldritch and wordless choir, it features multiple images of ancient standing stones, variously shown as ominous looming structures, with the sun refracting over them or in a layering of the past and present as they are pictured next to local village housing.

In these days of instant online access to knowledge about almost all culture, it can be appealing not to know about a piece of culture, but rather to enjoy and soak it up, without being overly informed about it.

In a connected manner, at times it can be interesting not to watch the series itself but just to let it and what it represents exist in the mind only; in this sense title sequences can act as hints or clues to these imaginary, unseen stories and allow the imagination to create the actual series, its tales and imagery.

Sometimes a programme or series itself feels like a separate piece of work to an imaginary version or one that was viewed long ago in youth, the images seen on rewatching bear only a passing resemblance to stored memories of the series.[2]

This author's interest in such introduction/end title sequences largely halts at programmes recorded around 1980. In a more easily definable sense, this is possibly because after around 1980 British fantasy and science fiction television began to try and compete with the slickness and spectacle of cinema blockbusters but generally could not match them, often because of budgetary restrictions and in the process it lost some of its own character or mystery.

But there is something not quite definable at play there also; compare the title sequence for the mid-1980s Tripods with its move towards a more contemporary slickness and the one for the late 1960s The Owl Service and its handcrafted, folkloric feel.

The first is part of now, of today, of here, the latter is from then, before and elsewhere.

Trying to work out why such things have become such icons or touchstones of something otherly, of hidden layers and meanings would appear to be quite a large part and parcel of the A Year In The Country journeying and cultural wandering.

Possibly the change in the two is because that point in time was a tipping point in society, its direction, aims, wants and needs; a move towards more individualistic concerns, accompanied by a move economically, politically and socially towards the right.

Programmes made up until that point somehow are imbued with an antideluvian quality, they are now broadcasts or remnants from an "other" time; in many ways, that is one of the defining features of what has become known as hauntology – a collective mourning or melancholia for this time before, these lost futures, this reaching for the stars (in a socially progressive sense).

Programmes made prior to around 1980 were produced before the beginning of the end of the sway of a certain kind of progressive modernism/utopianism thought and ideals, replaced by a monotheistic capitalist/scientific belief system.

In an interview with Michael Bonner in July 2013 for Uncut magazine, director Ben Wheatley said of series such as Penda's Fen, The Owl Service etc. that these were broadcasts which were:

> "...not afraid to put you through the emotional wringer. They were really impactful in a way that drama doesn't seem to be any more. There was no politeness about it. You felt your mind being scarred and you were never the same again afterwards... (The Owl Service) you wouldn't even fathom showing that to children now. That's what would pass as adult drama now, even quite difficult adult drama."

SKY IS ANOTHER OF those "Hmmm, what was in the water at TV commissioning meetings in the seventies to think that these were quite normal programmes for children's television?" series, which over time has grown layers of exoticism.

Of all such programmes it also perfectly captures a sense of 1970s grime and the anti-style of a country gone to seed via its parkers, flares and fake fur zip-up coat fashion.

It is a sort of rurally-set children's television version of *The Man Who Fell to Earth* (1976), with a cockney alien and ecological overtones which the promotional information describes somewhat esoterically as:

> "Out of the sky falls a youth, not of this place or time, 'part-angel, part-waif', a youth with powers he can neither control or understand... nature itself rejects him and takes on the cadaverous body of Goodchild in sinister personification of the forces of opposition... He speaks of time travellers 'Gods you call them' who had tried again and again to help the people of Earth... Sky must find the mysterious juganet, the cross-over point in time, that is the key to his return to his own dimension."

In a curiously forward-thinking manner, just to make sure that the programme would come to be connected to all things otherly Albion and hauntological, to quote one of the press releases, it was in part filmed on "such legend-rich locations as Glastonbury Tor, Avebury and Stonehenge".

Connected to such legends, although initially seeming to be nearer to some form of science fiction, the children's television series The Changes (1975) also eventually connects more with Albionic legends.

Spoiler alert: Please note that the following paragraphs reveal a considerable amount of the plot:

The series starts with a normal middle class family sitting at home as their daughter Nicky plans her homework; the weather has been strange and suddenly society is gripped by a form of madness which becomes known as The Noise, which makes the entire population destroy and fear almost all machinery and a pogrom of machine-orientated violence sweeps the nation.

The programme's narrative then follows the period after this and the journeys and experiences of Nicky who has been left behind by her fleeing parents.

As the modern cities become abandoned life returns in the countryside to an almost medieval way of life and one area which Nicky travels to is shown as being under the rule of a sword-wielding master of the village.

Black and chain-wearing louche beatnik styled robbers and brigands roam the land and at points the series wanders off into a milder version of *Witchfinder General* (1968) territory where those who are suspected of using machinery or even saying their names are seen as "wicked sinners" and considered to be witches.

In one of the memorable phrases from the series overhead electricity (and so on) cables become known as "the bad wires" and people are not able to pass underneath them as this brings a return of The Noise and the madness which compelled people to destroy technology.

The source of The Noise and the machine smashing/rejecting madness is eventually tracked down by Nicky and her companion to a form of sentient lodestone which has been uncovered in quarry workings.

Although it is not explained what this stone is or how it came to be, we are told that it had given magical powers to Merlin in ancient historical times and it is now trying to take Britain back to what it considers to be a better pre-industrial time by psychically inducing the rejection of machinery.

How on earth did this come to be made as children's entertainment? In particular the first episode where the madness has gripped mankind and the machines are being smashed in the streets: the scenes of which have an unnerving intensity.

The programme was originally made in 1973 and not broadcast until 1975. Possibly it was considered too depressing or prescient for a society that was reeling from a large amount of political, social and economic strife and the unravelling of a post-war political consensus.[3]

Connected to the above social conflict, The Changes could be seen as a reflection of some of society's fears of social breakdown at that time and the threats represented by a reliance on modern technology which needed modern fuel, which was at that time under threat due to a crisis in oil supplies.

The Changes is not an as inherently strange or exploratory programme as The Owl Service or possibly Children of the Stones but is still quite odd and worth a watch as it is an interesting document from and reflection of a particular time in British history.

Also programmes such as The Changes, the aforementioned Sky, The Owl Service etc. seem to have gained layers of otherliness with the passing of time and they now seem almost like occult (in the sense of hidden) artifacts and transmissions from some other stranger almost-parallel Britain and history.

That is possibly in part added to by the colours and nature of the images themselves; in particular with The Changes, which for a long time until a DVD release by the BFI in 2014 was not commercially available to rent or buy and the only way of viewing it were via the smudgy grey-green multiple generation ghosts of the original broadcasts.

THE CHANGES REFLECTS what seems to have been fairly prevalent topics within 1970s television; the undercurrents and flipsides of the landscape, of an air of unsettledness to rural areas accompanied by strands of folk horror.

Also, while not scientifically logical, the source of the rejection of machinery in society in the series seems to be more preternatural than strictly supernatural.

Along which lines the horrors and monsters under the bed explored in A Year In The Country have often tended to be more manmade or preternatural rather than directly supernatural; the ecological based disasters/dystopias such as can be found in *No Blade of Grass* (1970), the Cold War bunker which,[4] writer, illustrator and designer John Coulthart has said is "...a source of contemporary horror that doesn't require any supernatural component to chill the blood", the man-made end of days of *Threads* (1984) which Ben Wheatley has described possibly quite aptly as a horror film, despite its more overt speculative fact-based nature and his own *Kill List* (2011) more concerns itself with the evils of man and his occult machinations rather than those of phantasms and spirits.

Having said which, research for A Year In The Country repeatedly stumbles across the more ghostly and supernatural-concerned work of author M.R. James, largely in televisual form and via the referencing by other travellers in similar flipside pastoral cultural lands as A Year In The Country, rather than in their original printed form.

Along which lines, we reach the television play *The Ash Tree* from 1975, based on a story in M.R. James' 1904 collection *Ghost Stories*.

This shares some themes with Witchfinder General in its dealing with folk horror and persecution.

It tells the tale of an aristocrat who has inherited a country manor; the house has been cursed since his ancestor condemned a woman to death for witchcraft and it is discovered that an ancient ash tree outside his window is now the root of the curses.

M.R. James' short story was adapted for television by David Rudkin, who for a while seemed to be the go-to chap for otherly Albion-ic television and also wrote Penda's Fen.

In many ways The Ash Tree could sit quite comfortably amongst the not-so-salubrious fare that littered the faded cinemas of mid 1970s Britain; it has that nasty, unsettling feeling to it that a fair few cinematic releases from that period did, possibly reflecting a wider sense of corruption and malaise in society.

It is mildly surprising that it escaped onto television as it is a very adult piece of work: one which borders in part on exploitation cinema, albeit with an underlying arthouse intelligence.

It may have been the murky colours of the pre-DVD release transfer, but this is yesteryear pastoral England most definitely transposed to 1970s dissolution and grime.

There is little beauty in this landscape and its rolling fields. Bleak is a word that comes to mind; these are moors and feeding grounds full of judgement, punishment, voyeurism and unexplained carrion.

Wandering further along such pathways and television dramas which invoke a sense of "How did that happen? How was that allowed onto/ into mainstream television?" leads to 1974's Penda's Fen.

As with The Ash Tree and as mentioned previously this was created for television by David Rudkin, although this time it was his own original story and was directed by Alan Clarke.

While The Ash Tree is an unsettling film, it still exists and can be located within conventional film/horror narratives and genres. The same cannot be said for Penda's Fen.

This is a tale which takes in the revival of ancient pagan kings, hidden underground government facilities (cities?), left-wing truths, ranting and paranoia, substitute Mary Whitehouse-esque self-appointed moral majority figures, awakening sixth form adolescent sexuality, alternative religious histories and theological study, fancying your local milk man, demons, army cadet forces, William Blake's Jerusalem, the threat and worry of the never stopping industrial conveyor belt, returning dead classical musicians who wish to see the silver river and verdant valleys but who are actually staring at a flaking brick wall, the battle of religion against older gods, a birthday cake, adoption, fertility, almost breaking the fourth wall self-criticism about himself in David Rudkin's script, angelic riverside visitations and Kenneth Anger-esque phallic firework dreams.

Alongside which can be found the voluntary bodily de-appendaging scene which is a cross between some 1970s swingers get together, an episode of *Tales Of The Unexpected* (1979-1988), a folkloric gathering in The Wicker Man and who knows what else.

It could be a head spinning melange and collage of freakish, cult film making but it is not; although in its hour and a half (actually, its first half hour) it manages to have covered more topics than a whole catalogue of other films may do, this is a very cogent and coherent film which at its core deals with conformity, coming of age and mankind's sacred covenant with the land.

Red Shift from 1978 shares some similarities with Penda's Fen: it is a visionary take on the landscape and its stories and histories, older forms of worship, tales of coming of age and a priggish not always likeable teenage protagonist.

It is based on a book by Alan Garner, with a screenplay written by and collaborated on by him.

In it, three stories set in different time periods but with similar locales interweave and loosely interconnect; Roman and indigenous conflict, the English civil war loyalties/conflict and modern-day teenage trials and tribulations.

In part it could be seen as an exploration of the literary, intellectual and cultural idea that similar, interconnected things continue to happen in the same places over time, almost as though places become nodes or echo chambers for particular occurrences or a kind of temporal layering occurs: something which is also explored in Nigel Kneale's *The Stone Tape* from 1972.[5]

This connects with the sense of layers of stories and hidden histories (real or culturally imagined) that are recurring themes and ideas within A Year In The Country; a fascination with the patterns beneath or under the plough.

A particular touchstone for that sense of patterns beneath the plough and otherly landscapes is Alan Garner's *The Owl Service* book from 1967 which was adapted for television in 1969.

Very loosely and briefly, it is the tale of three teenagers who discover a mysterious set of owl and flower-patterned dinner plates in the attic and the magical ancient legend of the "Mabinogion" comes to life once again in their Welsh valley, with the story taking in supernatural fantasy, class struggle and adolescent permissiveness.

Accompanying the series was a book *Filming the Owl Service* (1970), which is long out of print and rare as hen's teeth to find second hand, which is a shame as it is a fine companion piece to the series, full of rather lovely photographs, artifacts, anecdotes, background story, prop sheets and designs from the filming and the series itself.

The book is split into three parts; an "Introduction" by Alan Garner in which he discusses the making of the film, some of what inspired the original book, the coincidences around it and so on, "Our Diaries" by his children who took nine weeks off school while it was being made to be on and around its filming and "Making the Film" by its director Peter Plummer.

Some of the points of interest from the book are:

1) The colours of the outfits of three of the main characters, Alison, Gwyn and Roger, were based on an older International Colour Code for electrical wiring (red, black and green). Although it was initially broadcast in black and white, a decision was made that if it was going to be filmed in colour, they would use colour to hint at the power the three could unleash.
2) Alan Garner looks surprisingly youthful in the photographs, as opposed to the bearded, grizzled chap one might imagine.
3) The spelling mistakes by the children have been appealingly left in the typed part of their diaries (so tomato soup becomes tomato soap).
4) It is easy to forget just how boring it can be to be a child; in the childrens' diaries one of the most repeated phrases and descriptions are variations on "I was bored"/ "It was boring".
5) When Peter Plummer introduced the actors to Alan Garner for the first time and asked if they looked right, Alan Garner's recollection of it was that it was a "nasty experience":
"I wanted to run. They looked too right. It was like a waking dream. Here were the people I'd thought about, who'd lived in my head for so long; but now they were real. I couldn't accept that they were only actors."
6) Alan Garner had based the part of Huw on Dafydd, an actual gardener from one of the locales of filming, but a Dafydd as he had imagined him being at the age of forty. When he saw them together he said that it "was like seeing father and son".
Apparently the two people in question when they saw one another said:

Dafydd: "I wish I was young and forty again."
Raymond: "Now I know what I'll look like at eighty."

The book leaves a sense that Dafydd was a very particular kind of person, one of those people who seem to have been part of the land forever, an archetype almost.

When the filming was carried out in the late 1960s, he was eighty one, while he first went to work at the location house in Wales in 1898, which seems an impossible stretch of time.

7) Alan Garner talks of the curious coincidences that occurred during and around filming.

At one point, unprompted, Dafydd Rees scratched the name "Blodeuwedd" on a piece of slate:
Alan Garner: "What's that?" I said.
Dafydd Rees: "A name."
Alan Garner: "Can you tell me about it?"
Dafydd Rees: "It's just a name."

Blodeuwedd is the name of a mythical character in an old Welsh legend which was a staring point for Alan Garner when writing the book; she was made from flowers and turned into an owl as a punishment after betraying and killing her husband with a lover. Connected to which, one of the iconic phrases from the book/series is the following:

"She wants to be flowers, but you make her owls. You must not complain, then, if she goes hunting."

Alan Garner: "The Owl Service is a kind of ghost story, in real life as well as on the film or page. Right from the start things happened that haven't happened with any other book I've written."

Peter Plummer refers to such coincidences as "selective perception" ie. You're working on an owl-themed piece of work, so you begin to notice owls in one form or another more often.

8) Alan Garner on writing the book:

"It seemed at times that I was discovering, not writing, a story: it was all there, waiting and I was like an archaeologist picking away the sand to reveal the bones."

9) On the last night of shooting the crew surreptitiously presented Peter Plummer with a brown paper package; it was a "jet-dark lambswool hat."

The accompanying note said "From your black sheeps" which seems rather apt and appropriate to the series and its stories.

10) The local fire brigade was hired to create the rain effects.

Alan Garner's children seemed to love that part (and even got to use the hose, snapping branches from a tree with it) and at one point comment on thinking that the actors do not know that pond water is being used.

There seemed to be a constant battle to not run out of water during the production, to create the correct seasonal conditions and struggling against the elements; reminiscent of tales from The Wicker Man and how extras had to suck ice cubes on supposedly sunny days to stop their breath showing in the cold air.

Alan Garner: "…we got there in the middle of May, it felt like the end of Winter…"

11) Alan Garner is one of the villagers in one scene in the series and apparently he was a foot taller than all the actual local people who were in the series and they all found it hard to behave normally when the man-made storm rain hits them.

Alan Garner: "…as soon as the solid water hit us we all gasped and yelled, and looked like anything but villagers out in a storm." Dafydd: "We must be dumb and waterproof."

Alan Garner: "That scene is still odd, because I was about a foot taller than anybody else, and I look like the village freak – which may be what Peter was after all the time."

12) The end of Alan Garner's section is a quote taken from a letter sent by Dafydd, referring to the time during the filming and The Stone Of Gronw, which the production had commissioned to be

carved, prepared and set in place for the series:
"It was a good time... I have been to the stone. It is lonely now."

1. Such intro sequences are also discussed in Chapter 8.
2. Aspects of this are also written about in Chapter 44.
3. This is discussed further in Chapter 7.
4. As mentioned in Chapter 17.
5. Discussed in Chapter 40.

12

A Bear's Ghosts: Soviet Dreams and Lost Futures

There have been a number of books and photography projects which could be seen to document a form of former Soviet Union hauntology; work that often focuses on monuments and remnants of Cold War era striving, dreams and far reaching projects.

"A bear's ghosts" is a phrase which draws from the bear as a symbol of Russia and also possibly from the song *The Bear Ghost* by folk music reinterprators and explorers The Owl Service, written by Dominic Cooper and Steven Collins of the band, which entwines a spirit that is both uplifting and achingly melancholic.

Jan Kempemaers' *Spomenik* from 2010, contains his photographs of structures that were created in Yugoslavia in the 1960s and 1970s as memorials to the Second World War but which now apparently are largely abandoned.

These take a largely abstract, geometric, concrete modernist form and there is a brutalist beauty and fascination to them, while they also seem to have tumbled from both the future and the past; despite the all too real history which inspired them, they now seem almost like impossible fictions or props from the fantasies of a cinematic story.

That sense of the fantastic, of design which seems to belong to something other than day-to-day utilitarian use can also be found in Christopher Herwig's *Soviet Bus Stops* (2015) book.

The structures photographed in it could also be considered in the eyes of some beholders to have gained elements of being utilitarian or pragmatic accidental art.[1]

As with the Spomenik photographs, in Soviet Bus Stops some of the more architecturally brutalist designs appear to be artifacts from lost futures, of a time when an empire reached for grand horizons and even the stars.

Along which lines is Danila Tkachenko's *Restricted Areas* book from 2016, the photographs in which focus on abandoned hardware, secret cities and installations from the Soviet Union during the Cold War period.

The book includes images of experimental laser systems, former party headquarters, antenna built for interplanetary connection with bases on other planets which were planned for once upon a time, a city where rocket engines were produced which was closed to outsiders until 1992, the world's largest diesel submarine becalmed and landlocked, a former mining town which has now become a bombing trial field, a particularly striking amphibious vertical take-off aeroplane of which only two were built and discarded space rocket capsules.

Danila Tkachenko says of the places, structures, equipment, vehicles and mechanisms he has photographed:

> "Those places lost their significance together with the utopian ideology which is now obsolete. The perfect technocratic future that never came."

And as with Spomenik and Soviet Bus Stops the spirit of these photographs seem like a different time and place's hauntology: a differing but also partly parallel strand to that which has come about in the UK and the West and its sense of reflections on, mourning and yearning for a more utopian future which did not occur.

In Restricted Areas every photograph is of a snow-covered and bound scene but this is not referred to anywhere in the text. This lends a stark, isolated, naturally cleansed, rather beautiful and minimal aesthetic to the photographs, which enhances the sense of these being a form of monuments to lost dreams rather than discarded technology and infrastructure.

Connected to which, as with Spomenik in particular, there is a certain iconographic nature to them; their shapes, silhouettes and geometries seem inherently imbued with, to capture and distill a certain progressive, utopian, striving Soviet philosophy.

Today there is a considerable amount of photography out in the world and particularly online that focuses on derelict buildings, machinery and so on and which is sometimes referred to as urban exploration or urbex photography.

However, in amongst the masses of such photography, Ralph Mireb's images of abandoned and incomplete Soviet era space shuttles (which are a curious simulacra of the American space shuttle in terms of design and can be found at the website *Bored Panda*) stand out.

This is in part due to the sheer scale of the infrastructure and buildings that surround them which they document - the space shuttle hangar is many storeys high and dwarves the other structures nearby.

To view them almost beggars belief, even more so as they have been abandoned after such a huge amount of work and effort went into creating them.

In photographs that act as an accompaniment to Ralph Mireb's, Alexander Marksin has documented the discarded wooden wind-tunnel models of these space shuttles.[2]

Due to the materials used, these bring to mind thoughts of a folk art project rather than an institutionally and nationally funded attempt at space exploration, which is heightened as they have been left outside to age, weather, crumble and be slowly reclaimed and covered by nature.

In terms of vehicle design, in the Soviet Union there is a cul-de-sac that could well be called "The Shape of the Future's Past" which takes in abandoned Soviet era hydrofoils[3] and which were known as river rockets.

These were made from the mid-1950s to mid-1970s and viewed now with their sleek, finned, almost space vehicle like designs appear as prototypes for a mid-century modern, atomic age take on how the future was to be.

There is a bravery, an optimism, a genuine progressive modernism and venturing onwards and outwards to designs like these that seems to have been lost somewhere along the way, surrendered to a more day-to-day practicality in design.

These hydrofoils seem closer to something that you would see in a science fiction series such as *Space 1999* (1975-1977) and to belong to the realms of imagination rather than actual working transportation vehicles, although they were once upon a time just that.

Throughout this chapter a number of times I have referred to a sense of the science fiction-esque or fantastical, often accompanied by a grand sense of an empire and its once ambitions, which many of these photographs imply.

This is particularly captured by the cover of Rebecca Litchfield's *Soviet Ghosts*, a book released in 2014 which focuses on the extent of abandonment in the former Soviet Union and its satellite states in the Eastern Bloc.

In the book's cover image an abandoned and derelict circular stadium has been photographed, capturing the enormous scale and futurist grandeur of this structure.

The sense of dereliction is heightened by the grey, washed out haze that the photograph presents the stadium in.

This is given counterpoint, poignancy and a certain faded, stalwart sense of the empire it formed a part of and its once power and iconography by the Soviet hammer and sickle flag design at the centre of its ceiling; in the haze filled photograph of this derelict structure the red and yellow of this symbol understatedly seems to pierce the mists of a faded history.

To the Western eye, as is similar to varying degrees with much of the above photography and structures, it conjures more a vision of a *Flash Gordon*-esque empire and future than something grounded in the reality of a still relatively recent earthbound political, economic and societal system.

1. In this sense the appreciations and documentations of them in the *Soviet Bus Stops* book are not dissimilar to that carried out by websites such as *The Telegraph Pole Appreciation Society* and *Poles and Pylons* in the UK.
2. The images of which can be found at the *Urban Ghosts* website.
3. Photographs of which can also be found at Urban Ghosts.

13

From "Two Tribes" to *WarGames*: The Ascendancy of Apocalyptic Popular Culture

FROM AROUND 1980 to the mid-1980s there were a fair number of music singles released which explored and/or protested against the threat of nuclear war, and which made it to the higher ends of the official national British music sales chart.

Because of the high profile nature of the music charts in the UK at the time, this placing meant that such records were a large part of the national conversation and consciousness and also that they may have sold hundreds of thousands, or more, physical singles. The commercial success of some of these records is highlighted by the list below, which shows the UK chart positions of singles that dealt with such apocalyptic themes:

Blondie - "Atomic" (1980): No. 1
Nena - "99 Red Balloons" (1983): No. 1
OMD - "Enola Gay" (1980): No. 8
The Pirahnas - "Tom Hark" (1980): No. 6
Jona Lewie - "Stop the Cavalry" (1982): No. 3
Frankie Goes To Hollywood - "Two Tribes" (1984): No. 1
Nik Kershaw - "I Won't Let the Sun Go Down on Me" (1984): No. 2
Strawberry Switchblade - "Since Yesterday" (1984): No. 5
Ultravox - "Dancing with Tears in My Eyes" (1984): No. 3

* * *

Musically these end of days pop songs took in a variety of styles and aesthetics, including the catchy, bouncy earworm nature of Nena's "99 Red Balloons" and The Piranhas "Tom Hark", or the equally sing-along-able but slightly melancholic pop of Strawberry Switchblade's "Since Yesterday".

The cinematically dramatic "Dancing with Tears in My Eyes" was a song based on Nevil Shute's 1957 novel *On the Beach*, which told the story of how people planned to live through the end of times brought about via wind carried fallout in a country that has avoided the main devastating nuclear attack.

OMD's "Enola Gay" took as its subject matter the dropping of the first atomic device in a conflict situation and pop pin-up Nik Kershaw in "I Won't Let the Sun Go Down on Me" considered the ending of three hundred million years of history in but one minute during a nuclear conflict.

Jona Lewie's "Stop the Cavalry" was more a general anti-war song but one which reflects on the ongoing nature of conflict and loss over the centuries, while also containing a sense of time schism in its mixed references to earlier twentieth century and Cold War conflicts.

Blondie's "Atomic" took a lyrically minimal almost abstract approach to the theme, one that invokes dramatic dread and glamour, accompanied by a post-apocalyptic disco video and mushroom cloud single cover.

IN TERMS OF CHART success Frankie Goes To Hollywood's "Two Tribes" was probably the daddy of them all, in the UK at least and it spent nine weeks at number one. It opens with the sound of air raid sirens and features a voiceover that recreated Cold War Civil Defence films.

Lyrically it deals with the ultimately futile nature of conflict and superpower Cold War posturing (which was given further expression in a video which featured dopplegangers for the real life USA and Soviet political leaders battling in a wrestling ring).

The background to the release of the above records in 1980-84 was that this was one of the heightened points of the Cold War and a reaction to an international defence policy that seemed to "subscribe to the point of view that the more dangerous we make the world, the safer we are".

Essentially the thinking behind this was the more weapons and in particular nuclear weapons the other side possess, the more we will obtain, which led to an arms race, stockpiling and a deterrent which relied on a fear of mutually-assured destruction for both sides if there was a conflict.

The above quote is from a documentary which is part of a 2016 UK television series, *Trailblazers*, that was narrated by one time glam rock star and Slade frontman Noddy Holder and had the intention of examining "the key moments that have shaped musical history".

There is one episode that focuses on the above loose gathering of chart topping protest pop: something of a surprising cuckoo in the nest amongst the more obvious looks at disco, funk, punk and goth.[1]

Although the description of the episode at the time of its broadcast talked about the evolution of such protest songs "...from western swing and country to gospel, jazz and rockabilly", actually it largely focuses on early to mid-eighties UK chart pop.

One of the most fascinating sections is where Trevor Horn, who was the producer of Frankie Goes To Hollywood's Two Tribes and the co-owner of their record label ZTT, talks about the Civil Defence voiceover parts of the single.

Apparently it went something like this:

Paul Morley (who was loosely and variously the philosophiser, organiser and provocateur behind ZTT) had a bootleg of the UK Government's Civil Defence *Protect and Survive* information films.

These were intended for television broadcast in advance of a nuclear attack on the UK.

They utilised animation to instruct the public on how to build DIY shelters in your home, deal with fallout, identify what different warning siren patterns indicated and so forth.

With hindsight they may have been an exercise in the government needing to appear to have some form of public instruction they could use, but the practical defence effects of the advice given is probably at best negligible or woefully inadequate, involving as they did advice along the lines of whitewashing your windows and leaning a mattress against a wall to shelter behind in order to protect against explosions with megatons of power.

At the time of Two Tribe's recording these films were classified, although today they are freely available on well known commercial internet video platforms and can be bought on DVD.

With their classified status in mind, rather than steal or sample the voiceovers from them, they hired Patrick Allen who had recorded them for the actual government broadcasts.

Around then he was a nationally-known figure as he also did well known television commercials such as for Barratt Homes, so his use in these films was possibly intended by the authorities as a way of providing a reassuring voice.

It cost ZTT around £1000 to hire him: a figure which seems low now. When they showed Patrick Allen what he was to read, he said:

> "I don't think I can do this. Where have you got this from? You know I had to sign the Official Secrets Act before I did this?"

And then apparently he went:

> "F*** it, I'm going to do it. You know you missed a few bits out. There was one bit that particularly upset me…"

(That bit, if you should wish to know, concerned disposals. Let us not dwell on this.)

These releases seem about a million miles away from popular music entertainment today. Such music releases can now be seen as part of a wider sense of the then-alive and well functioning of the circuit between the experimental, the avant-garde and the popular.[2]

In an interconnected manner, at the time the functioning of that circuit meant that the pop charts could also include the likes of Kate Bush's single "Breathing" from 1980.

While this did not quite reach the Top 10 (peaking at No.16, although the album it featured on went to number one) it took as its subject matter the decidedly non-mainstream theme of a mother worried about passing the fallout from a nuclear explosion to her unborn child.

Alongside which, further breaking from the conventions of what may be expected in a commercially successful pop song, it features an extended unsettling, drifting spoken word passage that describes in a scientific or documentary manner the characteristics of a flash from a nuclear explosion.

It was not just within the realms of mainstream pop music that such apocalyptic themes were explored with resounding commercial success around the early to mid-1980s.

The film *WarGames*, released in 1983, focused on themes connected to worries about Cold War nuclear armament computer based control systems gone awry and was that year's fifth highest grossing film in the USA.

It was largely aimed at a young adult or teenage audience and it shares some aspects, tropes and archetypes with classic John Hughes and other similar teen comedies and dramas from around that time. However this is not so much about being a geek and an outsider and maybe getting the girl, this is about being a geek and an outsider and getting the girl but to a background of computer hacking and apocalyptic mutually assured destruction via superpower conflict caused in part by that hacking.

It does not just share some aspects and tropes with those John Hughes comedies, it also shares a main actor in Matthew Broderick, who played the loveable goof-about seize-the-day-er in the 1986 film *Ferris Bueller's Day Off*, which Hughes wrote.

The characters played by Matthew Broderick in both films share the same resourceful computer hacking skills that enable him to outstep and outsmart the systems created by adults.

In Ferris Bueller he changes his number of absent days on the school computer.

While in WarGames he changes his grades via the school computer but also almost instigates worldwide destruction and conflict when he hacks a defence computer, which is in charge of planning and launching a US attack against its enemies.

Broderick's character is looking for the new unreleased games of a home computer game company when he connects via the modem and computer in his bedroom to this defence computer.

The computer begins playing a simulation of those possible attacks but cannot distinguish between games or reality and thinks that to win it must literally carry out and launch an attack in the real world.

Alongside worries about nuclear conflict, another period curio aspect of the film is the seeming omnipotence of the young hacker and his ability to do more or less anything and to break into any system from his normal family home.

This ties in with a period media obsession with the hacker as part of a lineage of youthful folk devils.

In previous eras such folk devils included the likes of the much more easily identifiable biker or hippy who generally adopted and dressed in styles which were markedly differently from the mainstream, whereas the hacker was considered threatening in part because of their potential relative visual and stylistic normality and hence anonymity.

There seems to be an ongoing theme of young adult fiction and films dealing with dystopian and/or apocalyptic scenarios.

The 2008 onwards *The Hunger Games* book and film series is a more contemporary example of this and has been notably commercially successful, while John Christopher's *The Tripods* book series (1967-1988) and its accompanying 1980s television series trod related ground.

What is different with WarGames is that it does not imagine a future fantasy despotism or alien invasion which is brought down by resourceful teenagers but rather the apocalyptic threat it reflects on was very real and present in the world and popular consciousness.

However, in line with those other fictions, WarGames also seems to have at its core a form of wish fulfilment or empowerment of the teenager as the one who will save the day, who will beat the evil power or who has the right-headed way of looking at things rather than the pigheaded (or sometimes more or less absent) adults.

WarGames has been described as "popcorn friviolity", which would seem to imply that it is just escapist, throwaway fun that sat alongside other such escapist, throwaway fun of the time.

Such ways of seeing things are possibly part of cultural reviewing and consideration whereby it can be hard to admit to "worthy" work or that which deals with serious issues as also being the f(un) word.

WarGames is fun, a thoroughly enjoyable and entertaining film but it does also fundamentally deal with one of the serious issues of its day.

It, along with the earlier mentioned apocalyptic pop protest songs, shows that teen or youth-orientated commercially successful entertainment and explorations of a serious controversial real world subject or debate are not necessarily mutually exclusive states.

Alongside its more escapist entertainment aspects it is also an underlyingly tense film, in part due to its presentation and plotting but in large part because of the reality of the threat it deals with.

Even now that is the case but back in 1983 when the Cold War was at one of its peaks this aspect is likely to have been particularly heightened.

Although it could be considered to be not purely a period film in terms of the conflict systems and weapons it considers.

On rewatching the film it is strange to think that many of the instruments, mechanisms and associated infrastructure from the Cold War are quite probably still out there. Or rather the phrase should probably be "under there" as they are often placed below ground for protective and stealth purposes (as indeed is much of the technology and equipment of WarGames; several of its big set pieces and locations are in underground bunkers and control or launch centres).

It is as though the game has been put to one side of the collective consciousness but the pieces have not been cleared from the chess board, more that they have been swept under a literal and figurative subterranean covering: semi-forgotten but not gone.

1. The goth-focused episode is worth watching if you can find it, in part to hear Noddy Holder say in his inimitable manner "Goth, not me guv" and describing Madchester-related bands when signalling the end of mainstream goth popularity as "Baggy-panted vampire hunters".
2. As a concept this is related to observations by lecturer and writer Mark Fisher, also discussed in Chapter 15.

14

Christopher Priest's *A Dream of Wessex*: Twentieth Century Slipstream Echoes

Christopher Priest's 1977 novel *A Dream of Wessex* came to this author's consciousness via a trail of cultural breadcrumbs dropped by Rob Young in his book *Electric Eden* (2010),[1] which explores interconnected and underlying lines of folk and rural orientated British music and culture and how it has been handed down and transformed by successive generations.

It is featured in the later "Toward the Unknown Region" section of the book wherein the lines through an otherly Britain he has drawn and explored wander towards an almost maelstrom gathering of the more hauntological concerns and hidden landscapes of the likes of exploratory record labels/projects such as Ghost Box Records and English Heretic, public information films that have gathered layers of uncanniness over the years, Oliver Postgate's gently off-centre animations, the unsettled televisual pastoralism of *Penda's Fen* (1974), *The Stone Tape* (1972) and *Children of the Stones* (1977) and related folk horror-esque work.

Including *A Dream of Wessex* in amongst such work seems particularly apt as though it was written before the term or concept had been created, at points it reads like part of a manifesto from or description of a release by a hauntologically-inclined record label; the text talks of spectral versions of oneself, time being deposited like layers of sedimentary rock which could be excavated via imagination and the muddy remains of the twentieth century being scattered like shipwrecks across the landscape.

Alongside which one of the main strands of the book involves time-travelling ability developed by participants whose minds have been electronically pooled but which is nearer to a visualisation via technological dream projection equipment.

In such ways, A Dream of Wessex connects with a hauntological sense of spectral, misremembered and reinterpreted histories and culture and the related creation and exploration of parallel worlds.

The book is also curiously prescient of modern day escaping into a virtual digital, social media world; the plot involves a group of researchers in an underground centre who join a scientifically created group projection of a future Britain, which is being carried out in order to try and learn about and provide solutions to modern day problems. This virtual world eventually becomes more attractive than the real world, its participants not wishing to leave and this created world possibly becomes self-sufficient/creating.

Essentially A Dream of Wessex narrates a mass dream or hallucination, which makes its inclusion in Rob Young's book at the Ghost Box/hauntological juncture all the more fitting; such activities form part of what he has called experiments in consensual hallucination, whereby the participants willingly allow themselves to become immersed or even subsumed in the dream like atmospheres, phantasms and worlds that particular cultural activity can at times create.

It could also be linked to another of the concepts/phrases which I came across via Electric Eden; that of imaginative time travel, which is used to describe voyagers in folk and other cultures when they interact with and attempt to visit or summon elements of other times through their creative work and ways of living.

Connected to such experiments and activity, the reference within A Dream of Wessex to time being deposited in a similar manner to layers of sedimentary rock and its excavation via the imaginations of participants in a mass dream has parallels with cultural tropes within hauntological realms.

In such work past culture is often explored, mined, reformed and repurposed and used as elements within new cultural artifacts.

Within hauntological-related work there is also often a deliberate mis-remembering of the past, filtering it through your own personal vision, reimagining it in your own form - which is mirrored by the researchers in A Dream of Wessex creating and shaping their own version of the future in their mass projection.

A version of such cultural reforming can be seen in the work released and created by Ghost Box Records, which conjures a world in some imagined past circa approximately from the early 1960s to the late 1970s, but which rather than being overly time period specific is possibly nearer to a never-never land parallel world slipstream.

A journey to the Ghost Box-created world finds TV station idents, educational broadcasts, public information films, modernist intents, utilitarian library music soundtracks and an overly picture perfect village parish life having somehow intertwined to variously become exercises in mind control, forms of transmission for hidden/occult messages, a yearning for lost futures and a quietly carried out Midwich-isation.

The cover artwork of the earlier printed editions of A Dream of Wessex further reflect and forebear that Ghost Box/hauntological world and intertwining.

The original hardback cover from 1977 published by Faber & Faber is quite a traditional landscape painting by Paul Nash but knowledge of the plot of the book and its appearance in the "Toward the Unknown Region" section of Electric Eden seem to infer a subtle sense of otherliness to it.

The original softback cover from 1978 released by Pan Books features a depiction of a happy couple ensconced amongst the idyll of a rural landscape but then wanders off to more *Sapphire & Steel*-esque hauntological territory; they are sitting on an incongruous maroon fabric stool that would be more fitting in a gentrified parlour, their outlines glow and their featureless faces reflect only a further imagined idyll, while far off in the distance behind them a red sun hangs over what appears to be some kind of futuristic, scientific building.

In this sense the cover's layering of the known, even comforting with elements of the unknown and unsettling atmospheres could be seen as a prescient reflection of some of the defining aspects of what would later come to be thought of as hauntological work.

1. Rob Young's book is discussed further in Chapter 1.

15

Sapphire & Steel and *Ghosts in the Machine*: Nowhere, Forever and Lost Spaces within Cultural Circuitry

Sapphire & Steel was a British television series, broadcast from 1979 to 1982 and was created by Peter J. Hammond. It starred David McCallum and Joanna Lumley, who played the two interdimensional operatives of the title, travelling through time and place and guarding the correct and continuing flowing of time.

In the series it is explained that Time is similar to a progressing corridor that surrounds everything but there are weak spots where Time, which is implied to be a malignant force, can break into the present and take things or people.

Alongside this, we are told that there are also creatures from the beginnings and ends of time who roam the corridor searching for the same weak spots to break through and then wreak their own version of havoc.

Very little is explained or revealed about Sapphire & Steel's backgrounds and while they take on the form of and appear as human, although not overly dwelled on they are beings of another type, being described as elements (hence their names).

They seem to be quite fond of humans and to have a sense of duty of protection towards them. but this is accompanied by a quietly superior air, almost as though they are helping slightly less evolved pets.

Their methods do not seem rooted in scientific, technical and logically conventional techniques and indeed, as with Nick Whitfield's 2010 film

Skeletons which features a duo of operatives who also operate using not all that dissimilar methods[1] and in terms of current scientific theory the premise of the series is nearer to an alternative take on super or preternatural forces.

If and where their techniques do have a scientific air in a contemporary sense, it is science that is beyond human knowledge at this time and seems to have an almost abstractly ad hoc aspect. Accompanying this, the actions and effects in the series are expressed more impressionistically rather than being concerned with high-end visual realism.

Creatures who have broken through the corridor of Time may only be represented as moving spots of light on the floor; Steel caught in the time trap of a crashing fighter plane only has his predicament represented via his stance and audio effects.

However, they are no less effective for this and can be positively chilling, possibly as they leave space for the viewer's imagination to fill in and expand on what they are shown.

This form of presentation also segues with the aspect of the series whereby different areas of Time break through into and exist in an at-times hidden manner within the modern day, expressing a sense of related layering and interweaving.

Spoiler alert: If you plan on watching the series, the following section reveals details of its ending.

I FIRST BEGAN TO watch Sapphire & Steel before the first year of A Year In The Country, and finished it during the second year. I had also watched some of it when it was originally broadcast, but only episodically. In the days before the widespread availability of home video recorders and long before online catch-up television, my viewing of the series would only happen every other week as its broadcast clashed with a series that somebody else wanted to watch, meaning that the two different programmes would be watched on alternate weeks.

However, I had learned how the series ended as during that extended watching and rewatching I read Mark Fisher's *Ghosts of my Life* book from 2014, that loosely focuses on hauntological-related themes and which opens with the ending of the series; Sapphire and Steel are left stranded in a roadside cafe that is suspended in space and their betrayers tell them:

"This is the trap. This is nowhere, and it's forever."

It is truly chilling as an ending to a series and as no further episodes of the mainstream television programme were commissioned (although it has been continued in more niche-orientated audio books), it genuinely seems as though they are trapped throughout all time.

As a series it contrasts with sections of modern drama in that there is not excessively kinetic movement from one location and big-bang moment to another.

Compared to much of modern day television it feels curiously almost soothing for not having that constant fast paced action. At the same time it does not feel as if the viewer needs to recalibrate to the rhythms of previous eras television to appreciate it, in contrast to say some of 1970s television drama.[2]

As with the final series of *Quatermass* from 1979, this is television which stands up well as entertainment, as well as being of interest due to gaining cult status and/or becoming cultural reference points.

Sapphire & Steel was a curious choice for prime time broadcasting; as Mark Fisher says in The Ghosts of my Life, this was science fiction without many of the expected trappings of the genre such as exotically different alien beings, spaceships, gadgets and advanced weaponry and it did not meet its audience halfway by providing thorough explanations for its world, story and characters.

Compared with today's sometimes carefully-targeted genre series which are often fan pleasing rollercoaster rides of plot movement that rarely step outside of expected comfort zones, it is genuinely odd to think of how a series which was none of those things could end up as mainstream fare and on the front of the *TV Times*.[3]

In some ways it could be seen as challenging television due to its lack of explanation of the whys and wherefores of its world and participants and its final unresolved plotline, which as with the lack of overly detailed and high end special effects, left space for the imagination of its viewers to roam.

The earlier mentioned opening chapter of The Ghosts of my Life is called "The Slow Cancellation of the Future" with Sapphire and Steel's casting out and possible betrayal "by their own side" being used as an analogy or introduction to some of the themes of hauntology; its sense of futures lost and of time/cultural time leeching forwards and backwards.

Accompanying that, Mark Fisher has also considered how we are possibly going through a period where there is a sense of loss of loss.

This is a side effect of the contemporary endless and precise archiving and replication techniques which are available via digital technology, which is in contrast with previous eras, where sometimes for example television broadcasts were performed live and not recorded at all, recordings were wiped or due to the fragile nature of older recording media they have degraded over time.

There has also come to be a romantic attachment to the markers of the decay, loss and degradation of recordings from earlier eras, for example the crackle of vinyl records, whether actual or applied retrospectively, as signifiers of certain atmospheres to contemporary recordings.

In line with such considerations, one of the things which is striking when watching Sapphire & Steel is that despite it being available on the more contemporary digital technology of DVDs, it is particularly not scrubbed up and restored – there are glitches, banding, small transmission-breaking-through crackles of interference at the edges of the screen, light trails and so on.

Often a good, sympathetically-done high definition restoration on more visually opulent archival film and television is to be appreciated, but with Sapphire & Steel such a process may well be inappropriate; the unrestored marks and infractions feel like an inherent part of the series, its spirit and aesthetic.

In these days of exact duplicatory ease, there is something intriguing about these particular "faults", they are the ghosts in the machine, as it were. Which brings me to *Ghosts in the Machine.*

This was a 1986-1988 late night programme on the UK's Channel 4 television station (one of but four channels at the time) which was dedicated to showing experimental/avant-garde video work: things you would be more likely to see in a gallery setting than via the mainstream television broadcast infrastructure.

It was non-populist television within a populist framework: a phrase that could also be used to refer to Sapphire & Steel.

At times there would be advert breaks with no adverts. Presumably this was because of a mixture of the late hour and Channel 4's then-still minority output remit. Advertisers probably could not see the marketing potential for fizzy sugared water after a 10-minute almost-still framed broadcast of a pond which showed reflections of people who were not there diving in.

It all seemed quite thrilling at the time: a glimpse into obscured culture that it is difficult to imagine being seen in amongst the transmissions of one of the big broadcasters today, no matter how late the hour. Mark Fisher has also talked about:

> "...the breaking of the circuit between the avant-garde, the experimental and the popular."[4]

Ghosts in the Machine was a brief moment when there was a spark generated by a few hair thin strands of connection in that circuit. And although Sapphire & Steel is not necessarily avant-garde, with its exploratory nature and the way in which it did not pander to audience expectations, along with Ghosts in the Machine it serves as a reflection of a time when there was more space within mainstream broadcast culture for such things than exists today.

1. Discussed in Chapter 4.
2. Something discussed further in the Chapter 8.
3. This was a massively mainstream in nature and circulation television listings magazine in the UK during the 1970s, one of only two which were widely available.
4. These comments are also discussed in Chapter 5.

16

Kill List, Puffball, In the Dark Half and *Butter on the Latch*: Folk Horror Descendants by Way of the Kitchen Sink

As mentioned in Chapter 6: "Folk Horror Roots...", which focuses largely on cinematic work from the late 1960s to later 1970s, folk horror is a film genre which as a cultural strand has created ever-growing reverberations and led to and/or inspired more recent work.

One such piece of work is Ben Wheatley's thoroughly unsettling film *Kill List* from 2011. As a film it is an intriguing, fascinating, inspiring piece of work. An online discussion about the film said "some pieces of culture are the thing that they purport to be about"; this is a film about evil.

Visually, if not thematically, it shares similarities with the grittier side of social realism British cinema. For a large part the world it represents, although about the lives of somewhat shady mercenaries, is presented in an every day, social realist, kitchen sink manner.

It does not feel like an esoteric otherly world, at least initially; people are shown having dinner, a couple argues about money and so forth. But something else lurks and creeps in; a symbol is scratched behind a mirror, a descent begins and the mercenaries are drawn into an arcane, hidden world and system.

In many ways the film feels like a sequel to 1973's *The Wicker Man,* or at least of its direct lineage or spirit, exploring the themes of that film but through a modern day filter of a corruption that feels total and also curiously banal; there is a sense of occult machinations and organisations but also of just doing a job, of the minutiae of it all.

Although initially set in more urban environments, the film travels to both subterranean and rural areas, presenting characters, folkloric elements and costume which seem to be descendants of or from The Wicker Man but shown through a very dark, nightmarish, hallucinatory contemporary filter.

Whereas in The Wicker Man the isolated society it presents is one set in a rural island idyll, in Kill List the abiding memory is a sense of the actions of the participants often taking place amongst empty, overcast, overlooked, neglected or discarded areas of capitalism and industrial society's edgelands and hinterlands.

The film utilises tropes from more recent horror and possibly voyeuristic exploitational film but seems to layer and underpin this with what psychogeographic thought has called "the hidden landscape of atmospheres, histories, actions and characters which charge environments": occult in both the literal and root meaning of hidden.

Mr Wheatley, you have made a fine piece of culture and have captured something indefinable, but it is not an easy piece of work to have around hearth and home.

Continuing on from Kill List, kitchen sink or realist folk horror is a description that could be applied to other films such as Josephine Decker's *Butter on the Latch* (2013), Alastair Siddons *In the Dark Half* (2011) and Nicholas Roeg's *Puffball* (2007).

These films take some of the recurring themes of folk horror (precised by Adam Scovell, author of the 2017 book *Folk Horror: Hours Dreadful and Things Strange*, as featuring landscape, isolation, skewed moral beliefs and a happening or summoning) but which strip away some of the more fantastical presentation and sometimes stylisation that can be found in The Wicker Man or 1970's *Queens of Evil* [1] and utilise a more "rooted in the real world" approach.

PUFFBALL IS UNEVEN in tone on various levels while also being somewhat intriguing. Set in a remote part of the countryside, it is a television-esque kitchen sink folk horror film that mixes *Grand Designs* with the music of Kate Bush and *England's Hidden Reverse.*[2]

In the film new age-ish imagery intermingles with "are-they-real or not?" folkloric and witchery shenanigans, tales of fertility battles, fertility ending with ageing and the slick yuppie-like outsiders gutting and rebuilding a cottage that was previously the site for intense local loss in a possibly inappropriately modern, minimalist, over-angled style.

In some ways it feels like the story of the old ways battling with the new: of the arrogance of money and man trying to push out the mud and nature of the land.

It is reminiscent of the *Play for Today* television drama *Robin Redbreast* from 1970[3] in the sense of the entrapping of an outsider in fertility rites and rituals and the use of a slightly simple man of the land for those ends.

Puffball adds a graphic, almost dissolute sexuality to that realism. This is not an easy film in parts: it is both unsettled and unsettling in various ways.

As an aside, it is loosely connected back to early 1970s folk horror by the appearance of Donald Sutherland, and being directed by Nicolas Roeg, it is but a hop, skip and jump from them to The Wicker Man via Nicolas Roeg's 1973 film *Don't Look Now*, in which Donald Sutherland stars and which was released cinematically as part of a double bill with The Wicker Man. In Puffball he makes for a striking figure, appearing as an almost slightly deranged happy old owl, albeit one in respectable business garb.

Further connecting Puffball to kitchen sink, the film also features the bird-like late beauty and fascinating screen presence of Rita Tushingham, who appeared in *A Taste of Honey* (1961), which is known as one of the classic 1960s kitchen sink/British new wave films; here she is all staring eyes and grasping country ways.

Throughout the film Kate Bush's song "Prelude" from her 2005 album *Aerial*, which features the angelic voice of her son accompanying her piano playing, appears and reappears, interconnecting the themes of the film and its stories of progeny to come and those lost.

Puffball is also further connected to Kate Bush's work through two of its actors: Donald Sutherland appeared in the video for her 1985 single "Cloudbusting", while one of the film's lead actors is Miranda Richardson, who was also one of the main cast members in Kate Bush's *The Line, the Cross & the Curve* film which accompanied her *Red Shoes* album from 1994.

The film also has the more exploitation friendly title *The Devil's Eyeball* (puffballs are large round white fungi, also known by this other name).

The imagery which accompanies The Devil's Eyeball version of the DVD release makes the film look nearer to a cheap b-movie, teenage friendly take on say the 1984 gothic fantasy-horror film *The Company of Wolves*, which is in part an adult take on the fairy story *Little Red Riding Hood* and could be considered an early example of folk horror with its tales of deceitful ravenous wolves in the wood.

In the Dark Half takes some of the tropes familiar from British social realist cinema such as a rundown estate on the edge of the countryside, family loss or dysfunction and a sense of social depravation or lack of chances to escape but wanders elsewhere with them.

It is not quite magical realism, but rather the subdued, downtrodden landscape is given a subtle sheen which creates a sense that you are looking in on a magical otherly world.

There are folkloric, borderline folk horror elements to the film, but it is not so much those which create the sense of a world with its own rules and even magic.

Rather via its visual presentation there is a certain lush, soft beauty to the rundown estate and the nearby countryside: a refreshing view of such things in contrast with gritty, realist and sometimes-dour cinematic presentations of similar locales.

This is partly due to the visuals of the film which are quietly sumptuous via the noteworthy lenswork by Spanish cinematographer Neus

Ollé, who director Alistar Siddons approached to work on In the Dark Half as he said that he thought the viewpoint of somebody from outside of England would bring something unusual to the visual aspects of the film.

However, in that lush beauty there is a sense of something else, something unsettling but the terrors in the film are understated and underlying rather than relying on more obvious visual shocks.

Which brings us to Josephine Decker's *Butter on the Latch.*

This film was discussed in the BFI's *Sight & Sound* magazine, with the headline "Dark Pastoral" and with "Lovely, dark and deep" written below a picture of a solitary wooden shack-like building in an isolated moorland landscape, with two female figures approaching it from the edge of the frame.

It is an intriguing image and pair of descriptions which, while not overtly signalling such things, seemed to conjure up a dreamlike, rather classy take or variation on folk horror.

Along with the above, a well-known online commerce site has this description of the film:

> "At a Balkan folk song and dance camp in the woods of Mendocino, California, Sarah reunites with her old friend Isolde and with a song she learned years before about dragons who entwine themselves in women's hair and carry them off through the forest, burning it as they go."

On watching the film digitally via a mainstream film streaming service (at the point of writing it is not available on DVD/Blu-ray) it is clear that anybody buying or renting this online and expecting conventional mainstream fare in any sense may be more than a little disappointed.

It could possibly be called a "slasher in the woods but without the slashing" – and is all the more disturbing for it (a note on such could well be sent back in time to the likes of the earlier mentioned Queens of Evil, 1974's *Symptoms,* 1977's *Suspira* and much of what has come to be known as giallo cinema).

Through many hours of watching, the viewer's mind can become programmed to expect cinema to travel down certain routes, particular actions to follow particular setups.

While Butter on the Latch interacts with cinematic tropes and conventions, it beats its own fragmentary path through them; the film is imbued deeply with a sense of dread and dysfunction and following those just mentioned conventions there's a sense of waiting for something terrible to happen in a conventional thriller or slasher manner.

Although the film may follow some of those expected cinematic routes, it is not presented in a manner that could be closely associated with standard cinematic expectations.

As a moment or two of calm amongst that dread, at points the film may just stop, pause and focus on close ups of woodland foliage. There is an entrancing beauty captured in such moments: you hope to remain ensconced in them but in this tale that is not how things are to be.

This is a form of folk horror where "folk" could be taken as implying "being from the wild woods"; these are woods that seem both tamed and untamed, connected to civilisation and yet those within it have also crumbled away from it.

These elements of Butter on the Latch connect with defining aspects of folk horror referred to previously: a sense of isolation and places where that isolation has come to mean that the norms, boundaries and safety nets of wider society are no longer fully present.

In terms of the film's aesthetics, the phrases cinéma vérité or realist documentary comes to mind, in the sense of it being made without frills or technically advanced artifice; although it is a fictional film, it is set in an actual folklife centre and features what appear to be non-actor participants and performers.

As a cultural intertwining aside, the music that accompanies the film and which is played in the camp is to the untutored ear in part not far removed from the stately, elegiac, otherly album of Bulgarian folk songs

Le Mystère des Voix Bulgares which 4AD released in the 1980s. While the film is also reminiscent here and there of the lower-fi aesthetics of David Lynch's 2006 film *Inland Empire*; Hollywood but at a far, dark remove.

The hand-held documentary feel is complimented or should that be fractured by surreal flashes of staring faces in the woods and other intriguing, hypnotic, yet terribly unsettling images and sounds, often with a more overtly folk horror/horror aspect; such split second moments, even if you pause or try to watch the film frame by frame are hard to quite fathom, explain or take in. To again quote Sight & Sound magazine:

> "Decker creates a weave of woozy camera movements and abrupt cuts that at once trouble and open up the viewer's perception."

Often today films are lauded as/for being independent cinema but essentially they are still quite conventional with maybe just a few quirks or less corporate funding (which is not meant as a criticism, more merely an observation).

However Butter on the Latch is a very different piece of work; this is genuinely experimental and exploratory cinema, an art piece but still definitely a cinematic film rather than being created for the gallery, low budget without being a B, C or Z-movie. And as with In the Dark Half, it is gritty without being social realist. It has an abstract, undefinedly unsettling atmosphere and is not always a conventionally easy-viewing experience, but nevertheless remains intriguing throughout.

1. A film which is discussed in Chapter 23.
2. *Grand Designs* is a long-running British television series that documents people spending often large sums of money custom building unusual homes for themselves and their families, *England's Hidden Reverse* is a 2003 book by David Keenan that focuses on the work and music of Coil, Current 93 and Nurse With Wound and posits the idea that they represent the real English cultural underground. The soundtrack to Puffball features Coil and Nurse With Wound, with the music to the film all sinister portents and drones that veers upwards and outwards, venturing into more normal climes and back again.
3. Discussed in Chapter 11.

17

The Quietened Bunker, Waiting for the End of the World, **Subterranea Britannica,** ***Bunker Archaeology*** **and** ***The Delaware Road*:** Ghosts, Havens and Curious Repurposings Beneath our Feet

ABANDONED AND DECOMMISSIONED bunkers are a subsection of utilitarian brutalist architecture that has come to gain totemic significance and to have a form of romance attached to them.

This can take a hauntological form where Cold War bunkers in particular have come to represent and be symbols of the spectres of history.

This connects with a central defining tenet of hauntological strands of interest: explorations of and fascinations with lost futures and areas of culture, artifacts, buildings, institutions etc. which are imprinted with spectres of those lost histories.

In this sense such bunkers are physical embodiments of the (thankfully) lost futures of end of days conflicts: the unsettling and disquieting counterpart to social and municipal brutalist buildings from a similar epoch and the yearning for lost progressive utopian futures that they can represent.

Generally we tend to think of Cold War bunkers, particularly those built by governments, as being located in the countryside and intended more for use by high end and/or control personnel.

However, a nuclear attack bunker exists buried underneath Germany's capital city Berlin, which was intended for use by the general population.

This is a somewhat spectral reminder of the Cold War, in both a hauntological and fear-instilling manner.

Or as writer, illustrator and designer John Coulthart has said bunkers are:

> "...a source of contemporary horror that doesn't require any supernatural component to chill the blood."

This Berlin bunker contains outdated technology but is still fully functioning and maintained. It was designed to hold 20,000 people in the near dark, in almost total humidity and without medical care. The air filters were designed to operate for only two weeks, which would not have been sufficient time for contamination levels outside to fall before the bunker's population had to leave.

It features row upon row of metal bunk beds and is not a fun place to visit, even for less than an hour.

As part of a bunker tour, visitors are shown a short video that features the attack sirens sounding and the bunker door slamming shut.

It serves as a stark reminder of the realities of these structures and the futility of their use as a form of defence; a very physical representation of the Cold War dread which underpins much of hauntology.

Connected to that sense of futility or delusional projections of their effectiveness, in 2014 as part of *A Year In The Country* a themed album called *The Quietened Bunker* was released.

This featured work by Keith Seatman, Grey Frequency, A Year In The Country, Panabrite, Polypores, Listening Center, Time Attendant, Unknown Heretic and David Colohan and interpreted the album's theme via recordings that included field recording subterranean ambience, paranoid industrial distortion, Radiophonic inflected electronica and elegiac end of days sequences. The accompanying notes are as follows:

> "The Quietened Bunker is an exploration of the abandoned and/or decommissioned Cold War installations which lie under the land and that would have acted as selectively populated refuges/

control centres if the button was ever pushed.

These bunkers could be seen as once modern fortresses - reinforced concrete and blast doors replacing moats and stone battlements.

The intention was that they would form part of a network of civil defence and management, accompanied by government-issued *Protect and Survive* leaflets/broadcasts that would have offered advice on how to protect home and hearth via little more than whitewashing windows as blast protection and forming a shelter by leaning mattresses against an inner wall of your house.

Looking back, such preparations can seem a reflection of some kind of madness or delusion in the collective consciousness and the halls of power - a tilting at windmills that was necessary to protect national psyches from the reality and aftermath of the sudden use and descending of mechanisms with almost indescribable destructive power.

Now it can all seem like a dream from another world, one where for a number of decades populations lived under the day-to-day threat of total annihilation and where millions was spent on this network of shelters and defences; preparations to allow fiddling once all had burned, such bunkers possibly being nearer to utilitarian national follies than fortresses - indeed, today they are as likely to be signposted tourist attractions as operative defences.

The Quietened Bunker reflects on these chimeric bulwarks and the faded but still present memory of associated Cold War dread, of which they are stalwart but mouldering symbols."

This album is part of a lineage of work that explores, is inspired by and documents bunkers, shelters and related infrastructure.

The book *Waiting for the End of the World* by Richard Ross published in 2004 is part of this lineage. It contains photographs of active and decommissioned bunkers and shelters around the world, both those built by governmental/military organisations and by private individuals.

One intriguing thing about some of the photographs of domestic shelters are the details of the way they have been made to feel homely and the amount of aesthetic consideration often given to their entrances, in the face of and opposition to what their occupants would be faced with if their intended purpose was ever called upon.

While many of the institutionally-built shelters are shown as harsh, utilitarian or crumbling places, this is contrasted by the entrance and blast doors for one Swiss public shelter which have been painted a somewhat incongruous seeming bright, friendly welcoming pink.

Rather than being purely documentary in nature, Richard Ross's book belongs more to the world of fine art photography in that it is a photography project which is underpinned with a sense of the creative or personal expression of its author.

In this instance Richard Ross says that he wishes to make the shelters and their present status real and tangible by presenting them as visual images rather than as more abstract intellectual ideas.

As is also referred to in the above notes to The Quietened Bunker, he comments on their ineffectiveness as a logical solution or salvation, in particular due to the minute number of them that exist in comparison to the size of population.

However, he also found a sense of hope and optimism in their repurposing as clubs in St. Petersburg, Russia and how these have become places where people go to celebrate life rather than anticipate destruction.

Other photography-based work which explores such buildings and installations is more strictly documentary in nature, in particular that done by the British based Subterranea Britannica society. Subterranea Britannica's members:

> "...study and investigate man-made and man-used underground places - from mines to railway tunnels, military defences to nuclear bunkers and everything in between."

They have published a number of comprehensive books featuring bunker-related work, including Nick Catford's *Cold War Bunkers* (2010) and Mark Dalton's *The Royal Observer Corps Underground Monitoring Posts* (2011).

The work in these books and by its members, which involves photography and text based notes and observations, is more a rigorous archival recording than the more expressive nature of *Waiting for the End of the World.*

Via its publishing activities, the collecting of archival material and photographs and notes from exploratory expeditions to locations by members which are viewable on its website, the society's work represents a comprehensive mapping of these often once secret or inaccessible to the public places and infrastructure networks.

A predecessor to the above Cold War bunker related lineage of work is Paul Virilio's book *Bunker Archaeology*, originally published in a French edition in 1975.

This collects his photography and writing on the abandoned World War II German bunkers and related installations that lie along the coast of France.

Along with their Cold War counterparts, these could also be filed as a form of brutalist architecture as they share a number of similarities in terms of the materials used and their aesthetics.

In comparison to many Cold War bunkers and structures, those in Paul Virilio's book seem to more inherently contain a curious and surprising, considering their nature, beauty or even poetry; they have a unifying flow or philosophy to them despite their once aggressive and defensive intentions.

The above refers to their aesthetics and artistic aspects rather than their political underpinning. However within the totalitarian regime that instigated them there was often something of an intertwining of such things.

Viewed now they seem to almost be a form of accidental utilitarian art: something they share with the likes of similarly appreciated pragmatic constructions such as telegraph poles, pylons, Soviet era bus stops or even library music.[1]

Although they were created with a very practical intent, looking at them now they seem nearer to monuments or tributes, reminiscent of the Cold War era Spomenik memorials that Jan Kempenaers photographed and which are collected in his 2010 book of the same name.[2]

With the structures in Bunker Archaeology, whatever their original intents, viewing them today they could be artifacts from an almost science fiction-esque future that never was, a form of hauntology possibly but one that steps aside from or precedes many of the more often referred to British cultural history related tropes.

That science fiction-esque quality seems particularly present in some of the structures that have been partly covered by or have sunk into the sand and their appearance brings to mind sentient or anthropomorphic crashed spaceships, alongside their actuality as bunkers and defensive outposts.

(The original *Planet of the Apes* film from 1968 swims into view with its mingling of crashed future/past visitors and part-buried monuments to mankind's folly.)

As with the earlier-mentioned, still actively maintained, Berlin bunker, decommissioned Cold War bunkers have also become part of the heritage tourist industry in the UK and as mentioned in the notes to The Quietened Bunker album they are "as likely to be signposted tourist attractions as operative defences".

They are even available to hire for events: one such of which is *The Delaware Road* event organised by record label Buried Treasure in 2017 and which accompanies their themed album of the same name.

This event was deeply interconnected with hauntological themes and tropes, featuring a number of performers whose work has been to various degrees linked with such areas of work including Dolly Dolly, Howlround, Radionics Radio, Ian Helliwell and Saunders & Hill.

It was described as an immersive mix of theatre, film and live music and some of the notes that accompany the event are reproduced below:

> "The Kelvedon Hatch Secret Nuclear Bunker at Kelvedon Hatch, in the Borough of Brentwood in the English county of Essex, is a large underground bunker maintained during the cold war as a potential regional government headquarters. Since being decommissioned in 1992, the bunker has been open to the public as a tourist attraction, with a museum focusing on its cold war history."

> "London, 1968. Two brilliant musicians create innovative sound using reel-to-reel tape. Whilst working for a large media organisation they stumble upon a conspiracy with seismic implications for themselves and for Britain. Exploring folklore, magic, propaganda, television & radio broadcasting, counter-culture & early, electronic music, The Delaware Road is an incredible, alternative vision of Britain during the second half of the 20th century."

> "This special performance takes place deep underground in a nuclear bunker, hidden in remote Essex woodland. The audience is free to explore the secret, cold war facilities where they will encounter a host of performers, experimental artists & musicians."

As with some of the bunkers in Waiting for the End of the World which have come to be used as clubs, this is a repurposing of such structures for entertainment or cultural purposes, albeit in this case a form of cultural exploration which explicitly refers to and explores the history of them rather than being more strictly hedonistic socialising and abandonment.

Returning more directly to the heritage and tourist industry repurposing of such installations, on British roads you can find official road signs that direct you towards the tourist destination of a "Secret Nuclear Bunker", often appearing on the same sign as one which also points drivers to an industrial estate and various towns.

Viewing these signs may bring kind of mental disconnect - a mixture of disbelief, humour and relief that we are no longer living in a political situation where these bunkers are considered necessary and possibly a touch of sadness, anger and grief for us having once done so.

In part this disconnect is due to the very Britishness of names like Chipping Ongar and Chigwell that the road signs also point to.

It may also be due to their sometimes positioning in amongst day-to-day normal housing or the gentle grey-green of the land, all of which are juxtaposed with these signposts to once end-of-days refuges.

Accompanying and interconnected with such road signs are the estate agent signs for when a decommissioned bunker has been made available for sale; the hoardings name the property for sale as a nuclear bunker and list its square footage and acreage of land.

Begging the question: is this a buyer's or a seller's market?

There is scarcity value to the property but presumably only a very limited number of potential buyers and allowable uses (data storage seems to be one such usage that is mentioned on these boards).

It would be interesting to see whether these installations are listed on general commercial property websites, so that your search results might bring up a warehouse for rent, listed as having plenty of onsite parking and then a former secret nuclear bunker listed as razor wire and emergency air filtration system included.

1. Discussed in Chapter 32.
2. Discussed in Chapter 12.

18

From *The Unofficial Countryside* to *Soft Estate*: Edgeland Documents, Memories and Explorations

EDGELANDS IS A WORD that refers to the edges of towns and cities that are neither urban nor rural; transitional, undeveloped or developing areas such as the land surrounding power stations, scrublands, wastelands, semi-derelict areas, semi-industrial areas and so forth.

These are often the places where society creates, stores, repairs, discards, forgets about and disposes of the things it physically needs and they can also be starkly aesthetically neglected, though in contrast and in part because of that neglect or overlooking can also become something of a haven for nature and wildlife.

Edgelands contain many of society's overlooked and often unsupervised nooks and crannies and so can seem to represent an ideal playground for a child (although they may not seem quite so ideal to parents due to them often containing various hazards and dangers).

Edgelands are random places and fascinating for a child: for myself they included building a dam across the river next to an old crystal deposit encrusted railway tunnel, a concrete military pillbox sitting incongruously at the edge of a field, an overgrown and more or less abandoned local graveyard where you could scare yourself by moving and peering inside the walls of old monuments.

Or a road that had broken up and collapsed down a hillside where if feeling intrepid you were able to pry the cats-eyes[1] from the remains of the middle of the road, the craters on hillsides where you could excitedly scavenge rusted machine remains, thinking they were sites where planes had crashed (they may have been discarded agricultural equipment, but these remains could have been aeronautical in origin as historically planes had crashed nearby).

Alongside these more rural edgelands lie actual edgelands: places that could have been real life 1970s public information film settings (instructional government sponsored films intended for television broadcast that told of the dangers to be found there).

I also found myself playing among humming electricity pylons and tumbling amongst the abandoned fridges and washing machines on a hillside which led down to a river that would change colour depending on what was being pumped into it upstream.

For myself, such youthful edgeland playgrounds also took in an edge of town decommissioned airforce base, which had become a semi-developed camping park complete with can, bottle and possibly spectre-filled air raid shelters.

In later years they would include wandering on grey Sundays through the local industrial estate, where a coffin factory shared space sandwiched between fields and the main road with a poultry-processing establishment, which I would walk around to the soundtrack of suitably upliftingly depressing music on a borrowed portable cassette player.

Marion Shoard was the first person to use the term "edgelands" to describe these areas in her *Edglands* essay from 2002, where she eloquently describes and defines them and considers how they are often overlooked by society:

> "Britain's towns and cities do not usually sit cheek by jowl with its countryside, as we often casually assume. Between urban and rural stands a kind of landscape quite different from either. Often vast in area, though hardly noticed, it is characterised by rubbish tips and warehouses, superstores and derelict industrial plant,

> office parks and gypsy encampments, golf courses, allotments and fragmented, frequently scruffy, farmland. All these heterogeneous elements are arranged in an unruly and often apparently chaotic fashion against a background of unkempt wasteland frequently swathed in riotous growths of colourful plants, both native and exotic... Huge numbers of people now spend much of their time living, working or moving within or through it. Yet for most of us, most of the time, this mysterious no man's land passes unnoticed: in our imaginations, as opposed to our actual lives, it barely exists... As we flash past its seemingly meaningless contours in train, car or bus we somehow fail to register it on our retinas."

In a continuum from Marion Shoard's observations, an extensive body of literature and creative work exists which has focused on these hinterlands.

One of the early and most renowned documents or celebrations of such overlooked, often unloved parts of our world was Richard Mabey's *The Unofficial Countryside* book, originally published in 1973 (and reissued in 2010 by Little Toller Books, who specialise in work which takes in a gentle flipside of rural, pastoral and landscape concerns).

The Unofficial Countryside records Richard Mabey's explorations and wanderings through edgeland areas and the natural world, which has made a home in places that had previously often been considered inauspicious for plants and wildlife such as inner city car parks, gravel pits and rubbish tips.

Rather than being purely a natural history document, within the book he also proposes another way of seeing and experiencing nature during our daily lives, whether wildflowers glimpsed from a commuter train, fox cubs playing on a motorway fringe or a kestrel hawking above a public park.

The social, political and economic strife of the UK at the time of its original publication makes its subject matter of plants and nature creeping and surviving through broken concrete, covering bombsites, thriving in cities and the associated sense of neglect and collapse somehow rather appropriate.

Edgelands - Journeys into England's True Wilderness is a 2012 book by Paul Farley and Michael Symmons Roberts and is a literary, poetic exploration of such areas, in which the authors document their travels, personal memories and connections to these transitional landscapes, taking in along the way childhood dens, container ports, wastelands, ruins, mines and the endpoints for society's automobiles.

In a more audiovisual manner the 2013 film, music and photography project by Karl Hyde and Kieran Evans' *Edgeland/The Outer Edges* presents a psychogeographic expressive, creative and documentary wandering through what feel like semi-uncharted lands and lives, ones which are overlooked, strewn with debris and contain a faded battered beauty amongst the mixture of nature and pylons.

Edward Chell's 2013 *Soft Estate* also makes use of multiple forms, including a book, traditional gallery exhibiting and what are effectively returning to their source installations. It takes as its subject matter such edgeland places when they are found at the side of motorways.

The phrase soft estate refers to the description given by the UK Highways Agency to the natural habitat that the motorways and trunk roads it manages occupy; an often unstopped-on hinterland that most of us only view as a high-speed blur from the corner of our eyes as we travel past these autobahn edgelands.

Soft Estate interacts with and documents these verges and landscapes, sometimes in a quite literal sense as some of the work is printed using road dust from such places, other work uses (presumably) engine oil, features plant life illustrations from these verges laser etched onto brightly chromed exhaust pipes or uses the same materials and colours as road signs.

In his paintings of the tubing which protects sapling trees (many millions of which have been planted on such lands), the mind's eye sees them rather as gravestones.

Indeed there is a ghostly, spectral quality to these paintings; they have a hauntological aspect in that although they are created in contemporary times, they also seem like documents of modernity's future and past.

Alongside which they also capture the spirit and point at which nature tumbles alongside and into mankind's march of progress and there is a meditative, calming sense to them; they ease the soul and provide a moment's respite.

The Soft Estate book is also a collection of essays and effectively an exhibition catalogue, albeit one which exists as a handsomely produced artifact in its own right.

The book includes a piece of writing by Richard Mabey and the inclusion of his writing here can be seen as providing a continuing line from and through considerations of edgelands in their various forms.

Intriguingly, some of Edward Chell's work has been installed in Little Chefs, which are British roadside family cafes/restaurants.

For many British children, these provided a first taste of what are now regarded as American-style burgers and fries. In the 1970s and 80s (and possibly later) in Little Chefs these were served on a plate with knives and forks in what was nearer to a traditional restaurant setting rather than eaten by hand in a burger bar or cafe as would become standard with burgers in later years; along with the nature of edgelands themselves, such places, presentation and foodstuffs can be seen as another transitional/liminal point.

On now-rare sightings of Little Chefs, they feel like endangered species: a quaint remnant of times gone by before the ubiquity of transnational chains and the utilitarian installations of motorway service stations.

It brings a smile to think of Edward Chell's work in them, which seems like an apposite, humorous coming together of cultures.

1. Reflective glass road markings that originated in the UK, before being adopted worldwide.

19

The Ballad of Shirley Collins and *Pastoral Noir*: Tales and Intertwinings from Hidden Furrows

Shirley Collins is known in part for her contributions to the English folk revival of the 1960s and 1970s; beginning in 1959 she released a number of solo and collaborative albums with amongst others her sister Dolly, Dave Graham and Ashley Hutchings/The Albion Band.

She also worked with Alan Lomax on various projects including folk song collecting in the Southern States of the USA in the late 1950s, which she wrote about in her 2005 book *America Over the Water.*

After 1982 Shirley Collins lost her singing voice due to what has been considered psychogenic dysphonia: a condition which affects the throat and which is associated with psychological trauma. Although she lectured, wrote and appeared on radio she did not release another album for several decades until 2016's *Lodestar.*

Prior to that new album Rob Curry and Tim Plester began work on a documentary of her work and life called *The Ballad of Shirley Collins,* which at the point of writing was nearing completion, with an accompanying trailer having been released.

The tone and presentation of the trailer and related publicity appear in part to show the film as reflecting how Shirley Collins and her work now seem to be intertwined and connect with modern day tropes, themes and interests in what could variously be called underground, neo or wyrd folk, folk horror and a sort of Arcanic Britannia.

In particular this is the case with images, sequences and characters within the trailer which are of a folk horror-esque or otherly folkloric nature (Nick Abrahams' video for Shirley Collins' version of "Death and the Lady" from the Lodestar album, released in 2016, also explores similar territory).

This positioning amongst such strands of folk is also made quite implicit by naming Shirley Collins as "The High Queene of English Folk" in the trailer, with its connotations of an almost occult, arcane take on such things.

The definitions, phrases and cultural strands wyrd folk, folk horror and the like did not overtly exist or at least had not been specifically named as such when Shirley Collins was performing and recording in earlier decades.

However, looking back at her recording of the traditional folk song "Poor Murdered Woman" (as featured on her 1971 album *No Roses* and the Bob Stanley-curated compilation *Early Morning Hush – Notes from the UK Folk Underground 1969-1976* released in 2006,[1] although it was inspired by true events, listening to it today with its dark unsettling tone it could well be seen as a pointer or harbinger for the darker elements of folk and folk horror.

Moving towards such strands and areas within and around Shirley Collins' work may also be connected back to David Tibet of Current 93's championing of it for a number of years and his releasing a compilation of her 1960s and 1970s recordings called *Fountain of Snow* back in 1992.

Current 93's "idiosyncratic meeting of old English folk, apocalyptic Christianity, and haunted horror" (to quote Louis Pattison writing at the *Bandcamp* website) has been called neo-folk, a form of often dark, experimental folk music which emerged from post-industrial circles.

Such neo-folk could also be seen as a further forebear for contemporary interest in wyrd folk and related folk horror-esque music.

Those post-industrial strands of experimental music also include Nurse With Wound and Coil, which while musically different and not necessarily folk-orientated, has been described and connected as being "*England's Hidden Reverse*" by David Keenan, in the title of his 2003 book of the same name in which he writes about their work.

That title creates and captures a sense of the hidden, flipside, underlying strands and patterns of culture which their work often seems to reflect and explore – which also connects back to the likes of wyrd folk and its exploration of similar areas and undercurrents within a more pastoral, landscape and rural based context.

Alongside the connection to David Tibet, such strands are further connected with Shirley Collins' recent work due to Stephen Thrower and Ossian Brown performing on her new album, both of whom have worked with Coil.

They currently work together as Cyclobe and their releases mix and combine aspects of folk or traditional music and instruments amongst other elements including drone, audio collage, soundscaping and electronic instrumentation within an experimental or exploratory context.

In a further intertwining of the underground, darker, flipside and undercurrents of folk-related culture, Ossian Brown compiled a book released in 2010 called *Haunted Air* which collects found photographs of Halloween from previous eras.

The images in Haunted Air, despite them having originally been family snapshots etc., over time have often gained a genuinely unsettling, otherly air.

Such a gathering and layering of the uncanny over time is also present within The Ballad of Shirley Collins trailer; at one point a framed photograph is shown of Shirley Collins and her sister Dolly standing either side of what is either a folkoric totem or possibly somebody in a traditional folkloric ram's head costume.

Once upon a time, although possessing a certain inherently odd or eerie aspect due to its intrinsic nature, this may well have been a more standard, typical example of folklore costume.

However, in the overall context of the trailer and the above cultural points of connection it seems to belong to considerably more shadowed, unsettled furrows.

Interconnected to such shadowed furrows, writer, artist and curator Justin Hopper used the title *Pastoral Noir* as the name of an exhibition he curated at Wood Street Galleries in Pittsburgh, USA in 2016, describing it as being a collection of avant-rural work by British and Irish artists:

> "...whose work is situated in the edgelands between what we once called human and the natural... Pastoral Noir will look at artists whose work calls into question the dichotomies between past and present, city and countryside, natural and man-made, within the landscape of the British Isles.
>
> Through their visual, sonic and sculptural investigations into the English landscape, the artists in Pastoral Noir have discovered a dark and eerie place. Using science and language, memory and myth, these works immerse the viewer in uncanny landscapes both real and imagined."

The work shown included Tessa Farmer, Jem Finer, Ghost Box Records, Tony Heywood & Alison Condie, Autumn Richardson and Richard-Skelton and could be considered an exploration of where the further reaches of folk and pastoral culture meet, intertwine and interact with what has come to be known as hauntology.[2]

The use of the phrase pastoral noir may be part of a seemingly wider, ongoing process of experimenting with and searching for names that could possibly serve to encompass and define such intertwined cultural explorations.

However aesthetically and on first glance there could appear to be a disjunction between the words pastoral and noir, their inferences, history and cultural reference points.

To a degree that sense of disjunction depends on how you consider or define the word "noir"; in large part it is a very city bound, often cinematic and fictional crime-related particular style and aesthetic, that brings to mind Raymond Chandler-esque stories of almost knight in shining armour, mystery solving private eyes and a particular related set of period signifiers and imagery.

However, mystery and crime fiction editor Otto Penzler takes the following darker view of the characteristics of noir:

> "...whether films, novels or short stories, are existential, pessimistic tales about people, including (or especially) protagonists who are seriously flawed and morally questionable. The tone is generally bleak and nihilistic, with characters whose greed, lust, jealousy and alienation lead them into a downward spiral as their plans and schemes inevitably go awry... the likelihood of a happy ending in a noir story is remote... It will end badly, because the characters are inherently corrupt and that is the fate that inevitably awaits them."

In fact, over the years, the use and meaning of noir has become something of a confluence of the two.

If you should focus on or subscribe more to Otto Penzler's bleaker, nihilistic definition of noir then pastoral and noir may well have a number of links within the darker narratives of some traditional folk.

These could include Shirley Collin's earlier mentioned "Poor Murdered Woman" and its desolate, dark and unsettling tale. While traditional song "Cruel Mother", as performed by Shirley Collins, Steeleye Span and The Owl Service amongst others[3] and its particularly brutal tale of the desperate actions of a mother deserted by her lover and subsequent damnation, could in a different context and era well be the plot to a noir-ish film or novel (albeit with a supernatural element).

1. Discussed in Chapter 2.
2. That meeting and interaction are discussed in Chapter 4.
3. Discussed in Chapter 37.

20

"Savage Party" and *Randall & Hopkirk (Deceased)*: Glimpses of Albion in the Overgrowth

NOW, ONTO *HOLLYOAKS*. No, don't run for the hills…

In 2012 in the earlyish days of planning for *A Year In The Country* there was a trailer being broadcast for an episode called "Savage Party" of the British television youth-orientated soap opera Hollyoaks.

The trailer is basically a high street-esque take on some of the visual language, themes and tropes of the flipside or undercurrents of folkloric culture expressed in the likes of *The Wicker Man* (1973): a glimpse of Albion in the cultural overgrowth, a step through the gates into the secret garden (with spangly hotpants as your attire).

It shows the young folk entering a gated slightly magical-seeming woodland; they are often animal masked, behorned and May Queen crowned and enter an unsupervised carnivalesque atmosphere which seems to subtly hark back to earlier almost pagan times. This is accompanied by flickering projections, preternatural weather, torchlit processions and a subtle sense of dread to come for some of its inhabitants.

The trailer's soundtrack is Stealing Sheep's "Shut Eye" (2012), which is a lovely catchy sort of psych-folk indie-pop song, with the band's music reminding me in a way of a more youthful, British Coco Rosie (the sister duo who were loosely connected with American freak folk in the 2000s, along with the likes of Devandra Banhart and Joanna Newsom). And yes the trailer is a simulacra of folklore-inspired culture but still enjoyable.

This brings into play notions of authenticity; what they actually mean, why we place such a high value on authenticity, which is such an elusive and intangible thing but at the same time often seems very apparent when it is there and when it is not.

For some reason this promotional video blurs those lines a touch. It is joyous, ridiculous, a copy and also created with some sense of love or passion for its source material, even if that is but a flickering, passing moment of interest.

All stories are created or summoned forth from imagination at some point, even the most precious and longstanding folkloric tales probably originally stumbled out of the mind/s of individuals but somewhere along the line they have put down roots and become thought of as authentic.

The Wicker Man is a prime example; this was a fictional film created with quite a pile of cash by one of the moneyed sides of the culture business as a commercial project and the music was created by a band put together for this purpose but it has become an authentic totem of a particular kind of otherly Albion and folklore.

Aside from such things the Savage Party trailer is perhaps something of a guilty pleasure but a pleasure nonetheless.

(Curiously in 2016 there was a "Halloween on Hollyoaks" trailer which drew from one of the other more flipsides of filmic culture, Italian supernatural horror and interconnected giallo, and was basically a homage to Dario Argento's *Suspiria* film from 1977 - although this trailer seemed a little more clumsy, a little less layered than the Savage Party one.)

The appearance of such less thoroughly travelled themes in mainstream culture can seem like something of an unexpected treat when it is treated in a respectful manner and done at least reasonably well.

Along which lines, a soft spot should be reserved for the turn of the millennium remake of television series *Randall and Hopkirk (Deceased)* that was broadcast in 2000-2001, and which was produced by Charlie Higson, who also wrote and directed some episodes, and starred comedians Vic Reeves and Bob Mortimer alongside Emilia Fox and gloriously white-haired former Doctor Who Tom Baker.

It is a series which concerns itself with a still-living private investigator who is visited, helped and hindered by the white-suited ghost of his former partner (the deceased of the title) and it is not a million miles away from the likes of *Doctor Who* in its mixing of fantasy and science fiction in a mainstream setting.

Yes, it is cheesy. Yes, it has that curiously dated appearance that cultural work from the 90s and around then currently has; not yet old enough to have gained a patina of retro fetishistic kitsch, not quite modern enough to fit with current tastes.

Yes, Vic Reeves and Bob Mortimer's acting is not necessarily that of high-end thespians but it is good knockabout fun. It is nothing too challenging but it often shows a great love for a whole slew of fantasy, television, literature, crime horror and science fiction films etc. from years gone by in the way that it references and draws from them.

The episode *Man of Substance* in particular, which seems to predate Edgar Wright & Simon Pegg's *Hot Fuzz* film of 2007 by a year or few in a number of its themes, borrowings and the story of a sleepy country idyll gone bad and is rather folk horror-like in its setting and plot.

It begins somewhat noirishly with a red silk clad femme fatale giving a private eye the glad eye and purr in his office, before it wanders off to a classic chocolate box English idyll of a village; all tea rooms, commemorative tea towels and an avuncular British bobby on the beat (who appears to be the living incarnation of a mechanical laughing policeman that would have once been found in a seaside amusement arcade). This is a neat, quiet and tidy piece of heritage real estate.

However, not so surprisingly things are not quite what they seem (spoiler alert about now).

The village has a dark secret or two and quite quickly it becomes apparent that something is not quite right in this particular chocolate box and the village is revealed as having a kind of parallel world existence.

Its population have been trapped in between life and death, unable to leave the village since the days that a pestilence had caused the demise of a considerable percentage of the English population a number of centuries previously.

(I guess we should have known something was not quite right when shown the unsettling monument on the way into the village that looked as though it should have been on the cover of one of the *John Barleycorn Reborn* series of dark Britannica compilation albums of wyrd, exploratory, underground etc folk that were released by Cold Spring beginning in 2007.)

Along the way towards the almost taking over the world shenanigans that the villagers get up to, the episode wanders into the territory of and borrows from:

The Wicker Man, with petal scattering woodland nymphs dancing through the churchyard. 1970s and early 1980s British horror portmanteau films such as *The Monster Club* (1981) and one of their "you're never going to escape from the village" plots. Medievalistic fetishistic pleasures by way of *Curse of the Crimson Altar* (1968). A touch of Hansel and Gretel and the fattening up of the chosen calves.

The somewhat unpleasant punishments of the incarcerated via *Witchfinder General* (1968) or its less well-known brethren *The Bloody Judge* (1970). Possibly even a touch of *Penda's Fen* (1974) and its sense of the mythic and mystical in the landscape and returning kings. And then back to The Wicker Man, as the fool becomes the king for the day (and eternity) during a local festival in service of the community's ends where a pyre is made for a sacrifical burning.

And just having Tom Baker, possibly still the archetypal Doctor Who, in amongst it all makes the episode fundamentally interconnected in the minds of watchers of a certain vintage with particular culture and tropes.

Oh and that is before we get to Gareth Thomas, who once starred as a freedom fighter in the cult science fiction series *Blake's 7* (1978-1981), who here plays a real ale pushing pub landlord who later appears in his festival garb only to be revealed as a centuries-old medieval lord of the manor.

Randall & Hopkirk is not necessarily as dark but thinking back this episode may have shared some ground with the similar time period's *The League of Gentleman* series that was broadcast from 1999-2002 and its mixing of horror and comedy in a rural setting gone bad where "You bain't be from round here" is the general refrain.

At the time of the Randall & Hopkirk remake's transmission the revival and growing interest in all things Wicker Man and folk horror-ish had not yet fully gained pace and yet here many of its themes and interests were looked to as inspiration for peak viewing entertainment.

JUST PRIOR TO its broadcast the The Wicker Man soundtrack had been first released in 1998 via the efforts and investigating of Jonny Trunk and Trunk Records and this is thought to have been one of the sparks that ignited that growing interest.

However, the number of different references to fantastic fictions from before that time in the series suggest its creator had a knowledge, interest and love of such things that stretches back some way.

For example the episode *Fair Isle* is set on an isolated island called Strait Isle which has its own laws and ways of doing things, produces its own unique foodstuff under the direction of an eccentric lord ruler and includes high jinx with the locals in a very local hostelry, all of which further echo The Wicker Man.

That episode also features Doctor Who-esque folkloric costumed creatures, ecological worries that have shades of the series *Doomwatch* (1970-1972), transformations which echo Ken Russell's *Altered States* film (1980), a hiding of relics which harks back to *The Raiders of the Lost Ark* (1981) and even an "I would've got away with it if it wasn't for you pesky kids" *Scooby Doo*-esque unveiling of the baddie.

As with Savage Garden, Randall & Hopkirk provides further glimpses of the flipside and undercurrents of folkloric culture in the cultural overgrowth and is also something of a guilty pleasure but a pleasure nonetheless.

21

Uncommonly British Days Out and the Following of Ghosts: File under Psychogeographic/Hauntological Stocking Fillers

Because of their titles, the two books *Bollocks to Alton Towers* (2005) and *Far from the Sodding Crowd* (2007) on initial sighting could well be just another in a long line of Christmas market throwaway fodder.

In fact, despite their jokey titles, some of the marketing and the paperback editions' jokey covers featuring garden gnomes there is something more to these particular books than is often found in such things.

Essentially they are guidebooks for, as their subtitles say "*Uncommonly British Days Out*"; the books are documents of the authors' Jason Hazeley, Robin Halstead, Joel Morris and Alex Morris' wanderings to often small, individual or family-run museums, visitor centres, follies, unofficial non-tours of television series recording locations, neglected or unloved public art, bygone defence of the realm installations and the like.

To mention but a few examples, in amongst the books are an appreciation of restored once-were-the-future 1960s diesel electric railway routes, the craftsmanship and pre-digital marvels of Keith Harding's *World of Mechanical Music* and its often-metallic melody machines, the possibly slightly eccentric, particularly focused collections of The British Lawnmower Museum and Barometer World, the decommissioned but still maintained Kelvedon Hatch Nuclear Bunker and so forth.

Generally they focus on attractions and places to visit that are off the beaten track, that seem in part to hark back to a gentler, more communally-spirited, sometimes progressive time or ethos and as they progress the books become an exploration of a semi-lost or overlooked British landscape and its cultural markers.

Be warned: reading them may cause you to plan a slightly panicked journey across the country, hoping that the places and attractions featured are still there to see and enjoy.

In Mark Fisher's Ghosts of my Life book published by Zero Books in 2014, which is loosely concerned with hauntological themes, the titles of the chapters that directly focus on the sometimes called hauntological work of Ghost Box Records instigators and recording artists The Focus Group, Belbury Poly and The Advisory Circle are "Nostalgia for Modernism" and "The Ache of Nostalgia" and these books put the reader in mind of such things.

In Chapter 3: "Hauntology: Places Where Society Goes to Dream…" there is a list of some of the defining characteristics of what has come to be known as hauntological culture. Part of which is that it is:

> "Music and culture that draws from and examines a sense of loss of a post war utopian, progressive, modern(ist?) future that was never quite reached."

In many ways that seems to be a subtly underlying theme of the Uncommonly British Days Out books; they are imbued with a quiet anger at the loss of what in some ways could be seen to be terribly British decency and politeness but could actually be seen to be an ire at the steam rolling, this way or the high way tendencies of the modern (but dominantly not modernistic) world.

There is a sense in the books of a Britain that is haunted, harried, hurried by some kind of potentially overwhelming loss but wherein there are little corners or enclaves of individuality, resistance and eccentricities.

At one point the text says "You are following the ghost of something interesting, and it left ages ago."

Which brings us back to hauntology and Mark Fisher's following observations:

> "The artists that came to be labelled hauntological were suffused with an overwhelming melancholy.
>
> "As to the deeper cause of this melancholia, we need look no further than the title of Leyland Kirby's album: *Sadly, the Future is No Longer What it Was.* In hauntological music there is an implicit acknowledgement that the hopes created by postwar electronica or by the euphoric dance music of the 1990s have evaporated – not only has the future not arrived, it no longer seems possible. Yet at the same time, the music constitutes a refusal to give up on the desire for the future. This refusal gives the melancholia a political dimension, because it amounts to a failure to accommodate to the closed horizons of capitalist realism.
>
> "Haunting... can be construed as a failed mourning. It is about refusing to give up the ghost or... the refusal of the ghost to give up on us. The spectre will not allow us to settle into/for the mediocre satisfactions one can glean in a world governed by capitalist realism.
>
> "The kind of melancholia I am talking about... consists not in giving up on desire but in refusing to yield. It consists... in a refusal to adjust to what current conditions call 'reality' – even if the cost of that refusal is that you feel like an outcast in your own time."

The above observations could well describe much of both the spirit of these books and the people and places they feature in their pages. Yes, within the books such views are filtered through a more mainstream and humorous lens and language than Mark Fisher's but there is nothing wrong with a good old laugh or two.

At the point of writing the paperback editions of the books are still in print. If you should buy those then at some point a small fraction of the cover cost will hopefully work its way to the author.

However, the hardback editions seem more in keeping with the spirit of the text. Particularly the first book and its depiction of a wood framed Morris Minor car on a white sea edge clifftop, with a classic seaside striped lighthouse just visible in the distance. As with the books in general it seems to conjure a quiet sense of melancholy without being chocolate box-like.

22

Gone to Earth: Earlier Traces of an Otherly Albion

GONE TO *EARTH* IS A FILM from 1950 directed by Michael Powell and Emeric Pressburger, based on the 1917 novel by Mary Webb. It is also known as *The Wild Heart* in a considerably re-edited version created at the instigation of producer David O. Selznick after a disagreement and subsequent court case between the directors and him.

In the film Hazel Woodus, played by Jennifer Jones, is a beautiful but innocent young woman who lives in the Shropshire countryside in 1897 and is very steeped in an older more rural way of life and lore. She loves and understands wild animals and whenever she has problems, she turns to the book of spells and charms left to her by her gypsy mother.

In some ways it is a caddish melodrama, with the untamed main female character marrying the local priest (the "good man") but being lead astray by the archetypal baddie, the local squire.

However, while containing elements of more mainstream cinematic fare of the time it also contains a non-populist or exploratory nature presented within a populist framework.

As you watch the film you can feel it straining at its period restrictions in terms of sexuality, desire, faithfulness and respectability, accompanied by expressions and considerations of sin, acceptance, redemption and retribution.

The ending is a genuinely shocking, decidedly not happy ever after conclusion, one that was clearly not focus grouped for approval.

That sense of shock is heightened by the film being very quickly over in terms of run time after the ending; in contrast to modern films where 5-10 minutes of credits rolling up the screen is not uncommon, here there are very few credits and therefore little time at the film's tail end to reflect and take things in.

As a film it also appears to be a forebear of later culture which would travel amongst the layered, hidden histories of the land and folklore, showing a world where faiths old and new are part of and/or mingle amongst folkloric beliefs and practices. Accompanying which, in the world of Gone to Earth (and it is most definitely its own world) the British landscape is not presented in a realist manner.

Rather it has a *Wizard of Oz*-esque, Hollywood coating of beauty, glamour and quiet surreality which in part is created by the vibrant, rich colours of the Technicolor film process that it shares with that 1939 film.

Often cinematic views of the British landscape are quite realist, possibly dour or even bleak in terms of atmosphere and their visual appearance and so Gone to Earth with its high end Hollywood razzle-dazzle which is contained in its imagery is a precious breath of fresh air.

The film's elements of older folkloric ways and its visual aspects combine to create a subtle magic realism in the film and the world and lives it shows, conjures and presents.

It also creates a bucolic dream of the countryside, particularly during the "Harps in Heaven" song and sequence.

In this section Hazel Woodus is pictured singing on the crest of a hill in her Sunday best dress and bonnet, accompanied on a full size harp by her father.

There is something wonderfully incongruous about this top-hatted, neckerchief-wearing local chap carrying a full size harp through the countryside, avoiding the pitfalls of abandoned mines along the way.

The song itself is reminiscent of "O Willow Waly" from the 1961 film *The Innocents* in that it has a similar haunting quality and a purity of voice that stops and captures you in your tracks.

While it is a scene from a fictional film it also contains a sense that it is a documenting of an alternative or lost way of life, geographically not too distant from today, but in spirit far removed.

It brings to mind Rob Young's writing on Peter Kennedy and Alan Lomax's folkloric documentary *Oss Oss Wee Oss* (1953) in his article "The Pattern Under the Plough" for the August 2010 issue of *Sight & Sound* magazine due to its creation of a peculiarly elsewhere seeming atmosphere in amongst a traditional British landscape:

> "...one of the strange survivals whose actual date of origin is almost impossible to trace, but whose very alienness points to an England from which modernity is almost insulated... manages to make this tiny fishing village appear as peculiar and exotic as Haiti in Maya Derren's films of voodoo rituals..."

In some ways the air of not-quite-real-ness that can be found in Gone to Earth makes it seem like a forerunner to the more adult fairy tale side of the Czech New Wave (especially *Valerie and her Week of Wonders* from 1970 and possibly *Malá Morská Víla/The Little Mermaid* from 1976 that are discussed in Chapter 45: "...Non-Populist Pop and Cosmic Aquatic Folklore") and also of the style, character and imagery of a younger Kate Bush, of a free spirit cast out upon and amongst the moors.

The connection between Kate Bush and Gone to Earth is also further entwined in that her 1993 album *Red Shoes* takes its title from and was inspired by Powell and Pressburger's 1948 film of the same name, which was also an influence on her 1993 film which accompanied the album *The Line, the Cross & the Curve.*

In a further interconnecting of later music, David Sylvian's *Gone to Earth* album from 1986 took its name from Powell and Pressburger's film and it is possible to trace a line from my interest in Sylvian's work and what grew into *A Year In The Country.*

Towards the later 1980s I was somewhat enamoured and intrigued by his 1987 album *Secrets of the Beehive* and the textured, layered nature based imagery of the cover by Vaughan Oliver and Nigel Grierson working as 23 Envelope, alongside being drawn to his 1986 single taken from the *Gone to Earth* album, *A Little Girl Dreams of Taking the Veil.* Both of these seemed to sidestep the sometimes-brash mainstream bustle of culture and attempt to create some kind of respite or repose.

Along which lines his and Kate Bush's work are also linked in amongst related cultural and literal landscapes by Rob Young in his *Electric Eden* book from 2011, in a section also titled "Gone to Earth" which in part could also be connected back to some of the themes of Powell and Pressburger's film:

> "In the changed, materialistic Britain of the 1980s, the ideas about myth and magic, memorial landscapes and nostalgia for a lost golden age were banished to internal exile, but scattered links of the silver chain glinted in the output of certain unconventional pop musicians of the time, most notably Kate Bush, Julian Cope, David Sylvian and Talk Talk."

At the time of writing the film of Gone to Earth is only available in a pre-widescreen television unrestored format.

Taking into account the esteem in which its directors are held this is somewhat surprising although may well be due in part to the dispute between the directors and producer.

Due to its somewhat ravishing and entrancing visual nature it is a film which would particularly benefit from a good, sympathetic restoration brush and scrub up.

As a final point the "Harp in Heaven" scene is one of the only times I know of, that the word "nesh" has been used in film. It is a very localised English phrase that means you are weak, delicate or feeble and that you feel the cold easily.

23

Queens of Evil, *Tam Lin* and *The Touchables*: High Fashion Transitional Psych Folk Horror, Pastoral Fantasy and Dreamlike Isolation

There is a mini film sub-genre of pastoral fantasy, with at times elements of folk horror, wherein late 1960s and turn of the decade high fashion mixes with grown up fairytale high jinx, wayward behaviour and sometimes a step or two or more towards the dark side, all carried out in dreamlike isolation in the woods and pastoral settings.

The three main films aligned with such things are *Queens of Evil* aka *Le Regine* or *Il Delitto del Diavolo* (1970), *Tam Lin* aka *The Devil's Widow* (1970) and in a more loosely connected manner *The Touchables* (1968).

All three of these films draw from, to varying degrees, some of the often defining themes of folk horror: being set in rural places and buildings where activities and rituals can develop or take place without easy escape to or influence from the outside world, normality and societal norms.

In all three films there is more than a touch of Hansel and Gretelisms about the way their victims (the word is used loosely here as it is not always clear cut how willing at various points they are in their own capture) are treated and kept in these remote country or woodland settings; pampered yes but also possibly fattened for the pot.

Transgression is a word that comes to mind when describing them and despite its initial more escapist, fairytale and dreamlike cabin in the wood setting, visuals and story, Queens of Evil becomes a very transgressive, unsettling film as it progresses.

The film was featured on BBC Radio 4's *Film Programme*, which although it can take trips into some of the outer reaches of film, the appearance of Queens of Evil was something of a surprise as this high fashion, woodland folkloric critique of power and psychedelic idealism belongs to particularly more outlying areas of cult filmdom.

Its plot follows a handsome young freewheeling hippie idealist who comes across a house in the woods after he has been involved in a road accident where a materially wealthy gent was killed.

Living in this house are three young women who take him in, charm, nurture, seduce and confuse him. Everything is rosy for a while but there is something off-kilter about the setup and he cannot quite seem to leave.

It is an at points chimeric fantasy which is largely set in sharply stylish but indolent, tree-inhabited period interiors and is full of late 1960s ethereal high-fashion along the lines of Ossie Clark and Celia Birtwell's work from then and also incorporating the period folkloric-meets-psychedelia imagery collecting of website *Psychedelic Folkloristic* and its reflection of a relatively brief point in time around the later 1960s to early 1970s when fashionability turned towards folk and pastoral concerns.

In terms of other reference points it creates a sense of a gently decadent grown ups version of a tea-party in the woods, a dash of *Snow White* (at one point somebody says "It's just like Snow White's house" about the cabin in the woods), a bit more of a dash of Hansel and Gretel and its tales of leading astray, more than a touch of the earlier mentioned and loosely interconnected kidnapping and pop-art pastoral playground film The Touchables, alongside the social critique and/or dreamlike qualities of some of Czech New Wave films such as *Daisies* (1966) and *Valerie and her Week of Wonders* (1970).

In fact although Italian the spirit it conjures could well belong to that cycle of fairytale like Czech films.[1] It has a similar playful, childlike idyll and sometimes-dreamlike quality to it but if you should go into the woods today, well, let us just say you may well be hiding behind the sofa by the end.

Tread carefully is sage advice. It is playful in parts but this is most definitely a film for grown ups and not always an easy piece of celluloid to watch.

Pastoral giallo might be another appropriate genre title alongside folk horror as it was produced in Italy at a similar time as some films which have been connected with the giallo genre and as with a number of those Queens of Evil combines thriller, horror, mystery, supernatural and more visceral moments in a stylish and stylised manner.

It could well also be appropriate to include *The Wicker Man* (1973) as another reference point.

In both films there is a similar sense of game playing, of leading a worldly innocent through a set of rituals and of differing levels of power and control in a rural setting.

Also, in common with that towering relatively modern folklore tale, apples and symbols of temptation play a part in this game.

And as with The Wicker Man, this is a tale full of its own and borrowed mythology, which seems to exist and be told in a world of its own imagining, where the outside rarely intrudes.

By the end you realise that this sometimes fairytale fable is actually a quite severe satire or critique on society, of those in higher echelons of power and also the decadence and potential corruptibility of the psychedelic/free love movement and its associated idealism.

In many ways it is a story of a culture tottering right on the edge of when the utopian, carefree, sundrenched dream of the 1960s was about to fall into the darkness of its own dissolution in the following decade (*Liege & Lief* becomes Comus, to draw parallels with folk music's progression at the time).

In terms of this loose mini sub-genre of pastoral fantasy, The Touchables is more rooted in the later part rather than the tipping point of that 1960s dream, although it does represent a world and culture which seems to have become untethered and possibly one which lacks a moral centre.

It is a very modish tale of a group of stylish sixties women who live in a huge see-through plastic bubble in the middle of the countryside who kidnap a pop star as "a temporary solution to the leisure problem" and in order make him their plaything.

Mixed in with this are the stealing of a Michael Caine dummy, gangsters, wrestlers with rather refined aristocratic tastes, a fair bit of high-fashion styling and a fine pop-psych title song by Nirvana (the 1960s band rather than the later Seattle based grunge group).

Essentially, at heart it is a caper romp but one that is more than one remove from the mainstream and quite surreal in its setting and the mixture of elements it contains.

It is a film which in part evokes a sense of how did they get the money to make it, due to its left-of-centre nature. Well, maybe it was partly because it was made during a peak of interest in all things youth and "Swinging London", at a point when money was quite possibly being thrown at anything that might make inroads into the pockets and pounds of a younger music and fashion-orientated demographic.

Also being directed by photographer and designer Robert Freeman, who worked extensively with The Beatles during 1963-1966 including photographing and designing a number of their album covers, may possibly have helped add kudos and aided the practicalities of seeking funding.

The Touchables is a more a playfully, surreally adult pastorally-set fairytale or fantasy than the more overtly folk horror Queens of Evil (although it does have some quite shocking moments in amongst its escapist visual confections) but as mentioned earlier it mirrors some of the elements of that film; in both stylish late 1960s women kidnap a pretty boy to live in their own rural dreamlike domain.

It was not a surprise to discover that The Touchables was based on a script by Donald Cammell (with a screenplay by Ian La Frenais), as in part it represents a proto, more pop-art, possibly light hearted take on *Performance* (1970), which he wrote and co-directed.

As with The Touchables, Performance also incorporates a theme of a popstar living in an enclosed bubble world, although its setting is in some ways more prosaic as it involves a former popstar who lives a reclusive, isolated life in a London flat rather than in a rurally set large-scale see-through plastic dome as is the case with The Touchables.

Alongside this and as a further point of connection, both films also intertwine professional gangsters and related criminal activities within these secluded worlds.

One intriguing aspect of The Touchables is that there is not even an attempt to explain how the stylish group of female kidnappers' bubble or lifestyle are afforded, nor why there seems to be no outside comment or interference by mainstream society, authority etc. about their quite frankly rather unusual giant blow-up see-through home that is sitting in the middle of the countryside, complete with jukebox, canopied merry-go-round etc.

This aspect of non-explanation it shares with Queens of Evil, although in that film there is the possibility that its main characters' lifestyle is afforded by those further up in a related hierarchy who wish them to carry out their manipulative intentions.

If ever a film seemed custom-made for a high definition brush and scrub up restoration it would be The Touchables. The BFI's *Flipside* strand could well be an appropriate home in that it has created a space for high end reclaiming and restoration of the more cult and forgotten side of cinema, which The Touchables would fit rather well amongst.

At the moment the version/s that can be seen have a colour palette where the hues seem quite muted and so there is the possibility that it was actually intended to be more a pop-art dazzle of colour, which would possibly suit the film more.

This is something which, at the time of writing, it currently shares with Queens of Evil, which is only viewable in a somewhat blurred, multi-generation version, which is a shame as both films are something of a visual delight.

However, the third film of this mini sub genre Tam Lin has been released in a high definition restored form, albeit only as a USA, locked to Region A Blu-ray and DVD.

It is curious film which as with Queens of Evil and The Touchables does not easily fit into any particular mainstream genre; it is a loose modern adaptation of the traditional folkloric tale and song "The Ballad of Tam Lin", relocated to the country home of an almost mythologically wealthy older woman which is peopled by various late 60s hipsters, hunks and prepossessing actresses of the time (including Madeline Smith, Joanna Lumley and Jenny Hanley) and soundtracked by British jazz-folk band Pentangle.

Hollywood legend Ava Gardner stars as that wealthy, older woman, alongside a dapper Ian McShane who plays a young man that catches her eye and Stephanie Beacham as the innocent from the world outside.

It was directed by Roddy McDowell, who is possibly most famous for playing the lead simian character in the *Planet of the Apes* films that were released from 1968 to 1973.

This was the only time he directed which is a pity as this film shows that he had considerable promise in that area.

The plot involves an immensely rich older lady Michaela Cazaret, gathering up hip young things to come and live, play with and amuse in her country mansion; her actions seems like a scooping up or pied piper-esque leading as she heads a convoy of cars through roads walled by pylons into her country lair.

Cue childlike games (how can a game of frisbee seem so very odd?), partying, pleasing of the senses, imbibing and so forth.

As just mentioned she has a particular soft spot for one young gent named Tom Lyn (Ian McShane), taking him into her bed and possibly her cold heart.

However, he falls for an innocent from outside their bubble world – the vicar's daughter played by Stephanie Beacham – and tries to escape from the clutches of Michaela, which displeases her somewhat and his life and freedom become rather fraught.

It was released in 1970, the same year as Queens of Evil, and along with that film this is also all high baroque dandyism and decadence turning towards something somewhat darker.

In Tam Lin there is a sense of playful opulence and a mod/post-mod sharpness to the style which could be compared and contrasted with say the murk, grime and tattiness of the also sub/counter culture orientated folk horror related film *Psychomania* which was released in 1973.

They are separated by but a few years but are worlds apart in terms of the aesthetic style, societal/economic conditions, atmosphere and possibly optimism that they represent or portray.

As with Queens of Evil, Tam Lin is set at the very tipping point of a transitional, liminal period; a time where the psychedelic, hippy, free-living of the 1960s is about to turn inwards and curdle.

Tam Lin seems to express the end of that point in history's utopian dream more overtly or implicitly when one of the sacraments of that era, psychedelic substances, are used as a form of weapon, hounding and destruction and also when the freedom loving hipsters become a hunting mass-mind pack.

The main films focused on in this chapter all present bubble-like worlds, literally or otherwise but whereas in The Touchables and Queens of Evil there is not an obvious source of financial, practical sustenance for these ways of life, in Tam Lin it is commented that Michaela is:

> "...immensely rich. She can afford to live in her dreams and she takes us into them for company."

Although The Touchables is more rooted in the real life fantasia of pop-art psychedelia, in Tam Lin and Queens of Evil there is a "Do they or don't they?" about the female protagonists possession or not of magical powers.

Are they merely manipulative or something more preternatural?

In Tam Lin the young hipsters are referred to as "covens" in the credits and it seems almost that Michaela weaves a spell of possession around her playthings (and hence the pied-piper siren like gathering mentioned earlier).

Queens of Evil probably feels more overtly ethereal and unreal in this sense; Tam Lin seems quite rooted in the real world and is in some ways is a more "normal" film but it is a world and celluloid story that is just askew in ways that are hard to quite put your finger on.

The phrase "magic realism" would not be out of place.

This askew normality is one of the things that makes Tam Lin such a curious film and slice of culture; it is a heady mix of mainstream talent and decidedly both mainstream and non-mainstream filmmaking.

This is heightened by the presence of a Hollywood goddess or legend in the main female role; Ava Gardner here has some kind of innate star or otherly quality that makes her seem separate, above and beyond the mere humans which she surrounds herself with.

And they are terribly disposable, these young pretty things, they are there but at her bidding and can be sent away just as easily, with Michaela stating at one point:

> "I want a party for all your special friends. I want a whole new world."

Tam Lin was also made at a high water mark of folk rock and the returning music refrain throughout the film is traditional folk song "The Ballad of Tam Lin" from which the film takes its inspiration, performed in the film by Pentangle and which infuses and intermingles with the more conventional music score.

The film's story follows that of its folk music forebear which with its fantastical tales underpins and layers the sense of this being an adult fairytale; in both the film and the song a young maiden (called Janet in the film and often also in the song) is drawn to a rake-ish rogue, nature takes its course and the ridding of the resulting child is narrowly averted.

However, the young man has been encaptured by a sort of queen (of wealth in one, of the fairies in the other) and he may well become a tithe or offering to differing hells (capricious whims in one, literal in the other).

Upon his escape and his lover's attempted rescue of him, he is turned into various beasts and even burning matter by his captors in order to make her leave him (via psychedelic ingestion in one, presumably magical powers in the other).

His form of transport for his escape bears the same white colour in both, though one is powered by a combustion engine, the other is of a more equine nature.

And in the end in both the queens of fairies and of wealth are angered by but acknowledge their defeat and his escape.

However, the film does not leave the viewer with the sense that this particular queen had permanently stepped away from the fray and the young lovers' lives; there is something genuinely unsettling and even subtly psychopathic or unhinged in the portrayal of Michaela's need for control.

Once again returning to the sense of an ending of an era and of a dream, in some ways the innocent Janet played by Stephanie Beacham is a representative of the normal, decent world outside this coven-ish pack and its ways; reflecting this, in the film it is said that they are and must be treated as scum and they appear to represent a dissolute, amoral gathering that needs to be escaped from.

1. Discussed further in Chapter 45.

24

Luke Haines: Our Most Non-Hauntological Hauntologist

MUSICIAN AND AUTHOR Luke Haines is a curious gent and his work is an interesting example of how pop/rock can be conjoined with a certain intellectual stance and influence and still be good pop/rock songs.

Along which lines it could be considered to be "non-populist pop" (to quote the sleeve notes to The Eccentronic Research Council's *Underture 1612* album from 2012[1]).

The term "pop" is used as two of the bands he was involved with, The Auteurs and Black Box Recorder bothered the singles charts in the days when such things kind of still mattered, while the songs themselves are often catchy.

However, his work also seems to largely exist in a genre all of its own, one without a particular name.

It is without a name as probably something appropriately descriptive would need to be multi-layered and include the likes of One Time French Breakfast TV Indie Popstar, Brief Top Twenty-er, Musical Dada-Pantomine Villain and Pop Culture's Hidden Undercurrents Explorer.

Which would be just a touch too long as a genre title for the racks of record stores.

As a background to the above possible genre title his band The Auteurs had a period of mainstream success in France which included Luke Haines appearing on breakfast television and Black Box Recorder's single "Facts of

Life" spent one week at number twenty in the UK singles chart. Although his work has a pop edge, it often also interacts with and explores more fringe or even experimental cultural areas, while he at times seems to position himself/be positioned as an arch observer or outsider, possibly even nemesis, to much of music and pop culture.

There has been a connection or few with his work and what has come to be known as hauntology.

The term "hauntology" is often related to a particular aesthetic and set of tropes, ie. a particular kind of often sample-led or analogue synthesised music and found imagery which draws on generally British library and educational music, public information films, TV and film soundtracks of the later 1960s through to the late 1970s, alongside a yearning for lost futures.[2]

If you consider hauntology in a more general sense to mean the present being haunted by spectres of the past then Luke Haines is probably one of the more hauntological musicians out there.

His music often seems to literally be haunted by the past - his own, society's, culture's and bogeymen-like figures or worries of one sort or another from previous decades.

Take the 1999 album *How I Learned to Love the Bootboys* by one of his previous bands The Auteurs, which he was the instigator/frontman of.

The lead track and single of the same year "The Rubettes" borrows liberally from 1970s pop ("Sugar Baby Love" by its namesakes in particular), there are marauding skinhead bootboys from a similar era, an ode to a 1950s pop rock band (the singer of whom is "dead within a year"), imbibements popular in other eras (Asti Spumante, known as a "noxiously sweet poor man's Champagne") and so forth.

Alongside the above, there is a sometimes a possibly recurring sense of the playground dread of an arty schoolboy looking back to the marauding dangers of his 1970s childhood.

Elsewhere, such as on his 2006 solo album *Off My Rocker at the Art School Bop* there are teddy boys discos and Vauxhall Corsas, "the three day week, half-day Wednesdays, the spirit of the Blitz" and an unsolved 1960s celebrity boxers death.

While in 2011 he released a concept album dedicated to 1970s and early 1980s wrestling, called in an "it does what it says on the can" manner *Nine and a Half Psychedelic Meditations on British Wrestling of the 1970s and early '80s*, which is a fine title and subject matter.

Between 1998 and 2003 Black Box Recorder, his trio with cohorts Sarah Nixey and John Moore, released three unparalleled albums which contained seething, brutally repressed, "now that the Empire has faded", "I know what you're doing in the afternoons", arch Albionic pop-noir.

They often sounded as though they were singing from some kind of brutal, sneering, imaginary 1970s English hinterland.

Their work could be considered its own unique take on hauntological work's creation of parallel worlds through a form of hazy misremembering and reinterpreting of previous eras and an associated sense of exploring resonant cultural reference points and atmospheres from the past and weaving with them to form new cultural forms and myths.

To a degree this connects with work that can be considered hauntological in a more conventional sense in that it puts me in mind of Rob Young's review of a Moon Wiring Club album in Uncut magazine, where he talks of the enclosed music being "slathered in the fiction that it comes from an older, weirder England".

His 2015 album *British Nuclear Bunkers* took him nearer to conventional hauntological territory, being a largely instrumental, Radiophonic-esque album which was recorded in part using (presumably, from his championing of them online around the time of the album's release) cheap tuppence ha'penny synthesisers.

Aside from the album's title, the titles of the tracks include "This Is the BBC", "Test Card Forever", "Mama Check The Radar at the Dada Station", "New Pagan Sun", "Deep Level Shelters Under London" and "Electronic Tone Poem".

What he brings to hauntology-related work is a playful, sometimes outright humorous take on such things; an absurdist and dada-like exploration of occult histories.

If you should look up the definition of dada you may find that it was an art movement founded on "irrationality, incongruity, and irreverence towards accepted aesthetic criteria", which sounds somewhat appropriate for Haines' work and might also be used to refer to his insubordinate to the cultural status quo stance as an author in the 2009 and 2011 autobiographical books *Bad Vibes* and *Post Everything* and possibly also at points his interviewee stance.

Along which lines, the video that accompanies British Nuclear Bunkers features him with only somebody wearing a gorilla suit for company.

They are pictured in a largely featureless room that implies a sense of it being part of a subterranean, not known to the public Cold War interrogation centre.

The gorilla squeezes lemons and plays an analogue synthesiser while Luke Haines, dressed in what appears to be a biohazard protection suit, practises what can only be described as occult pagan yoga.

This is accompanied by a misleadingly simple but surprisingly catchy mostly instrumental analogue synth track, the only vocals on which are the just once slowly stated and vocodered "maximum electronic rock'n'roll".

If Ghost Box Records' Belbury Poly and The Advisory Circle went "off their rocker together at an art school bop" they might just sound like this. Possibly.

Haines' 2015 album *Smash the System* seemed to also travel, in his own particular way, to the point at which hauntological concerns meet otherly folklore.[3] So, for example, while there are all kinds of pop culture titles and references to the album (Marc Bolan, Bruce Lee, Vince Taylor etc.) there are also tracks called "Ritual Magick", "Power of the Witch" and "The Incredible String Band".

The album has an archival photograph of morris dancers as its cover image and the accompanying video for the title track shows their contemporary equivalent on a slightly worrying and unsettling bender or borderline riotous fracas in an urban capital city setting (while the song also namechecks his love of The Monkees and The Velvet Underground).

The video also features gas masks and a tray full of shots for the Morris dancers to drink (for some reason the latter of which seems most unruly, unsettling and just a bit wrong).

One strand of contemporary reality television programmes show people not being able to handle their drinking or binge drinking in inner city areas, as such places are turned into near no-go areas of a Saturday night.

In some alternate universe the traditional folkloric characters in this video are what you would see if you tuned in.

Appropriate reference points may also include the arty-lairiness of Earl Brutus, with whom Luke Haines has at various points shared a designer and collaborator in the form of Scott King and possibly even the imagined troublesome youth cult of the film version of *A Clockwork Orange* from 1971.

The video is both entrancing and presents or creates a world that the viewer really does not want to step into and its fiction is only just burst at the end by the more normal smiles of a participant or two.

Preceding this album and video, there are glimpses of the flipside of Albion in his earlier work.

In particular there is a certain British nature or countryside brutality to the cover of How I Learned to Love the Bootboys.

It features a small gathering of sheep on a patch of desolate land next to the sea and crashing waves. There is red dye on the sheeps' coats and horns, which I assume are just farmers flock markings but they seem to conjure the edges of nightmares and the more troubled undercurrents of the land, hinting just subtly at a social realist take on the tropes of folk horror.

While the cover to the "The Rubettes" single from 1999 travels further along this path with its depiction of genuinely unsettling folk horror-esque masked men in black industrial protective weather proofs combined with Mr Punch-like outfits and masks.

They have parked their livestock van out in the countryside in the middle of nowhere and one of them peers out from the slats in its rear at the viewer with intentions that can only be far from good.

1. Discussed in Chapter 35.
2. Hauntology is defined and discussed further in Chapter 3.
3. An area discussed in Chapter 4.

25

Tim Hart, Maddy Prior and "The Dalesman's Litany": A Yearning for Imaginative Idylls and a Counterpart to Tales of Hellish Mills

It is wise to be wary of harking back to some imagined pre-industrialisation idyll; as someone whose thoughts are recorded in the 1969 oral history book *Akenfield: Portrait of an English Village* by Ronald Blythe says, the old ways which were often quite harsh at the time can come to seem like pleasant aspects of life and times as the years add a distance and rosy glow to them.

Having said which, the song "The Dalesman's Litany", as performed by Tim Hart and Maddy Prior on their 1968 album *Folk Songs of Old England*, which takes as its subject matter a yearning for a return to pastoral idylls and away from a life working in industry is an appealing thing.

Originally a poem by Frederic William Moorman written around 1900, it is a tale told by an agricultural worker who has to choose between a life with his beau on the land he loves and working in towns, cities and mines because the local landowner does not want married workers.

In the later 1960s when this song was released, an idyllic, pastoral view of Olde England alongside the use and reinterpretation of traditional folk music and lore were sometimes part of a more experimental, exploratory strand in music and culture which to a degree was intertwined with psychedelia and a "hippie" utopian viewpoint.

Over time however, folk music and culture came to be subsumed into a more twee, conservative, chocolate box viewpoint and at points it has been hard to disconnect it from such baggage and even taint.

However, although The Dalesman's Litany could in some ways be seen as part of a tendency to take the rough, almost documentary edges off such things and to romanticise past troubles and hardships, through its lamentative delivery it still carries an authentic, heartfelt resonance.

It is a very evocative recording due in part to that delivery and also the imagery it conjures of the tongues of fire thrust out by furnaces as the once dalesman walks the lanes of Sheffield at night.

The song imparts a sense of an aching yearning to return to the moor and leave the coalstacks, which makes the song a more personal counterpart to William Blake's "Jerusalem/And did those feet in ancient time" which was originally published in 1808 and its words of dark satanic mills; a text which was a reaction to the societal disturbances brought about by the industrial revolution.

As mentioned in the chapter 7: "1973: A Time of Schism and a Dybbuk's Dozen of Fractures", by the early 1970s the spirit of "hippie" utopian ideals, which backgrounded the era in which the song was recorded, had begun to turn sour and inwards.

Accompanying which, being drawn to imagined, bucolic idylls from times gone by, folk music and culture may in part have come to be a reaction to a period of social, political and economic turmoil within Britain, related energy shortages and electricity blackouts.

That yearning for simpler times could be seen as a form of escape or respite from such unrest and turbulence; just as the more pop confections of say glam rock provided a glittered, stack-heeled form of knockabout escapism from the day-to-day grit and grime of a country mired in troubles.

Indeed, The Dalesman's Litany almost seems like a subtle protest song aimed at the era of its recording, obliquely filtered via, to reference Rob Young's *Electric Eden* book (2010), a form of imaginative time travel, which further removes it from the more twee, romanticised side of folk interpretation and revival.

26

Katalin Varga, Berberian Sound Studio and *The Duke of Burgundy*: Arthouse Evolution and Crossing the Thresholds of the Hinterland Worlds of Peter Strickland

THE THREE FULL-LENGTH films which Peter Strickland has made so far: *Katalin Varga* (2009), *Berberian Sound Studio* (2012) and *The Duke of Burgundy* (2014), all create their own immersive worlds, often self contained and separate from wider reality and its markers.

Berberian Sound Studio is set in the enclosed world of a recording studio in 1976 and could be considered an homage to and a possible comment on that period's "giallo" and Italian horror film genres and their sometimes-questionable excesses.

As a loose definition, within cinema giallo generally refers to a sub-genre of work made largely during the 1960s and 70s, normally Italian or European in origin and which has gone on to gain a cult following. It usually has mystery or thriller elements, often combined with slasher and sometimes supernatural or horror themes and was known for being presented with distinctive, stylish aesthetics.

Berberian Sound Studio involves a garden shed-based British sound effects expert, played by Toby Jones, who travels to Italy to work on a film which turns out unbeknownst to him to be a disturbing giallo horror.

As time passes at the recording studio life and art implode and fall into one another and apart from going to his bedroom he does not seem to leave the studio complex.

His sanity crumbles and he becomes increasingly both part of and complicit in a culture and celluloid of misogyny, one which is masked and masquerading as art and the barriers between reality and unreality become increasingly blurred.

Alongside the link to giallo it shares a number of similar themes with David Cronenberg's *Videodrome* (1983); the stepping into an altered reality via recorded media and the degradation of its listeners, watchers and participants.

Although whereas that film has a certain ragged, driving, visceral, hallucinatory and at times street-like energy, Berberian Sound Studio has and creates a more subtle, phantasmagoric dreamlike atmosphere.

This is not a film which intrigues and draws you in through a plot arc, rather it is the imagery, experimentation, atmosphere and its cultural connections.

Indeed plot in a conventional, progressive narrative manner does not seem to be an overriding concern or intention of Peter Strickland's. As referred to previously, his full-length films so far have more been exercises in conjuring and creating particular worlds and atmospheres.

With Berberian Sound Studio the cultural connections include a soundtrack by Broadcast and design/film work by Julian House (variously of Ghost Box Records, Intro design agency, The Focus Group musical venture and sometimes Broadcast collaborator), with striking elements of its visual character being created by him.

These include the tape packaging, edit sheets etc. for the studio setting and as a film it is deeply steeped within such pre-digital recording technology, with its physical form and noises becoming an intrinsic part of the story and its enclosed world.

Julian House's work also includes an intro sequence for the film within a film called *The Equestrian Vortex*, which is the one Toby Jones' character is helping to create the sound effects for.[1]

Accompanied by Broadcast's music this uses found illustration imagery and creates an unsettling, intense sequence which draws from the tropes of folk and occult horror.

The film within a film is only shown visually by the illustrated intro sequence, with the violence and excesses of the live action parts only being expressed and implied by the sound effects that are created within the studio setting, guidelines given to the studio engineers or Toby Jones' character's repulsion or surprise at them.

Although he demurs at the extreme nature of some of the sequences he is expected to work on, this appears to be only in a British rather polite way.

His only connection with back home and a more morally grounded world being letters from his mother which are initially descriptions of bucolia but which later become their own form of dark horror.

Accompanying which during the film the interior world of the studio is only left when the film breaks through into the British countryside, which provides a brief relief via greenery and daylight. This is in considerable contrast to the corridor, studio, bedroom and nighttime courtyard where the remainder of the film is set.

As the film progresses, the nature of the work and the manipulative coercion, persuasion, denial or recalcitrance of the other staff seem to combine to corrupt him, to weaken and eventually remove any resistance he has to the nature of the work.

By the end of the film and as a sense of the demarcations between reality and fiction erode Toby Jones' character becomes as much a facilitator and collaborator in the imagined film's excesses as those around him.

Peter Strickland's intentions are unclear but the themes of Berberian Sound Studio seem to question the reasoning and motives behind the making of giallo and related horror film, its subsequent cult following and raising up as a form of artistic rather than possibly purely sensationalistic exploitation cinema.

If this is the case then it can be seen as a film which explores and debates viewers' and makers' complicit creation and enjoyment of such areas of film, ones which without that elevation could be considered in part to be curious and questionable forms of culture.

Following Berberian Sound Studio, Peter Strickland's next feature film was The Duke of Burgundy.

On initial glance and indeed for the first section of the film this appears to be something of a stylistically salacious piece of work, drawing from the more erotically-inclined side of the likes of director Jess Franco's films, which it is said in part to be a homage to.

Jess Franco was a Spanish film director, writer, composer, cinematographer and actor. He is known for having a prolific output of around 160 films released between 1959 and 2013, which often focused on exploitation genres. His work has gained a cult following, in part due to the exploitation elements of the films alongside his own at times distinctive film making style/aesthetics and also because his prolific output was largely made with little or no funding and has come to be considered a form of almost renegade or outsider film production.

However as The Duke of Burgundy progresses its cinematic journey is shown to not be an exercise in purely prurient cinema.

It is a tale where an almost *Famous Five*-like bucolic existence of bike rides, butterfly catching and picnics amongst the grass lives side-by-side with very specific, esoteric personal sexual needs, the strains that puts on a couple's relationship and at points a stepping into a darkly surreal fluttering, shattering night.

Although it concerns itself in part with the rituals of dominance and submission, ultimately it is a heartbreaking, moving film that focuses on the imbalanced needs, desires and even dysfunction that can take place within intimate relationships and has a Kafka-esque sense of unending, whatever the proclamations of a will to change that are made by one half of the couple.

It focuses almost exclusively on the lives of two female lovers, largely in the setting of one particular romantically and texturally ornate house and whose work involves the research, collecting and study of crickets and lepidoptera (butterflies and moths).

Although not explicitly explained, the wider world they live in seems to be largely concerned or even obsessed by such study, with their own lives revolving around little else (apart from boudoir activities).

Much of the decoration of the main house involves framed mounts of these creatures and the film will periodically focus on these and related images, creating a returning refrain and a near scientific but also reflective, expressive study of the beauty and decorations of nature.

As the couple's relationship becomes more fractious, at one point this imagery steps away from that calm, reflective presentation and a darkly surreal nighttime woodland wandering builds to become a multi-layered, intense consumption of the screen and one of the central characters.

Connected to the strife of the film's central characters, their conflicts and day-to-day nature of relationships, one of the reference points that Peter Strickland quotes in relation to the film is the 1979-87 British television sitcom *Terry and June.*

The Duke of Burgundy has much in common with such work in the way that it is an observation of the practicalities and unbalanced wishes and desires that can be present in relationships, of the sometimes petty, sometimes far from petty, annoyances and compromises that can be part of them.

Although in The Duke of Burgundy such things have an exotic setting and involve private, intimate rituals, ultimately some of the issues it considers are very similar to those in Terry and June; the frustrations of two people in their nightwear and pyjamas in bed.

As mentioned earlier in regards to Peter Strickland's work, this is not a film that overly concerns itself with plot.

It is more a creation of a particular esoteric, luxuriant, golden atmosphere and an almost fairytale-like world: a phrase used possibly more in a Czech New Wave film manner than its traditional use,[2] alongside a study of the push, pull, evolution, needs and conflicts of a relationship.

That world is one that you are drawn into without questioning the underlying infrastructure, logic, facts and figures.

For example, how do these people support themselves economically?

Why and how is the primary source of activity and even currency that of butterfly, moth, cricket etc. examination and collecting? Does the male gender still exist in this world as it is not shown?

Through the creation of its own sealed world such questions while intriguing do not seem relevant when watching the film and once you have stepped over the threshold of this imagined hinterland.

Its location and period are not made clear although it could possibly be some overlooked, bucolic area of Europe in an indefinable era, one which seems to nod towards possibly the 1960s or 1970s. It could also be today, although it is more a never-never time all of its own.

There is little or no modern technology nor many of the trappings of contemporary life and media in evidence; this does not just include digital devices such as computers and tablets but there also appear to be no cars, telephones, trains, television, radio, newspapers, magazines, music, more recently published books or modern kitchen appliances.

The only form of commerce shown involves a visit by a bespoke and rather esoteric furniture craftswoman, with shops and other retail outlets also being absent.

In this world the only recorded sound that is heard is that of field recordings of insects, played either via an unseen recording medium or at one point, in a rare appearance of electronic technology, a briefly and only partially seen record player of a fairly older vintage, while the connected speaker that is shown appears to be housed in a unique, almost handcrafted casing rather than to be of a modern design.

(In a further step aside from the real world, there are also no branded products shown, with the only departure from this being an imaginary exotic sounding perfume which is listed in the opening credits. This is a fitting touch for the film as it connects with the overall atmosphere and its sense of a certain sensuous and yet rather classily restrained decadence.)

Katalin Varga was Peter Strickland's first full-length film. Set in a contemporary period the films tells of a horse and cart journey and mission of revenge through the land by a mother, accompanied by her son who is unaware of the purpose of the journey.

Josephine Decker's *Butter on the Latch* film from 2013,[3] is more stylistically experimental but might well be an appropriate reference point for Katalin Varga; pastorally set work that wanders off the beaten paths of conventional cinema or indeed a slasher in the woods and the land without the slashing.

Katalin Varga could almost be a period film and in part it seems to be set in a generally pastoral world that may not have changed all that much since medieval times.

During the film it is physically jarring when the viewer sees a more built up area and modern buildings, or when a mobile phone ring tone is heard in the film, while a yellow plastic plate that appears at one point seems almost offensive in this setting.

The modern world often seems to only appear in relatively small details: the contemporary rubber car tyres on the cart that is used in the journey, haymaking carried out by hand while in the background is a building with a satellite dish.

It is similar to The Duke of Burgundy in that it creates the sense of an indefinable era, although in Katalin Varga due to the appearance of such occasional details as those mentioned above it is not such a hermetically sealed and created one.

However, despite the appearance of the modern or real world, this is still a film where you can often lose a sense of which era you are observing.

Katalin Varga does not necessarily have the more polished production sheen of the honey toned fantasy land of The Duke of Burgundy or the cloistered, contained and imagined interiors of Berberian Sound Studio but it creates a sense of its own world, time and place nonetheless.

It may in part be a side effect of that lack of sheen but it seems as though it could be some semi-lost European film from an unspecified point in time, possibly the 1970s, which although arthouse did not quite belong to the accepted, reputable canon of cinema.

The kind of a film that would have been screened at London's Scala cinema around the early 1980s to the early 1990s, which was something of a home for such things.

Peter Strickland's films bring to mind those kind of arthouse, sometimes transgressive films that have often gone on to find a cult following but have not always become mainstream critically acceptable.

For example films that would have once appeared in the pages of *Films and Filming* magazine which was published from 1954-1990; often European cult arthouse independent cinema, with leftfield, exploratory and sometimes transgressive or salacious subject matter and presentation.

Both when discussing his own work and in writing by others, there have been numerous mentions of such earlier films which are said to have fed into his and also of a sense of homage that his work contains.

For example the BFI's *Sight & Sound* film magazine called The Duke of Burgundy a "phantasmagoric 70s Euro sex-horror pastiche" and as referred to previously the likes of prolific fringe film maker Jess Franco are often referenced when writing about the film.

This sense of homage within Peter Strickland's films can sometimes be quite overt; in The Duke of Burgundy the earlier-mentioned night time dreamlike sequence which sees the screen and one of the main characters consumed by a rapidly layering collage of lepidoptera seems to quite directly visually reference experimental film maker Stan Brakhage's *Mothlight* film from 1963, which layered natural elements and insects to create a rapidly moving montage.

The connections to and lineage of such films via degrees of homage in his work can provide an intriguing cultural layering, acting as pointers to other areas of exploration and on this topic he has said the following:

> "The inclusion of an obscure reference done in an obvious fashion can be precarious in terms of what that reveals about a director's motivations. At worst, the act of homage is merely posing and diverting attention onto the director rather than the film, but when done organically and effectively, as with both Greenaway

at his best and Tarantino, it enriches the film and places it within a wider (albeit self-imposed) lineage that can be rewarding for the curious viewer."

Such earlier films as Mothlight and those of a Scala-esque nature can be culturally and/or aesthetically interesting and intriguing, they may also possibly have a great poster or soundtrack but they are not necessarily always all that easy to sit through in terms of also being forms of entertainment.

However rather than homage, Peter Strickland's films seems to more be an evolution of them, taking previous work as some of its initial starting points but then recalibrating their themes, tropes and aesthetics to create work which alongside it containing layered cultural points of interest can also work as entrancing entertainment (albeit that may also at times be more than a little unsettling).

1. This sequence is also discussed in Chapter 9.
2. An area of film I discuss further in Chapter 45.
3. Considered in Chapter 16.

27

General Orders No. 9 and *By Our Selves*: Cinematic Pastoral Experimentalism

General Orders No. 9 is a 2009 film by Robert Persons. As a very brief precis, the film takes the viewer on a journey through the transformation of a section of mid-Southern America (Alabama, Mississipi and Georgia) from a wilderness into its modern state and although not overtly stated or didactic it seems to be in part a mourning of the loss of wilderness areas and a connection to nature due to the encroachment of civilisation and urbanisation.

It is a non-narrative film, a form of expressive documentary with elements of experimentalism but it is eminently watchable and makes use of original location film footage, maps, vintage photographs, found objects and views of natural and manmade landscapes.

Despite a sense of a brutalising of the landscape via progress and the relentless march of freeways, there is a beauty to the film and much of what it portrays; many of the sequences seeming to be nearer to celluloid takes on fine art photography, with them lingering over the stillness of the subjects in the frame.

It could be thought of as a film which explores the hauntology of the Southern states; the land is seen to be littered with the remnants and spectres of mankind's industrial and technological endeavours – old factory installations, derelict mobile phone masts, rooms filled with discarded detritus and hundreds of scattered old books.

Adding to the texture and layers of the journey the film takes is an accompanying narrative by a voice which could well be announcing the end of days (it is reminiscent of God Speed You Black Emperors song "Dead Flag Blues" from their 1997 album *F# A# ∞*, which in some ways could almost be a companion piece to General Orders No. 9, with its sense of lyrically beautiful apocalyptic dread). A selection from the narrative is below:

"Why is the sign of the thing preferred to the thing itself?
We're lost without a map...
The lord loves a broken soul, let us hope we are well broken...
The city has none of the signs of the place and all of the machine...
You are not a witness to the ruin, you are a ruin, you are to be witnessed...
The only response is to refuse, to go to the ruins and sit amongst them..."

It could be placed very loosely amongst a strand of films that may be described as cinematic pastoral experimentalism. Along which lines is Andrew Kötting's film *By Our Selves* from 2015, which involves a re-treading of the wanderings which Northamptonshire nature poet John Clare undertook in 1841, as he went on a pilgrimage from a mental asylum to find Mary Joyce, the woman with whom he thought himself to be in love.

John Clare is played by Toby Jones, who is accompanied by a straw bear (a character from folklore, the costume of which involves its wearer being covered head to toe in straw), with director Andrew Kötting playing this part.

Alongside the film's depiction of John Clare's journey through the land are a number of separate sections where, for example, writer Iain Sinclair interviews Northamptonshire resident comic book writer Alan Moore (who describes Northampton as being so imbued with literary and poetic associations that it is "a kind of vision sump") and Toby Jones' own father appears and revisits his performance from a 1970 Omnibus documentary in which he played John Clare.

Possibly more appealing than the film's specific dealings with John Clare's story is its "folkloric in the modern day" imagery (for example Toby Jones in ramshackle period costume leading the straw bear through a field of crops under the gaze of pylons) and its exploration of the hidden, underlying layers and roots of the land's tales, people and history.

It seems to be very much an expression of those who are involved's love of and enthusiasm for exploring and delving amongst the interconnectedness of such things and by its nature is a literal psychogeographic wandering.

The film is connected to fine/experimental art in terms of its non-conventional presentation, narrative and form but also seems just as much to be about a bunch of mates mucking about and having a laugh while delving through those hidden, interconnected layers; a serious psychogeographic lark.

As a piece of work it has a certain arty accessibility and has had a reach out into the world that stepped beyond the more often strictly gallery based, well defined routes which such fine/experimental artwork may be expected to take.

Along which lines, alongside an exhibition and book, the film has had extensive cinematic showings, widespread mainstream and niche journalistic interest and a commercial DVD and Blu-ray release.

In terms of this wider release it links back, without being retro in nature, to a period or the spirit of a time when independent but relatively mainstream film and television production, broadcast and distribution could include the non-conventional and non-narrative but cinematically released work of say Derek Jarman and the broadcast on mainstream television of experimental video series *Ghosts in the Machine* (1986-1988).[1]

1. Discussed further in Chapter 15.

28

No Blade of Grass and *Z.P.G.*: A Curious Dystopian Mini-Genre

IN THE 1970s THERE WAS a curious mini-genre or gathering of doom laden apocalyptic, dystopian science fiction films, which warned of the dangers of ecological collapse, the depletion and battle for vital resources, out of control population growth and related ways citizens might be controlled and manipulated.

You could include *Z.P.G.* (1972), *Soylent Green* (1973), *Silent Running* (1972) and *The Omega Man* (1971) in amongst these, possibly in a more crowd and eye-pleasing way *Logan's Run* (1976) and you could draw a line from them to later British television series along similar lines such as *Noah's Castle* (1979), which also dealt with the effects of dwindling resources and the resulting societal breakdown.

These films varied in their depiction of what form such events would take place and included in Z.P.G. the ending of human reproduction to save resources and the replacing of living children with robot offspring alongside staged depictions of what life was once like, Soylent Green's food shortages, lack of plantlife, vegetables etc and a rather unusual closed food chain choice, Logan's Run's new age self-immolation rituals to keep the population ever young and an escape from the regulation of a domed city out into nature and Silent Running's shipping of the remaining plant life into space.

No Blade of Grass (1970), based on John Christopher's *The Death of*

Grass novel from 1956, was another such film.

This is a surprisingly bleak, brutal film (admittedly with some inappropriate almost sitcom-like music here and there and longstanding UK sitcom and soap opera actress Wendy Richards as a slightly out-of-place comic female character) about what happens when a new strain of virus kills the world's grass, related plants and crops.

It depicts a society where normal morality and rules of law almost immediately break down and life becomes more a *Lord of the Flies*, survival of the fittest and/or the best armed battle for food and control in the cities and amongst the fleeing gatherings of people in the countryside, while governments take to nerve gas bombing their own populations, killing hundreds of millions of people in order to have enough food for those who remain.

So, not all that cheery. Below is a look at some of what happens in the film when the veneer of civilisation does not so much fade but rather is rent asunder.

The title frames show a lone group of figures armed and on the run on a parched, cracked landscape, set against images of pollution and decay, which are soon followed by scenes of abundant food and conventional affluent middle class ways of life.

None of which lasts for long as the main protagonists flee a rioting city to try to reach the safety of a family member's remote farm, which leads them to at one point a violent conflict with a gang of bikers.

In the 1970s it often seemed to be wild gangs of bikers who were the recurring societal bogeymen that would take over when civilisation collapsed (John Christopher's 1968 novel *Pendulum* novel takes a similar line, while the 1973 film *Psychomania* sees the bikers become undead countryside hoodlums).

In No Blade of Grass this is shown to once again be the case; they are wrong 'uns make no mistake, en masse attacking refugees, although said refugees are shown to be no angels themselves.

Meanwhile those sometime symbols of bucolic English pastoralism, the good old tweed clad country farmer and the stone farmhouse become almost *Deliverance* (1972) style hijackers and scenes of troop insurrections.

While in the cities the dependable British bobby has become an altogether different gas mask wearing, gun-toting symbol of authority.

The spires of a land forever England now merely act as a backdrop to the chaos.

Although in some ways quite a mainstream, possibly even exploitation piece of cinema, throughout the film there are quite non-mainstream moments, presentation and commentary on what has led the world to this place: the action will stop and be replaced by non-narrative sequences and stills that show fields full of carrion, rivers strewn with dead aquatic life, smokestacks framed by leafless nature, rows of discarded cars are pictured on riverbanks, a luxury car is shown abandoned in the countryside as an advertising voice over says "You can do anything in a Rolls-Royce" while the almost unnoticeable specs of citizens fleeing the rioting and looting mobs in the cities can be seen on the hill behind it.

Alongside which inverted negative frames and flash-forwards show the horrors that have happened and are to come. The film also features a curiously out of place, upliftingly apocalyptic (two words you do not normally see together) string-laden and crooned theme tune sung by Roger Whittaker which is well worth a bemused listen or two.

Z.P.G. (WHICH STANDS FOR ZERO POPULATION GROWTH) is not as overtly apocalyptic, more being a depiction of a dystopian-regulated future. It was inspired by Paul Ehrlich's factual 1968 book *The Population Bomb* which warned of the potentially disastrous effects of mass resource depletion due to overpopulation, with a screenplay by Frank De Felitta and Max Ehrlich (the second of whom also published a novel based on the screenplay called *The Edict* in 1971 prior to the film's release).

The film seems reasonably obscure and overlooked but is somewhat intriguing, not least because of the cast which includes Oliver Reed, past his peak but still full of a glowering, brooding power, Geraldine Chaplin who is the daughter of bagged trousered celluloid tumbler and sometimes dictator botherer Charlie Chaplin and the bewitching, almost otherworldly luminescence of sometime *The Wicker Man* (1973)/Summerisle inhabitant Diane Cilento.

The setting is a massively polluted, smogbound Earth where natural childbirth has been banned for 30 years in order to try and preserve resources, with those who stray from these rules being punished in a particularly draconian manner as it results in execution, which slightly surreally and unsettlingly involves plastic domes printed with the word "Transgressor" being used as traps which are spray painted pink to hide the inhabitants who are then left to run out of air.

Couples are offered robot child substitutes, in a way that seems prescient of Japanese electronic Tamagotchi toys where the users had to nurture a digital pet but without giving away too much, not all citizens are obeying the "no children" edict.

One memorable scene from the film is Oliver Reed's day job in it; he is an actor in a museum that lets people watch how previous generations lived in the twentieth century.

The scene where he is putting in the hours at a simulated dinner party is a moment where the film seems to have stepped back through to almost today and it also seemed to connect it to other museums and repositories of previous times in other films in this mini-genre such as Soylent Green and Silent Running.

As a film, it is a good representation of a point in time when downbeat bleakness was often presented as part of mainstream entertainment, possibly reflecting the troubled times of the 1970s and the collapse of post-1960s utopian dreams which is mentioned elsewhere in the book.

It contains elements of B-movies and action movies but also possesses a certain intelligence and investigation within its genre tropes that put the viewer in mind of *Planet of the Apes* (1968) and the sense of "What have we as a species done?".

29

The Midwich Cuckoos and *The Day of the Triffids*: John Wyndham, Dystopian Tales, Celluloid Cuckoos and the Village as Anything but Idyll

Watching *The Village of the Damned*, the 1960 film adaptation of John Wyndham's 1957 novel *The Midwich Cuckoos*, it seemed like the perfect summing up of one of the themes of *A Year In The Country*; an imagined sense of an underlying unsettledness to country idylls, of something having gone wrong and rotten amongst the hills, valleys and sleepy local streets of this green and pleasant land. Below is a precis of the plot:

> A typical English village suddenly finds all its inhabitants have passed out and anybody who tries to enter the village or its surrounding lands also loses consciousness. The army and authorities are called in to try and find out what is going on.
>
> The villagers awake apparently unharmed and it would appear life can go on more or less as normal in these bucolic surroundings, but months later all the women of childbearing age find themselves unexplainedly pregnant.
>
> When born, these children all have similar piercing eyes, striking hair, advanced intelligence, powers of mind reading and control and possess a hive mind where if one of them learns something they all do.
>
> They are truly the cuckoos in the nest and their powers, possible

amorality and drive to survive threatens the village's way of life, its inhabitants lives and possibly mankind's rule and existence.

It is a film full of iconic imagery: nearly every scene arriving with at least one more: the early collapse into unconsciousness of that most British symbol of pastoral civility the bobby on a bicycle (bobby being a colloquial and possibly now period expression meaning police officer), nighttime mobs with burning torches and the children themselves with their emotional detachment, silver hair and glowing eyes.

In many ways it could be seen to be the flipside or even accompaniment to the film and television versions of Nigel Kneale's *Quatermass and the Pit* (1958-1959 and 1967 respectively).

Quatermass and The Pit is a post Second World War consideration of the battle for genetic superiority, purity and control as experienced in a then still recent historic conflict, while in The Village of the Damned an amoral, Aryan-esque race are seeded amongst the population, determined to survive and colonise whatever the cost.

Both Quatermass author Nigel Kneale and John Wyndham seemed to often specialise in tales where the landscape and rural areas were far removed from idylls.

For example, in John Wyndham's work there are the preternatural invaders of Village of the Damned and in his 1951 novel *The Day of the Triffids* survivors of a worldwide cataclysm take refuge in a rural cottage against predatory plants.

In Nigel Kneale's final series of Quatermass from 1979, rural stone circles are the sites of extraterrestrial reapings of the world's youth, the research conducive space that a country manor house should provide in 1972's *The Stone Tape* instead becomes the scene for an unearthing and return of spectral events and in 1968's *Year of the Sex Olympics* a remote rural island becomes a place to allow a television audience to voyeuristically view a family's tragedy and the danger they are placed in.

There is also more than a touch of horror fictions and film from both before and after its release to The Village of the Damned.

This includes shades of Frankenstein when the villagers take it upon themselves to form the aforementioned burning torchbearing mob in order to rid themselves of this technologically, biologically advanced new life form.

Also *The Omen* (1976), with its sense of a cold detached cuckoo in the nest, with telepathic or telekinetic powers beyond our ken or control and who will use those powers to dispatch any threat or adversary.

Viewed now The Village of the Damned has a number of a jarring or disjunctive aspects. The scenes set in the local village shop/Post Office look like a modern-day drama recreation of such things; it is full of the now simplistic looking boxes and cans of food from that era that we are used to seeing in slightly over neatly and tidily produced contemporary period drama productions; they do not look like they are real or truly existed.

Also, this is a world that seems to only be populated by upper middle-class figures of control and authority with perfect diction or the local pub drinking working class and the population is noticeably not at all ethnically diverse.

Which was possibly indicative of how things actually were then in such rural areas but to the modern eye it is a noticeably set, defined and delineated society.

Coupled with this the upper middle classes seem to take these frankly bizarre circumstances curiously in their stride and apart from the very occasional emotional outburst (mostly from a female and rarely the educated males) do not appear to get too disturbed, stressed or distressed about the fact that the women folk of the village have essentially given birth to and are being threatened by some unexplained, actually very other biological and possibly extraterrestrial force.

In the film such things are generally dealt with at the same level of emotional alarm and froideur as if it was merely some socially rather unacceptable gaffe.

Although these cuckoos are essentially a hive mind or colony, their leader or more vocal spokesperson is played brilliantly by Martin Stephens, just the touch of a smile playing about his lips as he stares otherwise without emotion at his mother after sending someone to a fiery departure.

He appears to have been the go-to young actor for such quietly unsettling preternaturalness in the early 1960s as he also appears amongst the reeds, willows, hauntings and transgressions of the 1961 film *The Innocents.*

Returning to the analogies with the then recent(ish) historical conflict of the Second World War, the way the British or at least the social class with authority deal with these invaders or colonising cuckoos, is shown to be very decent in comparison to how the rest of the world does.

Reason generally prevails and the British are for talking, consideration, study and compromise.

Elsewhere in the world where similar events have occurred, the film tells us there may well be brutality and the simple application of military force to deal with the problem.

I read John Wyndham's original novel of the film at a young age, when I was living in a tiny country village that was not too dissimilar to the book's setting.

In common with the book and film, although that village was most definitely a country idyll, it was surrounded by symbols of a readiness or defences against those who might be tempted to invade: low flying military planes flew overhead regularly as they practised avoiding enemy radar, there were abandoned concrete pill box defences in the fields, unexploded military ordinance would be found from time to time and the disposal experts would have to be called in and there was a map in the local information centre which the local youngsters considered near mythological as it apparently showed where aeroplanes had crashed during wartime.

Alongside which in and around my domestic home life and that of a friend's were two nuclear air raid warning sirens in the shape of smallish brown Bakelite boxes (literally sitting on a shelf and window ledge in the front room where my friend lived and in a small office in the forecourt of my house.)

John Wyndham's writing was a general background to such things and provided some early introductions to more grown up science and dystopic fiction, including a 1981 BBC television adaptation of his Day of the Triffids novel.

This series has an air of being genuinely unsettling, in particular the introduction, where green and blue tinted faces stare wonderingly at the cosmic light show which will make mankind blind, the brief terrifying attack by a triffid plant and the accompanying spectral choral soundtrack.

The disquiet is in part because plants are generally seen as a benign aspect of nature, so when in Day of the Triffids they are shown as carnivorous, poison-equipped hunters of mankind they seem all the more shocking. Also, there is something about the triffids in this version that is genuinely gruesome and unsettling.They do not look "real" in the way that digitally generated later versions may do but they do appear to be part of the real world.

30

Folk Archive and *Unsophisticated Arts*: Documenting the Overlooked and Unregulated

Folk Archive: Contemporary Popular Art from the UK is a book and exhibition from 2005, created and collected by Jeremy Deller and Alan Kane.

The Folk Archive collection is a gathering and documenting of creative work that could be loosely considered folk art from everyday life in the UK, part of which includes work which may have been created for utilitarian purposes or decoration such as cafe signs and often things which may not be considered art by its makers or wider society.

The phrase "folk art" often conjures or represents a particular quite well-defined, often rural or cottage industry aesthetic and has been frequently used to refer more to work from previous eras but The Folk Archive does not make such distinctions.

In the pages of the book you can find largely photographic images of tattoos/tattoo guns, artwork from prisons, burger van signs, illustrations painted onto the bonnets of cars and crash helmets, fairground paintings, sandcastles, cake decorations, Christmas decorations, protest banners, shop signs, decorative costume for a night out or a carnival, clairvoyant's hand created signs, crop circles and the trappings of what could be considered traditional folkloric rituals.

The use of the word "folk" in Jeremy Deller and Alan Kane's work presumably refers more to a sense of art from, by and for the people than to the roots of the word *folk*, which essentially refers to a sense of music and culture from the wald or wild woods.[1]

However the work contained in Folk Archive could in some ways still be considered work from the wild woods, in that this is unregulated art, work which sidesteps definitions and hierarchies surrounding what is allowed into the canon of art and high culture.

Jeremy Deller's work often involves, incorporates and is interactively accessible or co-created by the public.

In line with that, his work in the past has included taking modern music technology to record with retired musicians in an English seaside town, re-enacting pitched battles in political disputes in conjunction with those involved at the time and re-enactment enthusiasts, taking a bouncy castle version of Stonehenge around the country, a traditional brass band playing acid house records to a young dance audience or a procession through Manchester that incorporated everything from a local pensioner-friendly snack bar recreated on the back of a float to Manchester's musical legacy reinterpreted by a calypso band.

In a traditional library, the books of Jeremy Deller's work would generally be found in the fine art section but in reality his work exists separately to much of what surrounds it; it belongs to a genre unto itself.

Within his work there is a curious lack of ego; he is more of a creative enabler, curator and event organiser than an artist with a capital "A". In some ways, his work bridges the gap between what is known as fine art and accessible popular art.

The Folk Archive collection provides a pathway to a modern-day revisiting of some of the themes of Barbara Jones' *Unsophisticated Arts*, originally released in 1951 and republished in 2013 by Little Toller Books.

That book told the story of her explorations in the 1940s of everyday art throughout Britain and which took in some similar subject matter to that in Folk Archive: fairgrounds, tattoo parlours, taxidermists, house-boats, high street shops, seaside piers and amusement arcades.

Also in 1951 Barbara Jones organised the *Black Eyes and Lemonade* exhibition in the Whitechapel Art Gallery as part of the Festival of Britain, which in a similar manner to the Folk Archive presented creative work and objects which would normally not be included within the realms of fine art and associated gallery display.

In contrast to the photography of Folk Archive and the presentation of actual objects in the Black Eyes and Lemonade exhibition, the documenting and archiving of work in Unsophisticated Arts is carried out via Barbara Jones' illustrations.

Although it was intended as a recording of real life and day-to-day art, viewed now it provides a document of a fabled lost Britain; there is a certain whimsical fairytale like quality to the images of often ornately and elaborately decorated canal boat interiors, fairground rides, table cupboards etc.

1. Discussed further as a topic in Chapter 1.

31

Folkloric Photography: A Lineage of Wanderings, Documentings and Imaginings

THERE IS AN AREA of photography which concerns itself with documents of British folkloric rituals and costumes.

A starting point for such things is Sir Benjamin Stone's work in the late 19th and early 20th century, when he photographed British traditional customs, collected in book form in *A Record of England: Sir Benjamin Stone and the National Photographic Record Association 1897 -1910*, which was published in 2007.

The people, times and places in Benjamin Stone's photographs seem as though they belong to somewhere now impossibly distant from our own times.

The physiognomy of those portrayed, their stances and very being have gained layers of difference and otherliness as the years have gone by. There is a sense at times of them being photographs not from Benjamin Stone's land of birth but rather of them being documents of rituals in exotic foreign lands.

Alongside this they can also possess an air of surreality: in one photograph a stuffed figure is shown as if it is floating in the air amongst the foliage of a tree; dressed in a white flowing dress its face and hands are completely obscured or replaced by what appear to be harvest crops.

As an image it brings to mind more a sense of being from a fairy tale rather than 19th century reality captured via documentary photography.

Other photographs contain numerous stag's antlers worn as part of ritual costume.

This, along with the challenging stance and stares of their subjects, lend them a folk horror aspect, almost as though they are a glimpse forwards and backwards to the transgressive rituals of the villagers in 1970 *Play for Today* television drama *Robin Redbreast.*[1]

Benjamin Stone's work is an early point in a lineage that leads to more recent books which document British folkloric tradition, ritual and costume such as Homer Sykes *Once a Year: Some Traditional British Customs* (1977), Sarah Hannant's *Mummers, Maypoles and Milkmaids: A Journey Through the English Ritual Year* (2011), Merry Brownfield's *Merry England - the Eccentricity of English Attire* (2012) and Henry Bourne's *Arcadia Britannica: A Modern British Folklore Portrait* (2015).

As a starting point, Homer Sykes *Once a Year...* is a collection of photographs from seven years of journeying around Britain and was reissued in 2016 by Dewi Lewis Publishing.

As with sections of Benjamin Stone's work, some of the photographs in Once a Year have a genuinely eerie or unsettlingly macabre air, particularly the cover photograph of the original edition which features the custom of burning tar barrel-carrying in Allendale, Northumberland.

It presents a sense of a ritual that feels considerably separate to mainstream contemporary society and mores, whether at its original time of publication or today and although it is a documentary photograph, as with some of Stone's photographs, seems to hint at or lean more towards the fictional worlds and tropes of folk horror rather than the real world.

Once a Year also acts as a document of period 1970s detail and style, while also capturing the way traditional customs existed in amongst such things.

One of the key images in the book is of somebody completely enclosed in a Burry Man folkloric costume, which is made from sticky flower or seedheads, in a pub who is being helped to drink through a straw. It is a precise distilling and capturing of a particular moment in British life, full of subtle signifiers of a way of life which, while only being a few decades ago and not yet as inherently distant as the world captured by Benjamin Stone's photographs, still seems to belong to a world very far apart from our own.

In a number of ways Sarah Hannant's Mummers, Maypoles and Milkmaids is similar to Once a Year in that both books are documentary photography social histories of the ongoing observance and enactment of British folk rituals.

Although Hannant's photographs are in colour, some of the photographs could almost be exchanged from one book to the other, although they are set apart by subtle period signifiers and details.

As with Once a Year one intriguing aspect of this book is the way that these sometimes-arcane rites and rituals are pictured alongside and in contrast to symbols of modern-day life.

In Sarah Hannant's book this positioning and juxtaposing is shown in photographs which, for example, picture somebody dressed in a straw bear folkloric costume next to a local metro supermarket and a fluorescent-clad safety officer next to carnival float queens.

It is also given expression in her book through more subtle details such as a digital camera next to blackened faces, the modern eye wear of a traditional jester as he wanders down a country lane and possibly in the modern day physiognomy and clothing of the observers of burning tar barrel carrying.

Often the rituals pictured have a playful, dressing up, knockabout air but just once in a while something else seems to creep into the photographs, in particular in one photograph where the blackened faces of those engaged in and wearing the costume of folkloric rituals peer and appear through a pub window.

As with Once a Year, such photographs suggest the tropes of folk horror rather than being purely documentary photographs and they begin to hint at or conjure up an otherly Albion, slithers of a view through the portal as it were.

Alongside Once a Year and Mummers, Maypoles and Milkmaids, Merry Brownfield's Merry England is a book which utilises documentary photography via its photographs of its subjects in real world settings.

At first glance and from the book's cover, which features somebody dressed in traditional green man folk costume, it appears to be another book in this lineage, one which directly focuses on folkloric traditions and photographs of people in traditional folk costume forms the heart of the book with sections titled "Straw Bear", "The Castleton Garland Day", "Holly Man", "Mummer's Plays" and "Morris Dancers".

However, it also travels considerably further afield to encompass pop culture tribes and styles such as mod and people who appear to have tumbled from the page of *The Chap* magazine in "The Tweed Run" and "Vintage Style" sections.

Alongside which it also documents the city-based London East End tradition of pearly kings and queens, the comic convention-esque costumes of attendees to the World Darts Championship, traditional Billingsgate fish market bobbin hats and a number of possibly more contentious hunting and aristocratic areas.

Because of the way in which the book explores a breadth of different areas of traditional and celebratory wear it reminds me of Jeremy Deller and Alan Kane's Folk Archive book and exhibition from 2005,[2] being more a "from the people" view of things than specifically what could be considered folk aesthetics.

Henry Bourne's Arcadia Britannica takes a different approach to the above books in that, as its subtitle suggests, the book contains more formal posed portraits of those in folkloric costume.

The photographs are described as being "shot in the wild" at various events and festivals but apart from the occasional appearance of grass beneath the feet of some of those in the photographs, due to the use of a blank white backdrop aesthetically they could be studio portraits.

The white backdrop removes those in the photographs from the wider world and accompanied by the capturing of detail which is enabled by the formal posing and controlling of light sources it lends the project the air of an almost scientific recording of its subjects; through these choices of technique the book represents and contains a precise documenting of a particular point in folkloric time archived for future generations.

While the book largely focuses on those wearing traditional folkloric costume, although less so than in Merry England it also branches out further to include Pearly King and Queen costumes, while also taking in practising witches and warlocks (and in an interconnected manner includes an introductory essay by Simon Costin, who is the director of the Museum of Witchcraft alongside being the founder and director of the Museum of British Folklore).

All the above books and photography focus on the British isles but there are a number of books which carry out similar studies and documenting of folkloric rituals and costumes elsewhere in the world, one of which is Charles Fréger's *Wilder Mann: The Image of the Savage* originally published in 2012. This takes as its theme:

> "The transformation of man into beast is a central aspect of traditional pagan rituals that are centuries old and which celebrate the seasonal cycle, fertility, life and death."

Reflecting such transformations, generally the images in the book are of costumes where the human features of their wearers are no longer visible, being much more hidden than many British folkloric costumes.

Fréger travelled throughout Europe to document such rituals and while his project took him to the UK the costumes in his photographs seem to the untrained eye to largely be exotically foreign.

In British folklore-focused photography and books the sense of unsettling folk horror-esque undercurrents are more glimpses here and there; with Charles Fréger's images such atmospheres are much more prevalent.

Many of the costumes in his photographs could well be escapees or prototypes for the 1970s British BBC costume and creature effect department in terms of their design.They appear to be creatures from a forgotten *Doctor Who* episode from back then, possibly compatriots of the befurred yetis or abominable snowmen that had a nation's children hiding behind the sofa. One photograph in Wilder Mann pictures somebody smoking a cigarette, which should break the spell but it does not; the wearer's masked white costume, makeup, walking stick, stance and the way they are staring at the camera makes it wander off into some very odd almost slasher film territory and more childhood nightmares. These could be creatures from the television series *Sesame Street* turned into monsters, ones which have crawled from under the bed and out of the cupboards and are wandering the landscape freely.

THE IMAGES IN Wilder Mann and the above books of British folkloric rituals often focus on documenting rurally-orientated or located events and customs. Axel Hoedt's book *Once a Year* from 2013 shifts focus more exclusively to streets and towns, in particular the Swabian Alemannic carnival known as Fasnacht, Fastnacht or Fasnet, a custom in southwest Germany. The carnival is described in text which accompanies the book as being:

> "...when the cold and grim spirits of winter are symbolically hunted down and expelled. Every year around January and February processions of people make their way through the streets of Endingen, Sachsenheim, Kissleg, Singen, Wilfingen and Triberg dressed up lavishly as demons, witches, earthly spirits and fearful animals to enact this scene of symbolic expulsion."

The language used seems brutal and harsh; hunted down, expelled, expulsion, fearful.

To view these photographs is to step in amongst the denizens of a land far from the twee fields of folklore and carnivalesque dressing up.

The creatures his photographs capture (that particular word is used somewhat appropriately and possibly hopefully) seem like the darker urban cousins of Wilder Mann.

The images put the viewer in mind of folklore as rethought by club kids (think 2003 film *Party Monster*), while sharing a sense of Wilder Mann's 1970s Doctor Who-esque "how do we scare the heck out of people for relatively tuppence ha'penny?".

In Estelle Hanania's *Glacial Jubilé* book (2013), some of the European folkloric costumes and creatures from Wilder Mann seem at points to reappear and breach the rural/urban divide, but this time they can seem like alien invaders as they are shown advancing in formation across the landscape and then appearing in urban streets and shopping centres.

Alongside the rural/urban division that is at times present in such folkloric-based photography work there could also be seen to be further separate but interlinked strands, themes, atmospheres and approaches.

As mentioned above there is the more documentary-like photography which focuses on British folklore and that can be found in the work of Benjamin Stone and the books Homer Sykes' Once a Year, Sarah Hannant's Mummers, Maypoles and Milkmaids, Henry Bourne's Arcadia Britannica and Merry Brownfield's Merry England.

Alongside these in a connected but parallel strand are the photography books and projects which focus more on European and non-UK folklore such as Charles Fréger's Wilder Mann, his *Yokainoshima - Island of Monsters* (2016) which is a study of Japanese folkloric costume, Axel Hoedt's Once a Year and *Dusk* (2015) which takes his folkloric/carnival photographic studies to Austria and Switzerland and Estelle Hanania's Glacial Jubilé.

Both loose groupings of books and work are essentially photographic portraits and documenting of folkloric costume but just in different locations.

The European-focused books seem in part to be more a reflection of a fine art like take on photography, to be partly an expression of the photographer's own creative intent and stories as well as being documentary in nature; although being photography projects which focus on the real world, within them is often a sense of an intention to create a particular atmosphere or personal narrative that at various points interacts with or even to a degree supersedes the documentary aspects.

This fine art, expressive intent is given full reign in Laura Thompson's *Senseless* photography series from 2016 where she produced staged photographs of figures in the landscape dressed in costumes made from disposable manmade objects.

These photographs appear to recall European folkloric or mythical costume that may have appeared in say Charles Fréger or Estelle Hanania's work but filtered as though via a story of outer space creatures who are lost and wandering the earth.

1. Discussed further in Chapter 11.
2. Discussed in Chapter 30.

32

Poles and Pylons and The Telegraph Pole Appreciation Society: A Continuum of Accidental Art

THE INTERNET HAS given space, nooks and crannies to all kinds and manner of niche interests, and it's safe to say The Telegraph Pole Appreciation Society and its website is one of the more niche, even amongst the further flung of such crannies.

The Telegraph Pole Appreciation Society declares that its aim is to celebrate "the glorious everyday mundanitude of these simple silent sentinels the world over", which has a rather fine poetic lyricism and intent. Amongst its pages you will find numerous photographic documentings of telegraph poles, Pole of the Month, Pole Appreciation Day and reporting on photographic recordings of poles from around the world.

A sense of appreciation is woven tightly throughout its collecting and documenting work; though sometimes cast in jovial language, there is a genuine love for these utilitarian objects, an appreciation of their accidental art.

An accompanying but not formally connected website is *Poles and Pylons* (or to give its full name, *Telegraph Poles and Electricity Pylons*). At this site, communication poles and their lines of communication can be found alongside fellow land-striding brethren and their humming power carrying cables. It is possibly a more otherly/psychogeographical study and documenting than The Telegraph Pole Appreciation Society but both sites and their related activities complement one another somewhat; the flipside of one another's coins.

The images they contain can often be a literal expression of the juxtaposition of technology, modernity and the pastoral, of the old ways and the new, when they are photographed amongst the landscape. In this manner they connect with the cover image of the first printing of Rob Young's *Electric Eden* book from 2010 which depicts a farmer ploughing the land in a traditional horse-drawn manner under the gaze of electricity pylons.[1]

They also connect with hauntological takes on the landscape and edgelands, via the cautionary tales of public information films, wherein children were warned not to fly kites under electricity pylons because of the dangers this could bring about.

In a further hauntological manner to a degree they could be connected to the 1984 television programme *Threads* which depicts the aftermath of a nuclear conflict in Britain, taking its name from such lines of communication and how they bind our society together, allowing it to function and communicate and how easily disrupted such gossamer strands can be.

Further sites which act as archival documentation hubs and expressions of an appreciation of similar structures and aspects of infrastructure include *Disused Stations*, which focuses on closed British railway stations and *Subterranea Britannica*,[2] which documents often forgotten or decommissioned underground structures and installations such as Cold War Monitoring Posts and bunkers.

Sites such as these can also capture a sense of a lost age, of lost futures and a related melancholia or even paranoia at points with Subterranea Britannica. They can have a haunting quality that seems at points to conjure the spirit of a very particular time that now seems far, far away from our own, whether by documenting the no longer required structures of a formerly public owned railway system or the Cold War dread that can be associated with some of the infrastructure to be found at Subterranea Britannica.

The Telegraph Pole Appreciation Society and Poles and Pylons also remind us of Jonny Trunk's book collections of library music covers, *The Music Library* (2005 and revised in 2016).[3]

While library music was produced in the more overtly creative medium of music, it was still designed to serve a particular purpose, to be stock audio that could for example soundtrack or reflect particular moods in film and due to that utilitarian intent the appreciation of it has links with that of the more accidental art of poles and pylons.

Also, a line could be drawn from such things to Jeremy Deller and Alan Kane's *Folk Archive* book (2005) and exhibition, Barbara Jones *Unsophisticated Arts* book (1951) and the associated *Black Eyes and Lemonade* exhibition.[4] These focus on, document and serve as an appreciation of creative work from everyday life that may have been created for utilitarian purposes and may not be considered art by its makers or wider society such as fairground ride decorations and cafe signs.

Further lines could also be drawn to Christopher Herwig's *Soviet Bus Stops* book published in 2015,[5] in which he creates a photographic document and appreciation of Soviet era bus stops and their designs which seems to have a reach beyond their utilitarian purpose and to reflect the visions and far reaching striving of an empire.

These various sites, Jonny Trunk's library music books, Folk Archive, Unsophisticated Arts, Black Eyes and Lemonade and Soviet Bus Stops could all be seen as representing part of a continuum of collecting, curating and appreciating of work which was created with varying degrees of initial utilitarian and/or creative intent and which for some has come to contain or represent a more expressive or creative aspect than was necessarily intended in that initial intent.

1. The book itself focuses on the history and interconnecting undercurrents of pastoral and folk music/culture and is discussed further in Chapter 1.
2. Discussed in Chapter 17.
3. Discussed in Chapter 38.
4. Discussed in Chapter 30.
5. Discussed in Chapter 12.

33

Symptoms and *Images*: Hauntological Begetters, the Uneasy Landscape and Gothic Bucolia

The British Film Institute's *Flipside* strand of DVD/Blu-ray releases and cinema events began in 2009.

Its intention is said to chart "the untold history of British film" and it has taken in a wide variety of the fringes of film and cinematic work which for various reasons has fallen outside the critically accepted and/or acknowledged canon of cinema.

The DVD/Blu-ray releases have included what could be considered subterranean, exotica or mondo cinema, forgotten or lost film, arthouse and odd b-movies and occasional strands of unsettled or otherly pastoralism.

These cinematic outcasts have been sympathetically restored and released with extended extras and notes.

In 2016 the 1974 José Ramón Larraz film *Symptoms* was released as part of the Flipside strand of films.

As a brief precis of the film's history and plot, it was produced in 1973, came out in 1974, received a fair amount of critical attention and praise and then largely disappeared for the best part of forty years, apart from via privately circulated bootleg copies.

It is the tale of two young women who go for a break in a large rurally located house, wherein one of their mental states begins to splinter and fracture.

In a *Record Collector* magazine review from 2016 it was described as "...gothic-bucolic... the sort of thing that begat hauntology and Peter Strickland...", ending on "...it's a revelation".

The phrase gothic-bucolic connects with certain aspects of *A Year In The Country* wanderings, particularly in terms of views of the landscape that deal with an unsettled flipside or subterranean, darker-hued bucolia.

Peter Strickland does not appear to mention the film in any interviews, nor lists it as one of the films that he noted as having fed into, influenced or were an inspiration for his 2014 film *The Duke of Burgundy.*[1]

However, in many ways Symptoms appears connected with that film, seeming to be in part an unintended companion or sister piece.

The setting and setup is not all that dissimilar from The Duke of Burgundy; two women living in a relatively isolated rurally-set grand house that is decorated in a slightly faded, possibly slightly aristocratic or upper class, decadent or luxuriant manner and a depiction of the increasing tensions and dysfunctions of their relationship.

While the sense of connection and even sisterhood is increased by Angela Pleasance, who plays the lead in Symptoms and who bears a degree of physiognomic similarity to Chiara D'Anna who plays one of the main characters in The Duke Of Burgundy.

Both have a slightly unworldly, almost childlike air to them, although Angela Pleasance's character is more otherworldly than just unwordly, as compared to Chiara D'Anna's character's slightly brattish pique; Angela Pleasance's character feels nearer to *The Woman Who Fell to Earth.*

Symptoms also brings to mind the work of fashion photographer Deborah Turbeville and the use in her photographs of crumbling textures, decaying glamour and grandeur, alongside a certain shared languor to its characters and the use in both of edge of rural isolation settings.

Chapter 26, which focusses on Peter Strickland's work discusses how The Duke of Burgundy seems to exist in an indefinable neverland era: to take place in its own self-contained, quietly fantastical world, one where any possible external world or infrastructure are not seen and the markers and technology of contemporary life are hardly acknowledged.

In contrast Symptoms to a degree acknowledges the outside world and the contemporary time of its making: London and visitors from there are mentioned, or indeed they visit via car, the women travel to the local village for supplies and so forth.

However, their world still has the intensity of a couple alone, one which increasingly intensifies and collapses into itself, with anything outside of the house and/or their relationship being seen as and indeed feels like an intrusion.

To a large degree The Duke of Burgundy's pastoral idyll seems generally richly honey toned; mellifluous is a word that comes to mind but within this idyll conflict and imbalance between the two main characters builds into an unresolvable tension.

The rural location in Symptoms also has a certain entrancing beauty but it is a darker, more overshadowed gothic bucolia.

There is a calm present and the house's inhabitants go row boating on leaf-filled water and as in The Duke of Burgundy they also partake in carefree bike rides.

However, as in The Duke of Burgundy there is an ever-increasing build up of pressure and tension but with more literally fatal and psychotic results than the emotional wounds that are depicted in Peter Strickland's film.

Although in Symptoms there is an underlying sense of dread, the viewer can at points or to a degree relax, sink into and enjoy its views of nature and escape. Such elements are very much part of the film's enclosed, self-contained, claustrophobic world which is all overhanging branches and wooded enclosure rather than wide-open spaces.

Here and there light may break through the trees but it seems to only just be breaking through, to be almost battling or momentary.

And while the viewer can appreciate the natural beauty the film contains, it also instills a sense of "never has the British countryside been so quiet and calm and yet so unnourishing."

As mentioned earlier, Symptoms acknowledges the period in which it was set, including some slightly incongruous Carnaby-Street-become-tourist-attraction latter period hippie garments in an early sequence.

However, this is a film that is difficult to place in any particular era (something which it also shares with The Duke of Burgundy). This is particularly so once the participants are ensconced in the subtle grandeur, grounds and the nature which are part of and surround their house, which seems to a degree a timeless place that is separate from the contemporary world.

This lack of being able to fully place it in a particular era is despite its muted grey-green visual atmosphere: one that was rather prevalent in film and television from the period of Symptoms' production in the early to mid 1970s.

Accompanying which, the not being able to precisely pinpoint a decade when watching the film may also in part be due to a certain sharpness, glamour and style to the imagery that does not seem to fully belong to its time of production in the 1970s and that period's often gritty representation in British film, television and media of the time.

This dischronicity could also be due to the contemporary restoration of the film, as the related visual qualities can cause a certain sense of time period dissociation, possibly due to the push and pull of the aesthetics of technological processes from different eras.

Although it is not overly filled duration-wise with such things, this is a film that not so much wanders as lunges, sparks and darkly shatters into intense, particularly unsettling physical violence.

In one sense, although it is an inherent part of the film, this is when it is at its weakest – when it veers towards more obvious genre tropes.

It is a more interesting piece of film making when its deeply unsettled atmosphere is held at bay and its mystery is left intact rather than being given full unflinchingly brutish expression. Which is something it shares with that other isolated home in the woods gone awry 1970 film *Queens of Evil*.[2]

Associated posters and promotion from Symptoms' release often focused on those genre tropes but this is not precisely that kind of film; it is odder and more containing of its own character than such standard exploitative fare, there is a layering, intelligence and unspokeness in the film that seems to battle with and against genre expectations.

Symptoms shares a number of similarities with its almost cinematic period contemporary *Images*, a Robert Altman film from 1972: in both films the main female protagonists undergo extreme mental disturbance with somewhat deadly results, while living in largely isolated rurally based homes.

However, whereas Symptoms has a more subtly fractured dreamlike quality in the way it expresses such things and atmospheres, Images has a more overt, ongoing literal and graphic expression of those disturbances.

The plot involves a children's author Cathryn, played by Susannah York, who receives a series of disturbing phone calls at her home in London, which leave her in a state of confused disarray. When her husband comes home they decide to take a vacation at their isolated country cottage in Ireland, hoping that it will ease and calm her.

Once there Cathryn's mental state deteriorates, she begins to witness hallucinations or apparitions of people who are not there: past lovers, dopplegangers of herself and reality seems to crumble.

As a viewer it becomes difficult to decide and decipher what is real and what is not, with all such things seamlessly linking into one another and being presented in a largely realist manner rather than possible hallucinations being signposted by overt visual effects.

As with Symptoms it is a study of the fracturing of a mind in an isolated rural setting, amongst a landscape that should contain bucolic ease, escape and rest but that underlyingly could be seen to represent and capture a sense of 1970s psychic malaise.

In part that may be because despite the rural setting, both films have an understated murky, subdued colour palette, which as previously mentioned, seems to have been prevalent around the time of their making.

Also, within both films the interior scenes of the country houses are claustrophobic, confined, dark spaces, seemingly worlds unto themselves, decorated in what could be described as a gothic, bohemian, Hammer Horror mansion bric-a-brac style.

Symptoms is possibly more overtly claustrophobic, with its exterior scenes seeming to consist largely of overhung, sunblocking trees and vegetation, whereas in Images there are views of rolling moors and open hillsides but still within such shots there is little sense of ease and these landscapes and skies contain a foreboding, brooding sense of menace.

All three of the films discussed in this chapter straddle a line between arthouse, enquiring cinema and a certain exploitational sensationalism[3] although with Symptoms and Images this is more focused on violent acts and is possibly more unsettling or even distasteful in parts but intriguing nonetheless.

1. Discussed in Chapter 26.
2. Considered in Chapter 23.
3. Something that is also referred to in connection with Peter Strickland's work in Chapter 26.

34

The Spirit of Dark and Lonely Water: Public Information Films and Lost Municipal Paternalisms

The Spirit of Dark and Lonely Water is considered something of a "classic" public information film from 1973, some of which are renowned for having scared the heck out of a generation of youngsters through their forthright, graphic or unsettling atmospheres and depictions of potential dangers.

Public information films were a curiously blunt tool used to educate the population, often on matters of health and safety and were issued by the government-run and funded Central Office of Information in the UK from 1945 until 2005.

The structure, naming and concept puts me in mind of a previous era's underfunded, unsophisticated benign paternalism, of a "we know best" tea and limp sandwiches committee which was in charge of a sub-sub-Orwellianism, though it actually seems to have sprung forth in part from that previous era's social consensus orientated wish to help, nurture and protect its citizens.

To a certain degree such films have become iconic symbols of a particular era alongside related television broadcasts, series etc. which often seemed to have had a more unsettling and longlasting effect and impact on their audience than was possibly intended, having become a part of and also inspired a hauntologically-inclined collective memory.

As an aside public information films have been collected in various commercially released DVDs, including a series by the BFI. They are also featured extensively in the *Scarred For Life - Growing Up in the Dark Side of the Decade - Volume One: The 1970s* book by Stephen Brotherstone and Dave Lawrence, published in 2017 and which focuses on ongoing unsettled reverberations from these films and related period culture.

Revisiting The Spirit of Dark and Lonely Water, which was intended to warn children of the dangers of playing near water, there is a striking similarity with that other cultural artifact of 1973, *The Wicker Man*, at the point when Lord Summerisle tells Sergeant Howie of the characteristics he had that made him ideal as their sacrifice/source of plant renewal:

> "I am the spirit of dark and lonely water, ready to trap the unwary, the show-off, the fool..."
> (from The Spirit of Dark and Lonely Water).

> "A man who would come here of his own free will. A man who has come here with the power of a king by representing the law… A man who has come here as a fool…" (from The Wicker Man).

(Of course, adding some extra phosphorous, nitrogen and potassium to the plants nourishment via a good fertiliser along with, as suggested by Sergeant Howie, choosing plants appropriate for the local geography and climate may well have had a better chance of increasing apple growth on The Wicker Man's Summerisle island but probably would not have made for as good a story.)

In part, both films have come to signify or been repurposed to become part of a form of modern-day folklore.

The Wicker Man is more directly so in a folkloric sense, The Spirit of Dark and Lonely Water more in a hauntological manner.

The Spirit of Dark and Lonely Water is oddly almost comic as opposed to frightening, although that may in part be due to minds of a certain age connecting particular clothing aesthetics with knockabout 1970s children's shows.

However, what is striking is the scene which pans across rusted debris on a riverbank:

> "Under the water there are traps: old cars, bedsteads, weeds, hidden depths..."

There is something about this, mixed with the styles of clothing in the film and the sense of essentially playing on wastelands which remind us of just how foreign and far away a place the early 1970s are from today.

It invokes a sense of the journey that UK society has gone on, from youngsters playing amongst a culture's debris, in the muddy puddles and potential deathtraps of its discarded places and edgelands (although that word did not yet exist at the time of the film's release) to a time of much more intensified commodification and birthday trips to softplay centres and so on.

In that sense, the film seems like an antideluvian recording of a pre-Thatcher, pre-captalist realism and related monotheistic "the market is all time and forever" era.

It could be seen as a document produced during or transmission from one of the times when society was battling over its future shape, order and social consensus; hence the link to the themes and interests of hauntological study and work and associated yearnings for forgotten futures and municipally organised utopias.

Such themes and work appear to consider in part that maybe such paternalistic tendencies within politics and society were not such a bad thing, particularly in contrast with the in some ways harsher market-led times in which we live; a sense that what was once considered Big Brother was also possibly a more nuanced "big brother".

35

Magpahi, Paper Dollhouse and The Eccentronic Research Council: Finders Keepers/Bird Records Nestings and Considerations of Modern Day Magic

ALISON COOPER, who often records under the name Magpahi, creates work which feels as though it exists in and has tumbled from an indefinable fabled time and place of its own creation, work which at times seems to have been created by or also tumbled from arcane and lost music boxes.

Her recorded work includes the tremulously vocalled acid or psych-esque folk on the *Magpahi* EP compilation, released by Jane Weaver's Bird Records in collaboration with Finders Keepers Records in 2008, which is a gathering of imagined poems and tales told in folk music refracted through a filter of woodland fantasia.

The creation and transporting of its listener to an unknown or unknowable place can also be found in her more folk-orientated work as Magpahi on the album *Watchbird Alluminate* from 2011 where songs from Jane Weaver's *Fallen by Watchbird* album released in 2010 are reimagined or reinterpreted, on which Magpahi reinterprets "My Soul Was Lost, My Soul Was Lost and No-One Saved Me", imparting an otherworldly fabled atmosphere to the song.[1]

On *Devon Folklore Tapes Vol. IV - Rituals and Practices*, released by Folklore Tapes in 2012[2] Magpahi's contribution includes leftfield glacial otherly and exploratory folk pop, instrumentals and wordless singing as though captured by far away dusty recording mechanisms; in spirit it may not be a million miles away from work that say Broadcast or Cat's Eyes might have created for the insular dreamscapes of Peter Strickland's films.[3]

As Alison or A. Cooper and collaborating with fellow sometimes Folklore Tapes collaborator and co-founder of the Hood Faire record label Sam McLoughlin, she has released two volumes of folkloric soundscapes called *Natural/Supernatural Lancashire* and *Supernatural Lancashire Volume Two*, released in 2009 and 2013 respectively by Finders Keepers Records.

These are largely instrumental works (though just occasionally her voice will fleetingly appear) which create a soundtrack or an audiological tribute to the northern British Lancashire landscape and its stories.

"Natural Lancashire", the A-side of the 2008 album is referred to in accompanying notes as "a natural history reference work that is dedicated to the flora and fauna of the region" while "Supernatural Lancashire", the b-side "delves into the mysteries, myths and strange phenomena of the old county of Lancashire."

However, neither part is a straightforward pastoral view and on the Natural Lancashire side you can be immersed in the wheezing almost carny previous era world of "Stream Power" one second and then transported to the meadows via "Edder" the next.

This juxtaposition highlights the duality with regards to the landscape and nature contained within the records; they are pleasantly dreamlike and bucolic but also around the edges, sometimes much nearer in, there is something disquieting amongst the trees, beneath the meadows, at the edgelands of towns, cities and along the canalways.

In Chapter 9: "…The Imagined Spaces of Imaginary Soundtracks" music is discussed that is a soundtrack to an imaginary film, in particular *The Tales from the Black Meadow* (2013) and *The Book of the Lost* (2014). Without stating that it is such a soundtrack, *Supernatural Lancashire Part Two* can seem at times to create a soundtrack to an imaginary television series, one which was probably made deep in the deepest 1970s, aimed at children but which had arrived as a curiously unsettled and unsettling thing.

Some of the tracks invoke a sense of half-remembered or mis-remembered memories of such a programme and conjure the slightly smeared, grimy colours of faded spectral transmissions from another era, particularly on "Hexagons above Dovestones".

Alison Cooper has also released work in collaboration with Gwendolen Osmond as Crystal Mirrors on a joint Folklore Tapes/Hood Faire released cassette in 2014, alongside contributing tracks as Magpahi to the compilation *Mistletoe & Cold Winter Skies* released by Was Ist Das? in 2014 and several *A Year In The Country* released themed compilations including *The Forest/The Wald* in 2016 and *All The Merry Year Round* and *The Quietened Cosmologists* in 2017.

The Magpahi EP, Natural/Supernatural Lancashire, Supernatural Lancashire Part Two and Watchbird Alluminate were all released by Finders Keepers Records or its collaborative sister label Bird Records, which is run by musician Jane Weaver.

Both labels have proved to be a home for various often female-led or sung explorations of music that could very loosely be connected to folk but which wander amongst their own particular landscape of such things.

This has taken in both modern, newly created work and also the release of archival material such as "O Willow Waly" by George Auric taken from 1961 film *The Innocents* which was released on 7" by Finders Keepers in 2013.

Sung by Isla Cameron, it could be considered a precursor to the folk horror and soundtrack of the likes of *The Wicker Man* film from 1973[4] in the way that it draws from traditional music tropes to create beguilingly entrancing music which also summons a sense of the "other" out amongst rural climes.

Devon Folklore Tapes Vol. IV - Rituals and Practices, as mentioned earlier was a split release by Magpahi and fellow Bird Records-released Paper Dollhouse, whose 2012 album *A Box Painted Black* is an experimental piece of music but as with much of Magpahi's work it also contains an accessibility and/or a left field folk-pop sensibility.

This album was made by Astrud Steehouder working as solo artist; it has been described as "dark gothic minimal folk" and at the time she listed her influences as:

> "...bewildering post nuclear landscapes, bleak fields, forests, thunderstorms and archaic industrial objects in the middle of nowhere..."

All of which could make it seem that the album is quite a heavy, dark recording but though it has elements of such things, it is not a purely darkly toned record.

As with Magpahi's work, the album seems to belong to a time, place and landscape of its own. It comes across as having been recorded in some semi-lost wooden cottage, in an indefinable place and time and the noises and creaks of its habitat have seeped in and become part of the very fabric of the music.

As the songs begin they can feel like opening the shutters to the sun in that lost home, allowing a shimmering and golden but also quietly fractured and unsettling view of the landscape and the world it has created and in which it exists.

There is a dreamlike, subtly surreal quality to the music which recalls the flickering half memories of nighttime tales and journeys.

Along which lines, Paper Dollhouse in part take their name from the intriguing rurally-set 1988 film *Paperhouse* and its themes of childhood dreams and nightmares of drawings come to life, which was previously made as a television series in 1972 called *Escape into the Night*, with both being based on Catherine Storr's 1958 novel *Marianne Dreams*.

Bird Records also released the 2012 album *1612 Underture* by The-Eccentronic Research Council. This was a collaborative work by Adrian Flanagan and Dean Horner, who had previously worked in the fringes and left-of-centre areas of electronica and electronic pop via the likes of Kings Have Long Arms, Add N To (X) and I Monster, alongside renowned actress Maxine Peake.

1612 Underture is a concept album which takes the form of a spoken word, soundtracked travelogue play, one that sometimes moves into more overtly song based moments; it is said to be "one part political commentary and feminist manifesto and two parts theatrical fakeloric sound poem".

The album's subject matter is the historical persecution of the Pendle Witches in the early 17th century and as suggested by the word "fakeloric" in the album's description, throughout its observations on a contemporary voyage of discovery and pilgrimage it also interweaves historical events, folklore and imaginings and reimaginings of past events.

During the telling of its stories the album draws more than a few analogies with modern-day times: moral panics, folk devils and economic/political goings on and shenanigans then and now. All of which are wrapped up in a warm, woozy, acoustic and synthesized analogue take on hauntological folk music, primarily voiced by Maxine Peake.

The album was accompanied by an extended accompanying video/film by kluncklick (who also worked with Jane Weaver on her The Fallen by Watch Bird album from 2010[5]).

This is rather slickly done on a (presumably) shoestring and handful of pennies budget.

Although using footage of actual people, it is not dissimilar in a way to a semi-animated children's programme from years gone by, while also reminding us somewhat of Chris Marker's film *La Jetée* (1962) in that it is built up largely from still images rather than traditional movement.

You could call it a fumée: the comic strips that are put together using actors or the book adaptations of films that were made up of stills that in previous decades were published fairly regularly.

While the album's themes are quite serious and it is experimental in spirit, this is also a record which is deeply rooted in electronic pop and has been called non-populist pop.

"Another Witch Is Dead" is pop music, unabashedly so, including ear worm-like choruses, in particular the rhyming couplet "It's a middle class vendetta, on women who are better", which is a fine piece of class-related lyricism.

Today, often even within more leftfield music, it is relatively unusual to hear overt comment on class politics and relations and so in this sense 1612 Underture is somewhat refreshing. It also considers analogies with previous era's magic and belief systems and that of today, describing mobile phones as being "modern-day magic on a monthly tariff".

If we talk of previous era's belief systems it may well be in reference to spirits and fairies in the woods, invisible forces, deities and powers that had to be appeased.

During such times in history there were often a small cadre of priests, clerics, prophets, enchanters etc. who had an understanding of and influence on those spirits and powers and who often presented their world-views and/or core belief systems as unchallengeable.

This is in a not dissimilar manner to that of science today, which may allow for the challenging and evolution of existing theories and beliefs but only generally within the overall structure of pre-existing scientific systems, ways of thinking and viewing the world.

In earlier belief systems offerings were often made to the forces, deities etc. which they believed controlled the world, in order to hopefully gain favour and influence outcomes for the better.

All of which is now largely considered balderdash or at least looked on as quaint, untenable, unscientific or even irrational ways of understanding and thinking about the world.

Which may be to deny history and that contemporary ways of viewing, explaining and manipulating the world may well one day come to be seen as also quaint or founded largely in what at their roots could be considered fundamentally unknowable, just as with any previous system of explanation and belief.

Our modern, technological world is seen as being more purely logical, based on scientific fact and research which we often talk of quite knowledgably but the fundamentals of which in large part we accept more on faith than via a personal thorough, in-depth understanding.

Take for example the fact that most of the general public cannot see or truly follow the actions of the miniscule circuits, systems, molecules and electrons which make up and control our technology but we know they are there and they are doing their job.

Generally, within the context of modern society and its needs, such things work relatively well, with any aberrations referred to or trivialised as mere glitches or considered problems which can be solved with just one more set of steps and advancement in our knowledge.

Another example would be the premise that the universe and all matter, energy etc. within it is explained by science as just having magically appeared from nothing in what is known colloquially as the big bang; there may well be advanced theories that attempt to explain this but they could also be seen as a mystical, faith-based creation myth in scientific clothing.

We have our own clerics and high priests today, those who speak of the one true way of viewing existence but within our technological, scientific world they are more likely to be known as scientists, researchers, theoreticians and engineers.

Just as with previous eras, we could be seen to be making our own offerings to faiths and powers today but as The Eccentronic Research-Council point out it is more likely to be via the comparatively prosaic forms of the likes of direct debits which keep our mobile phones and their "modern-day magic" working.

1. Jane Weaver's work is also discussed in the Chapter 45.
2. Whose work is discussed in Chapter 41.
3. Discussed in Chapter 26.
4. Discussed in Chapter 10.
5. Their video work is discussed in Chapter 45.

36

Vashti Bunyan: From Here to Before: Whispering Fairy Stories until They are Real

WHEN I WAS PLANNING and researching in the run up to starting *A Year In The Country* and during its first year in 2014, I tried in vain to watch *Vashti Bunyan: From Here to Before*, the 2008 documentary about her fabled horse drawn trip across the country at the end of the 1960s and turn of the decade and the album she made at the time.

Other films and documentaries made by its director Kieran Evans, including the Saint Etienne and Paul Kelly collaboration *Finisterre* (2003), edgelands exploration *The Outer Edges* (2013) which was made as part of a wider project with Karl Hyde and dramatic film *Kelly + Victor* (2012) have all had fairly widespread releases in the cinema and/or on DVD.

However, From Here to Before although covered in the press to a certain extent seemed to have a fairly limited cinematic release and then, apart from a few clips that can be viewed online, it seems to have more or less disappeared from view and has never had a commercial home release.

In 2017 almost purely by accident as I was not looking for it, I stumbled upon the film and was able to watch it.

If you should not know about Vashti Bunyan and the subject matter of the documentary, below is a brief precis of the background to it:

Born in 1945, in the mid 1960s Vashti Bunyan worked with Rolling Stones manager Andrew Loog Oldham, released two singles which did not sell in great numbers and recorded further songs for Oldham's Immediate records which remained unreleased for many years.

After this she decided to travel with her boyfriend Robert Lewis by horse and cart to the Hebridean Islands to join a commune planned by a friend, fellow singer/songwriter Donovan. During the trip, she began writing the songs that eventually became her first album, *Just Another Diamond Day* which was released in 1970.

The album sold very few copies and Vashti Bunyan, discouraged, abandoned her musical career.

By 2000 Just Another Diamond Day had acquired a cult following and it was re-released, with her work and story becoming inspirational to a new generation of musicians, some of whom including Devendra Banhart and Joanna Newsom, who have been loosely connected under the label "freak folk".

After this re-release and a gap of more than 30 years Vashti Bunyan began recording again, collaborated with contemporary musicians and appeared live.

She released the album *Lookaftering* in 2005 and in 2014 what she said was to be her final album *Heartleap* (both on Fatcat).

Vashti Bunyan: From Here to Before accompanies her as she retraces the horse drawn journey she made with Robert Lewis and sets it against the backdrop of her first high-profile London concert and the associated rehearsals.

The film serves as an entrancing exploration of a youthful journey of exploration and searching and also an associated self-created almost parallel sense of reality.

Vashti and her partner appeared to want to step aside from mainstream society and the modern world's ways of doing things and to seek out some kind of rural, previous era way of life.

Watching the documentary it was as though they were searching for some pure, unobtainable dream, an escape, refuge and respite from the wider world.

To quote author Rob Young from his 2011 book *Electric Eden*[1] they seemed to be undertaking a form of "imaginative time travel", a wish to get back to the land and simpler ways of life, which seems to have been fairly widespread at the time within certain often folk leaning areas of culture and music.[2]

Just Another Diamond Day has become a totem and reflection of such yearnings.

This is due in part to the album's gentle farside of folk delivery and vocals, alongside the almost dreamlike bucolic subject matter of its songs and the evocative nature of her horse and cart journey when she began work on what would become the songs on the album.

Adding to this are the equally almost dreamlike, fantasy rural atmosphere conjured by the cover image of Vashti Bunyan in period rural clothing and headscarf, where she is pictured outside her cottage accompanied by painted animals.

However, as she says in the documentary:

> "The songs represented the dream. They didn't represent reality... I wasn't living in the... beautiful hills, I was living in my head."

Alongside recording Vashti Bunyan's thoughts and memories of her journey, life and work as she revisits places from her journey or prepares for a live appearance, contemporary interviews make up part of the film.

These include amongst others Andrew Loog Oldham, her 1960s producer Joe Boyd, Adem Ihan who is one of the musicians rehearsing with her for a live performance and artist John James who was a companion for parts of the journey.

The film also includes archival footage and photographs of Vashti and her partner in their folkloric, late 1960s-esque, gypsy like garb that they wore at the time.

This is clothing that at times is almost medieval and which accompanied by images of them travelling in their horse and cart shows the degree to which they lived out their dreams and attempted to remake their lives in the image of those dreams.

They were dedicated to the creation of those dreams in a very singular manner and in the documentary John James comments on how the "leaders" of the journey (by which I assume he means Vashti Bunyan and Robert Lewis) took the dedication, single-mindedness and purity of their quest very seriously with it gaining an almost religious aspect or puritanical zeal.

Vashti Bunyan comments on and illustrates this by saying how she would look disfavourably on people who for example went off to get a shop-bought chocolate bar and how she wanted everything to be as natural or what she thought of as natural, handmade or created by themselves as possible.

From Here to Before also effectively becomes a document of the landscape as it records her return to locations of her journey and a line could be drawn from its more rural views and capturing of their beauty and Kieran Evans later film The Outer Edges' exploration of edgeland landscapes.[3]

The realities of Vashti Bunyan and her fellow travellers' lives during their journey and after that are shown and discussed in the film were far from an idyll as much of it was physically and materially hard, reflecting the practicalities of long distance horse and cart travel in the twentieth century, particularly when undertaken with little financial cushioning, as was so in their case.

The refuge at the end of their horse and cart journey was a cottage in the Outer Hebrides which they eventually settled in for a while and which had a mud floor and a leaky thatched roof (although in From Here to Before Vashti Bunyan remembers being very appreciative after their horse and cart journey of the fact that it had a roof, whatever its condition).

The dream did not last, with her saying in the film that they felt that they were not wanted there and in contrast to her interests in the old ways of doing things the local people, particularly the young, were embracing modern ways and the coming of electricity, with the timing of her journey meaning that they arrived just as the old way of life was noticeably changing.

Although not made overly implicit in the film, it seemed that in part such things caused her to return with her partner to London.

This decision was also due to practical considerations about childbirth when she became pregnant and realising that no matter how beautiful the place and landscape, she actually wanted to be around friends and family (although she talks in the film about an ongoing journey and searching; they later moved variously to The Incredible String Band's Glen Row cottages, then Ireland and also back to Scotland but did not return to the cottage).

From Here to Before was made over four years around the mid to later 2000s, when interest in her work was flowering and she began to express herself again creatively in public via music and live performance and the film is a respectful observation of this period in her life and her earlier stories.

Vashti Bunyan's music of the time and her journey have created an iconic story, set of images and songs; a modern day fable or almost fairy-tale. The film is a reflection and exploration of this fable-like nature but it also captures the realities and hardships of their journey and subsequent home but without shattering the allure or spell of that dream.

1. Discussed in Chapter 1.
2. Explored further in Chapter 7.
3. That film is discussed in Chapter 18.

37

The Owl Service, Anne Briggs, The Watersons, Lutine and Audrey Copard: Folk Revisiters, Revivalists and Re-interpreters

On the way towards starting *A Year In The Country* the three albums I probably listened to the most were Jane Weaver Septième Soeur's conceptual cosmic folkloric *Fallen by Watch Bird* (2010), the acid folk compilation *Gather in the Mushrooms* (2004) and The Owl Service's *The View from a Hill* (2010).[1]

The View from a Hill could be categorised as folk but it has its own take or edge to it.

Many of the songs on it are folk or traditional music mainstays and both musically and visually it uses what could be considered standard tropes of folk music, folklore and culture but this is anything but a mainstream folk album.

The reasons for that are hard to fully define but there are other layers and intelligence to the album, a pattern beneath the plough as it were; it feels subtly experimental but still maintains its listenability.

The songs wander from the Archie Fisher-esque widescreen but intimate take on "Polly on the Shore", through to the "quite pretty but if you listen to the lyrics you realise that this is actually quite an odd story of attraction and paternalism" "Willie O'Winsbury" (and a reprise by way of 1973 film *The Wicker Man*'s "Procession" as if played by a New Orleans marching band), through to the spectral "The Lover's Ghost" (featuring vocals by former 1970s acid/psych folk band Mellow Candle member Alison O'Donnell) and the album also draws on the talents of amongst others The Memory Band's Nancy Wallace and The Straw Bear Band's Dom Cooper.

It ends with traditional song "Cruel Mother" which is astonishingly brutal and disturbing. Not because it is musically dissonant - it is actually wrapped up in a rather lovely musical package - but because its story of seduction and the desperate actions of an abandoned mother towards her children and their supernatural return and prediction of damnation is so unsettling.[2]

The album ends with the line from that song "'Tis we for heaven and you for hell" and as Steven Collins of The Owl Service says in the sleeve notes, what could come after that?

The band were formed by Steven Collins in 2006 and were active until 2016, with the band name being drawn from Alan Garner's *The Owl Service* novel from 1967 and its subsequent television adaptation from 1969.[3]

According to an interview with him in Jeanette Leech's *Seasons They-Change* (her 2010 book on the story of acid and psychedelic folk that is discussed in Chapter 47: "...Lost Focal Points and Privately Pressed Folk"), originally The Owl Service did not physically exist as a band but was more created by him as an imagined idea for his ideal folk band, one which drew its influences from a certain section of 1960s and 1970s British film and television and the sound of the English folk revival.

Apparently people became interested in this imaginary band when he posted about it online (although they did not know that the band did not exist) and began asking when they would be putting their songs out into the world.

From which the band became a real project, which is rather nice as a way of something starting.

I would not necessarily consider The Owl Service as overtly acid or psych folk: it is more a revisiting and reinterpreting of traditional folk and folk rock in a quietly left field or exploratory, respectful to but not hide bound by tradition manner.

In that sense of revisiting and reinterpreting, they could be seen to be carrying on another tradition that can be traced back to the likes of folk singer Anne Briggs in the 1960s and early 1970s.

As mentioned in Chapter 39: "…The Worlds and Interweavings of Kate Bush", Mike Scott of The Waterboys said that when Kate Bush's "Wuthering Heights" went straight to number one in the 1978 singles chart that it "was like an old British soul got returned to us".

Which puts me somewhat in mind of Anne Briggs and her music.

Her recordings were also some of the earliest I listened to when the roots and seedlings of A Year In The Country began to grow and develop in earnest.

Although connected with the folk revival of the 1960s, to a degree she was separate from it, somebody whose work and music trod its own path, the roots of which stretched backwards and forwards to old stories, today's stories and created its own particular place under the sky; to refer back to that Mike Scott quote, listening to her work is like hearing the return of an old soul.

There is a beauty, purity and transcendence to her music and her voice that quite simply stops the listener in their tracks.

As with Kate Bush, her work is characterised in part by a stepping back and away from the bright lights and hurly burly of public life.

Aside from a handful of collaborative and compilation appearances there are only three recorded solo albums and two EPs that document her music, with the third of those albums *Sing a Song for You* being her final album, which she recorded in 1973 but that was not released until 1997 after which she seemed to wish to largely step back from public view and performance.

Which brings us to another revisiting of folk music: *Travelling for a Living*, a 1966 documentary by Derrick Knight that focuses on folk band The Watersons, in which Anne Briggs briefly appears.

It was originally broadcast into the nation's living rooms by the BBC but for a long time after it rarely had an outing or outlet, only being available on an out of print video cassette and an also out of print 2004 Watersons CD box set called *Mighty River of Song* and more recently at the handful of British Film Institute Mediatheque digital film/television viewing installations that are available for use at a limited number of locations across the UK.

Fortunately, it has more recently become available to watch online via the British Film Institute's BFI Player.

The film follows The Watersons throughout their life on the road, playing their interpretations of traditional folk songs at folk clubs, recording in studios and at home in Hull as friends and other performers visit (including the earlier mentioned fleeting rare glance of folk singer Anne Briggs).

Although it was released in 1966, it seems to belong to an earlier much more kitchen sink, almost post-war period.

Often representations of British life and social history from that time focus on a swirling, colourful, pop-mod about-to-be-psych Swinging London metropolitan view of things.

Travelling for a Living presents a more gritty Northern contrast to that (although no less vital), an almost alternative history view of culture at that time which seems to have been semi-written out of popular cultural history.

However, quite possibly, the locations and music shown in Travelling for a Living were nearer to the day-to-day life of more of the nation than that of Swinging London; more backroom of a local pub than Kings Road high life club and boutique orientated.

The film provides a glimpse of a culture which, though it existed in what is now looked back upon as a time of swinging Britain etc., appears to be very separate from the more often considered views and aesthetics of that period.

This is a much more grassroots, kitchen sink, gritty culture and makes the viewer think more of the 1950s than the 1960s; all monochrome

Northern living and black-wearing beat style.

In a way it is reminiscent of images of the 1980s Medway garage punk scene, such as photographs taken by Eugene Doyen; it shares a similar sense of a culture that is occurring separately to the mainstream stories and histories of the time and as with his photographs contains a similar kitchen sink, no frills and fripperies aesthetic.

To which you could possibly add a touch of the minimal post-beat style of The Velvet Underground, although without the more arch self-consciousness.

The two groups were separated by geography and different musical aesthetics but they could be considered counter-cultural historical contemporaries, although The Velvet Underground have come to exemplify a particular kind of "cool" or "hipness" somewhat more than the other.

Along which lines the film is curious in part because it can be hard to connect the images on the screen with the music that comes from the speakers; on the screen are young, proto/post-beat looking performers in black turtle necks with swishingly angular bobs – cool if you like.

While the music is a particular strand of traditional folk that now seems at odds with the sometimes hip images and styles it accompanies in the film.

This disconnect between the images and the music may well be a side effect of the way in which over the years the music of this once non-mainstream, youthful culture has become tarred with the "uncool" brush and the documentary serves as an interesting insight into a time when that was not the case.

Although possibly this sense of hipness is also in part a side effect of just being young and cutting a dash at a particular age.

Alongside which lines, the accepted stories/history of coolness of the time when Travelling for a Living was made tends to be predicated towards pop culture rather than folk culture.[4]

So the once non-mainstream stories of say The Velvet Underground have been allowed and even welcomed into the tomes of canonised cool, while some of their then traditional folk singing contemporaries have been anything but.

Which in part highlights one of the pathways of A Year In The Country; exploring and discovering sometimes more widely overlooked tales from/ via the fields and pastures and taking a sometimes step aside from more well paved cultural municipalities.

Not necessarily in an either/or, good/bad, zero/one manner. More just casting a gaze and curiousity elsewhere.

Folk music is often associated with rural areas and tradition but in Travelling for a Living it is generally shown in amongst a Northern city setting.

The film features extensive evocative terraced house street views and makes a connection between The Watersons' music and the harsh realities of the local fishing industry from which some of the traditional songs they perform originated.

At one point their music producer talks about how all the other music that they have heard – Ella Fitzgerald, more contemporary work by the likes of The Rolling Stones, music hall, jazz etc. – edges into their music.

Pub singing could be added to that as their take on folk singing seems in part to have developed from and could be connected to the oral, communal tradition of pub singing. This developed in the local area after the war and the demolishing of the music hall, with the associated music moving into pubs; at one point Norma Waterson says of pub singing "This is our tradition, it's what we were brought up on."

The producer's words beg the question of how much The Watersons were replicating the past and how much they were creating their own take on traditional music:

> "This music doesn't exist today as a living form but only in odd corners of memory; selected, hidden in the early recordings, notes and jottings treasured in the collections of Cecil Sharp House. From these still warm ashes The Watersons created music which

is then seen to be very much alive."
(From the narration to the film).

There were relatively few recordings of traditional folk available at the time, it being more an oral tradition and often existing outside or before the widespread recording of music or only having been recorded in written form by the likes of folk music researchers and revivers such as Cecil Sharp in the early 20th century.

In the film The Watersons are shown visiting and listening to the recording archives of Cecil Sharp House, which is the headquarters of the English Folk Dance Society that Cecil Sharp founded in 1911 in order to promote traditional dances through nationwide workshops.

Therefore, reference points and memories of this earlier music may well have been fragmentary in nature and not have leant themselves to exact replication; possibly meaning that the traditional music performed by The Watersons back then was in part an almost hauntological, hazy remembering of folk music – one that is both a homage to earlier traditional folk and which has also to a degree over the years come to represent what traditional folk music sounds like.

Which brings us to Lutine, whose work is rooted in folk music but which also exists within its own landscape, creating work which draws from folk and other music but is not a recreation or homage.

If you should take sprinklings, seedings and pathways to and from the following then you may arrive at some sense of Lutine's work:

The songbird travellers and imaginers of Finders Keepers and Bird-Records, in particular Paper Dollhouse and Magpahi, the coruscating reimagined folk journeys of Espers, possibly the purity of the previously-mentioned teller and re-teller of old stories Anne Briggs, voices such as Audrey Copard from past revivals of folkloric music that seem to have stepped aside and into spaces of their own, the swooping ancient tellings of Dead Can Dance and Lisa Gerrard, the encompassing tranquil dramaticisms of The Cocteau Twins and their collaborative work featuring minimalist piano performed by Harold Budd.

Lutine's 2014 debut album *White Flowers*, released by Front & Follow, is reminiscent of a peak point of the label 4AD in the 1980s until around the turn of the decade, a time when it was a home for fragile, textured beauty and explorations, with its releases often being packaged, enhanced and accompanied by the equally textured and intriguing visual work of Vaughan Oliver and Nigel Grierson working as 23 Envelope.

A particular point of reference in terms of Lutine and that period of 4AD is His Name Is Alive and the ethereal beauty of their 1990 album *Livonia*. If you take one of the literal definitions of ethereal as being "something which is extremely delicate and light, in a way not of this world" then you may be heading towards the atmosphere and work Lutine create.

However, they do such work without wandering into pastures of tweeness or cloyingness and there is a shimmering seam of something far from such things that underpins their music.

That seam could not necessarily be described as a darkness but there is a subtle sense of stepping away from the light in their work.

"Dream pop" is another phrase which comes to mind and which has been mentioned in connection with Lutine and one which could also connect back to that 4AD/23 Envelope peak era of music and other fellow wanderers through chimeric soundscapes and melodic will-o'-the wisps such as Virginia Astley.

Lutine's is chamber music from a time neither then, today or tomorrow. Thoroughly modern and yet steeped in waters from previous eras, gently experimental but particularly accessible.

Which brings me to the just mentioned Audrey Copard and her 1956 folk revival album titled simply *English Folk Songs*.

There is a playful, sometimes cheerful, sometimes wistfully sad delivery to the songs on this album, with its 14 traditional folk songs being presented simply and in an unadorned manner, featuring just Audrey Copard's voice and sometimes guitar accompaniment.

It features the first recorded and commercially released version of traditional song "Scarborough Fair" which used the melody that was later used on the commercially successful version of the song released by Simon & Garfunkel in 1965.

English Folk Songs enabled this author to hear some of these songs' earlier incarnations and caused me to wonder how these versions may have somewhere along the line come to influence their future versions existences, revisitings and reinterpretations of folk music.

1. The first two of these are discussed in Chapters 2 and 45.
2. The song is discussed further in Chapter 19.
3. Discussed in Chapter 11.
4. Something discussed in Chapter 1.

38

The Seasons, Jonny Trunk, the BBC Radiophonic Workshop and Howlround: A Yearning for Library Music, Experiments in Educational Music and Tape Loop Tributes

One of the defining elements of hauntology is considered to be an interest in, and taking inspiration from, educational and library music from previous times, particularly the 1960s and 70s, alongside a similar interest in the work of the BBC Radiophonic Workshop.[1]

At this stage, it is helpful to provide backgrounds and definitions for both educational and library music and the BBC Radiophonic Workshop:

Educational music is generally that which was created to be used as a classroom aid and/or music created by children in an educational setting under the guidance of adults.

In the 1960s and 1970s it produced some remarkable recordings that if placed in a different context may well have been considered experimental or avant-garde work.

Library music, sometimes otherwise known as production music, is music which is available ready and licensable off the shelf in a similar manner to stock photography and is music that has generally been created quite specifically for that purpose and made available for use in adverts, films, television, radio etc.

In the period this chapter focuses on (and to a degree today) this music was almost exclusively only available from companies which were set up to deal directly with those involved in the production of television programmes, films etc. and not intended or marketed for direct retail sale to the general public and the pop music charts.

Some related library music work has now become highly collectible and/or influential and is sought out in part because of its scarcity and also because of its at times exploratory and innovative nature.

The BBC Radiophonic Workshop was established in 1958 to produce sound effects and new music for BBC radio and later television, and was closed in 1998.

During the late 1950s through to the 1970s in particular it was responsible for creating a body of renowned and technically innovative work, with this often being considered the "classic" period and the one that hauntological interest generally revolves around.

Often the sounds required for the atmosphere that programme makers wished to create were unavailable or non-existent through traditional sources.

This lead to some of those working at the BBC Radiophonic Workshop to explore new techniques to produce effects and music for their pieces utilising tape manipulation, experimenting with electronic music equipment etc.

Using such methods allowed them to create often unique soundscapes and music, notably the iconic theme tune to *Doctor Who* which was created electronically by Delia Derbyshire in 1963 utilising Ron Grainer's score.

Delia Derbyshire herself has become somewhat iconic as a member of the BBC Radiophonic Workshop and a musical explorer and pioneer. It is well worth seeking out *The Delian Mode*, a 2009 documentary on her life and work directed by Kara Blake if you should wish to know more.

One of the reasons for the connection between educational music and that of the BBC Radiophonic Workshop and hauntological areas of work is that it connects with a hauntological sense of a yearning for lost progressive futures associated with the 1960s and 70s.

Simon Reynolds describes this aspect of hauntology in the November 2006 issue of *Wire* magazine in his article "Haunted Audio", which focuses on Ghost Box Records and other hauntological-related work, as being:

> "A wistful harking back to the optimistic, forward looking, benignly bureaucratic Britain of new towns and garden cities, comprehensive schools and polytechnics."

Through its use in television broadcasts etc. library music was often widely heard but was effectively hidden in clear sight as it could not be bought or sought out through the same channels as pop music and apart from those who worked in connected industries access to information about the music, who it was by or what is was called was very limited or not generally disseminated.

It was further obscured by being created by often anonymous musicians who were not necessarily credited when their work was used.

In this sense library music from earlier decades could be seen as belonging to a flipside or parallel, semi-hidden history of music and to connect with a hauntological sense of hazily or misremembered cultural fragments from a previous time.[2]

During the 1960s and 70s library music covered a vast range of genres and sometimes contained a considerable degree of musical exploration, experimentalism or even avant-garde work. It lent itself to the discovering and use of innovative sounds and techniques in part as a side effect of looking to create work which would appear new and distinctive within its intended market and for its eventual public audience.

John Cavanagh who runs the Glo Spot label, which has reissued library music originally released by the company KPM has commented:

> "There's a striking originality to library records from that time because they were all about the search for new sounds. Back then, musicians weren't told what to do. Big companies also weren't so obsessed with focus groups and demographics, so musicians were allowed to have more open-ended adventures."

Much of this music from previous decades was released in only very small quantities, often on vinyl and as mentioned previously, it was not normally available for sale to the general public.

In part because of the resulting scarcity original copies of library music on vinyl have come to be particularly collectible, hard to find and often exchange hands for considerable amounts of money.

Due to these factors, it has become one of the few genuinely rare areas of culture, particularly in today's climate of almost everything being available online at the touch of a mouse button and so has become appealing to collectors who appreciate such scarcity and the extended searching which is often required to find such items.

This also creates a dichotomy and debate in terms of appreciating and collecting library music.

Tim Lee, MD of Tummy Touch Records which has reissued a number of recordings also from the KPM music library, has commented about this and the sometimes-associated snobbery around such music, saying that:

> "Library music was never supposed to be expensive. By its nature, it was utilitarian and designed to be used as cheaply as possible. People forget that these records were made to be used and heard often, rather than being treated like fetishistic objects. So by distributing these sounds to more and more people, labels like ours treat the music in a similar way to its initial intentions."

JONNY TRUNK HAS FOR a number of years been championing, compiling and reissuing library music via his Trunk Records label, journalism and broadcasting.

He seems drawn to, and expresses an appreciation for, such music for a number of reasons including its at times musically innovative and intriguing qualities, alongside the significance that its scarcity lends it and the investigative work required to find such music, while also wishing to extend its reach into the world by reissuing it.

The Trunk Records library music-related releases have included compilations of the work by different performers originally released by a particular company such as *The Super Sounds of Bosworth* (1996) which brings together work from The Bosworth Music Archive and *G-Spots* (2009) which is subtitled "The spacey folk electro-horror sounds of the Studio G Library".

They also take in related releases in an album such as *Dawn of the Dead* (2004), the soundtrack of which used library music in part from the Music De Wolfe label, alongside albums that focus on the work of one particular musician in this field such as *Stand by for Adverts* (2011), subtitled "Rare Jingles, Jazz and Advertising Electronics" and which features work by Barry Gray.

In a further appreciation, exploring and archiving of such work Jonny Trunk has also authored two editions of *The Music Library*, published by FUEL in 2005 and revised in 2016, a book which collects the cover art of library music.[3]

Curiously in a rounding of the circle manner, as the Trunk Records reissues are often available in limited quantities on vinyl, although not to the same degree as the original library music albums, some of the reissues can become collectible and exchange hands for relatively high prices.

This is pure speculation, but it is possible that the limited nature of these releases may be partly due to the practicalities and costs associated with producing extended runs of vinyl records or associated limited licensing agreements. It may also be due in part to an understanding and appreciation of how scarcity can be one of the factors that makes such music and releases appealing to certain collectors.

Another strand of the Trunk Records reissues focuses on educational music. One such record is *The Seasons*, which features music by David Cain of the BBC Radiophonic Workshop and poetry by Ronald Duncan. Originally released in 1969 by BBC Radio Enterprises, it was reissued by Trunk Records in 2012.

As with much of library music, the original version of the album, if you should be able to find one, is likely to cost you a fair few pounds and pence.

Listening to it is one of those "shake your head and be pleasantly slightly stunned" moments in culture.

The album was "designed to stimulate dramatic dance, movement, mime and speech" and was part of a series of radio broadcasts by BBC Radio For Schools called *Drama Workshop*, a creative drama programme for children in their first and second years of secondary school.

The album's songs (that word is used fairly loosely in this instance) are divided into twelve months and four seasons and to a minimal Radiophonic-esque musical backing it features poetry along these lines:

> "Like severed hands, the wet leaves lie flat on the deserted avenue. Houses like skulls stare through uncurtained windows. A woman dressed like a furled umbrella, with a zip fastener on her mouth steps out of number 53 to post a letter. Her gloved hand hesitates at the box. Then, knowing there will be no reply, she tears it up and throws it in the gutter. And autumn with its pheasants tail consoles her with chrysanthemums."

Which could be regarded as being a touch odd for a later 1960s psychedelic album or performance piece, let alone something aimed at schools.

The poetry goes on to say:

> "An empress with an endless train walks the broad valley, she holds no sceptre, wears no crown, moving so proudly. White swans and modest little boats follow her slowly, thus the royal cortege goes down to the indifferent sea. Her way is lonely."

Her way is lonely? Why is her way lonely? On his website Jonny Trunk says of it:

"...by the mid noughties it was coming across as a major influ-

> ence on retro futurism and the new fangled scene they named hauntology. This comes as no surprise as the album has several layers and levels to it; it is weird, spooky, unsettling, very British, has an unusual whiff of childhood to some, it comes scattered with pregnant language and is full of unexpected metaphors, pagan oddness, folk cadences and insane noises."

The hauntology reference is particularly apt as listening to it the music on the album sounds as if it could well be a Ghost Box Records release which had fallen backwards and forwards in time.

When the album was reissued by Trunk Records, Ghost Box co-founder Jim Jupp said at his Belbury Parish magazine website:

> "It's an album that's very much part of the DNA of Ghost Box: the perfect example of the spooked educational media we reverence and reference so often."

This connection is made more implicit by the reissue which features a Q & A by Julian House (the other co-founder of Ghost Box Records) with David Cain, while the sleeve notes were written by sometimes Ghost Box artist Jon Brooks of The Advisory Circle.[4]

The Seasons is part of a mini-genre of educational music-related oddness which as mentioned earlier also includes work performed by children themselves under adult guidance, examples of which have been issued on two other Trunk Records releases: Carl Orff & Gunild Keetman's *Music for Children/Schulwerk* and the compilation of work by different groups of schoolchildren *Classroom Projects*, both released in 2013.

Music for Children/Schulwerk compiles work that originated in the 1950s as part of a programme intended to help the co-ordination and development of children and contains the results of simple, melodic musical exercises that variously reflect playground rhymes and/or contain elements of improvisation and choral qualities.

Classroom Projects is subtitled "Incredible Music Made by Children in Schools" and includes a wide range of styles of musical work which Jonny Trunk describes as being:

> "...small primary school choirs or groups singing obscure folk songs to full-blown avant-garde experiments written and performed by children still at secondary or grammar school."

One of the best-known of all such recordings and albums is The Langley Schools Music Project *Innocence & Despair*, containing recordings from 1976-77 by Canadian schoolchildren reinterpreting the likes of David Bowie, The Carpenters and The Beach Boys in a somewhat unique and inimitable style and which was first released commercially in 2001.

As with The Seasons and some of the work on Classroom Projects, presented in another context Innocence & Despair would quite possibly have been considered experimental or avant-garde music.

It was a project undertaken by Canadian music teacher Hans Ferger, who said about it:

> "I knew virtually nothing about conventional music education and didn't know how to teach singing. Above all, I knew nothing of what children's music was supposed to be. But the kids had a grasp of what they liked: emotion, drama, and making music as a group. Whether the results were good, bad, in tune or out was no big deal - they had élan. This was not the way music was traditionally taught. But then I never liked conventional 'children's music', which is condescending and ignores the reality of children's lives, which can be dark and scary. These children hated 'cute.' They cherished songs that evoked loneliness and sadness."

WHICH BRINGS ME to *The School Is Full of Noises*, a documentary on the BBC's Radio 4 first broadcast in 2015. In it, poet, journalist, playwright, and broadcaster Ian McMillan considered:

> "How did tape loops, recycled everyday sounds and countless other weapons of the avant-garde find their way into school music lessons during the 1960s?"

As with Hans Ferger's comments above, the programme imparts a sense that the educators who used, employed and experimented with such techniques did so in part to get away from a particular view of making music that focuses largely on learning "proper" instruments and making music "properly" and the associated exclusion that can at times be associated with that.

To quote one of the documentary's participants, this was music education which:

> "...wasn't about privilege, it wasn't about instrumental lessons outside school, it was about something that everybody could engage with, understanding music from the inside... knowing what it takes to make a piece of music, that it's not something fully formed that exists in the world, it's something that you make."

Connected to the above comments, the programme also highlights how such work should possibly not be labelled as avant-garde or experimental music as that just seems to put it into a particular potentially excluding bracket – at its heart it is just music.

Such labels can be convenient as markers and may help give audiences reference points, which is good and fine along as they do not prove to be part of elitist barriers or marginalising.

As mentioned earlier Jonny Trunk is also a broadcaster, in particular being known for his long-running *The OST Show* on Resonance FM.

It is one of the avenues by which he explores his appreciation of and penchant for the often-overlooked nuggets of gold and sometimes tarnished with neglect areas of music, with this programme concentrating on films and television soundtracks, library music and other related work.

One of the things that makes it particularly tune-able into are the guests that he has along, who bring with them their own findings, collections and stories, all of which are added into an eclectically-flavoured musical stew.

Over the years these guests have included Jon Brooks of The Advisory Circle and sometimes Ghost Box Records, whose appearance was accompanied by a good deal of knitting and "doing" the actions to a mining safety song by once highly popular light entertainer and singer Max Bygraves.

They have also included the DJ and musician Andrew Weatherall, *Monsterist* illustrator Pete Fowler, Jim Jupp and Julian House of Ghost Box Records, Radiophonic Workshop explorer Paddy "*The Changes*" Kingsland, more Radiophonic exploring courtesy of David "The Seasons" Cain, Ian Hodgson of whimsical hauntological music and visual project Blank Workshop who releases records as Moon Wiring Club and some excellent delving and wandering through the undercurrents of music courtesy of Trish Keenan and James Cargill of Broadcast.[5]

There have also been a number of themed specials which have included shows on film composers John Barry and Ennio Moriconne, library music company Bruton Music, experimental film director Kenneth Anger, BBC Radiophonic Workshop member and musical innovator Delia Derbyshire and BBC Records.

A classic episode is the one in which Fenella Fielding, renowned as the iconic star of 1966 film *Carry on Screaming*, slinks and sveltes by and Jonny Trunk is genuinely impressed and starstruck.

During the episode she compares her "attributes" to Barbara Windsor's and The OST Show's assistant and engineer Robin The Fog has cause to mention that it has suddenly gotten very warm in the studio (cue steaming up of glasses and tugging of collar).

Generally the programme is something of a smorgasboard of musical delights and if you should have a spare hour or two and would appreciate a fair few "Oh, what's that, that's nice" accompanied by a sprinkling of "Ah, that's what that is" moments, then a quick pop along to The OST Show's weekly transmissions could well be just the ticket.

A number of the programmes have been archived online if listening via the traditional airwaves is not practical.

The OST Show has at times been hosted by the aforementioned Robin The Fog who releases records as one half of Howlround, working in collaboration with Chris Weaver.

Howlround came to prominence with their first album, 2012's *The Ghosts of Bush.*

This is a recording which documents the last days of Bush House, the once home to broadcasting stalwart the BBC World Service. It takes as its initial source material indoors field recordings which were captured late at night in the empty rooms and corridors of the building towards the end of the BBC's tenure of it and the resulting album is a culturally and musically fascinating and intriguing piece of work.

The album is a tribute to its subject from whence it sprang, one which is made up of many layers; whether literally in terms of the sounds it contains and how they were made, the history of where it was made or the Robin The Fog's own connection to the work (at the time he was a studio manager at Bush House).

Part of that layering process and how the recording was made comes about by a literal layering of sound. The record was created using only tape loop manipulation which utilised some of the last remaining of such machines in Bush House.

This process feels like an intrinsic part of the work and its cultural connections, a way of reflecting and capturing the spirit and history of the building, related institutions and their technological stories and legacy.

It also connects with a contemporary romance and at times nostalgia that has come to be attached to analogue technologies, something that is also expressed through and a partial explanation of interest and fascination with the BBC Radiophonic Workshop and its analogue based musical explorations and pioneering.

Robin The Fog has said of the The Ghosts of Bush:

> "These are the sounds the building makes when it thinks no-one is listening, the sounds of many sleepless nights spent isolated in a labyrinthine basement surrounding by a crepuscular soundtrack of creaks and crackles. It's an attempted homage to the work of the BBC Radiophonic Workshop who crafted the most incredible of sound-worlds from the most basic of sources. But mostly it's my way of saying goodbye to a building that I and so many people have loved. When talking of historic structures, the old clichéd approach is to wonder what one might hear if the 'walls could speak'. I like to think that with The Ghosts of Bush we come closer to hearing them sing: one last song about the passage of time and the impermanence of all things, with the ghosts of the machines joining in. The last hurrah of a bygone era, of obsolete equipment and of a studio that has since fallen silent forever."

When I listen to The Ghosts of Bush I often think of the distant howls of long-lost and departed creatures, huge as dinosaurs. Which in these days of almost ubiquitous free market culture, may well be somewhat appropriate as Bush House was responsible for transmissions from that possibly endangered philosophical idea, publicly owned broadcasting in the free market-orientated West. Which along with Robin The Fog's reference to it in the notes above, brings us back to the BBC Radiophonic Workshop.

As mentioned earlier the BBC Radiophonic Workshop connects with a hauntological sense of a yearning for lost progressive futures. It was one of those occasional, brief and often relatively small areas within culture where, partly through the effectively publicly funded space afforded it by the BBC and partly due to the explorations and curiosity of those who worked there, creative work was to a degree shaded from the sometimes restrictive or prescriptive pressures of commercial imperatives and able to burgeon and blossom into work which still resonates and inspires today.

1. The loose culture genre of hauntology is further defined in Chapter 3.
2. Discussed in Chapter 5.
3. Jonny Trunk's archival book work is also discussed in Chapter 46.
4. Ghost Box Records is discussed further in Chapter 5.
5. Whose work is discussed discuss further in Chapter 8.

39

An Old Soul Returns: The Worlds and Interweavings of Kate Bush

Drawing a line back from *A Year In The Country* to early discoverings of more experimental or left-of-centre forms of pastoralism, then on the way to the likes of *Bagpuss* (1974) and other Smallfilms produced work, then doubtless a dot would be marked on the said line, and a pause made for a cup of tea, to consider the work and interweavings of Kate Bush.

As mentioned in Chapter 37: "...Folk Revisiters, Revivalists and Reinterpreters", Mike Scott of the band The Waterboys said that when Kate Bush's "Wuthering Heights" went straight to number one in the UK charts in 1978 that it "was like an old British soul got returned to us".

That resonates in part because her work seems often to delve amongst and have roots in the myths and tales of the land, of its magic and mystery and belong to or draw from something deeper than the sometimes quite surface or more purely straightforward "Boy meets girl, love's great, love's hard, life's great, life's hard, let's have a party"- orientated realms of pop music.

This is not intended to be judgemental; there is nothing wrong with such things, particularly if space is also afforded to or for other types of work.

And make no mistake, this was pop music, if of an exploratory nature; in the earlier parts of her career Kate Bush worked within the realms of pop music, the charts and related work such as promotional videos. There were experimental elements to her work but such things were also generally intertwined with accessible and even catchy song structures and melodies.

For many people, the primary focus of Kate Bush's work is caught in the amber of the period during which she released her first five studio albums and the compilation *The Whole Story* (1986) and the surrounding visual work and imagery, which seem to channel those mysteries and myths particularly strongly.

From *The Kick Inside* (1978) to *The Hounds of Love* (1985), those five albums stand unparalleled and even after all these years they are impressive stuff.

It is curious when you look back at the early more traditional pop style promotion of those albums and their singles; when she was performing in the prosaic surrounds of a lunch time light entertainment programme in the later 1970s she was part of it all but also a space unto herself.

Although working within the realms of pop music and generally commercially successful releases, her work often explored themes which you would not normally expect to bother the pop music charts but these most definitely did, featuring numerous Top 40 or even number one hit albums and singles over the years.

As a small snapshot of such things, some of those themes included:

1) "Breathing" was a five minute single based around Cold War dread and the maternal passing on of radioactive fallout, which at one point wanders off into a public information broadcast about how to recognise the size of the weapon used in a nuclear attack.[1]
2) *The Ninth Wave*, the concept album side of The Hounds of Love album is in parts breathtakingly beautiful and takes in dreams of sheep, bucolic bliss, traditional folk jigs and a sense of the sun rising over the earth, while it is actually about somebody in the water, close to drowning and there is a genuinely nightmarish,

folk horror quality to it at certain points.
3) The single and video "Experiment IV" (1986) tells of scientists being asked to create a militaristic sound weapon, which results in the creation or summoning of a malevolent spirit that sets about devastating and doing away with the staff of the research establishment which brought it forth.

Looking back, when I first started to listen to Kate Bush and investigate her work extensively, it was one of the first times that I began to discover popular music and its surrounding culture that was truly layered, where you felt as though you were stepping into a semi-hidden secret world: one where not all the mysteries would be solved or knowable.

That sense of mystery was part of its power. Which brings us to the song and video "Cloudbusting" (1985) from The Hounds of Love album.

The song Cloudbusting and its accompanying film tell a cinematic tale in miniature of a father's attempt to create and operate a cloud-creating, steampunk-like machine, accompanied and aided by a son/daughter (although played by Kate Bush, the gender of the child is not completely clear in the video).

This experimenting is carried out to a background of intervention and hauling away of the scientist by governmental or secret service agents.

In the video, Kate Bush's character pulls a copy of a paperback called *A Book of Dreams* from her fictional father's pocket while they are on a hilltop and about to operate his cloudbusting machine.

This is essentially breaking the fourth wall in a metafictional manner as the book is a real world autobiography written by Peter Reich and published in 1973, which inspired the Cloudbusting song.

The image created a particularly potent cultural mystery that I was drawn to and wanted to solve and for many years afterwards this book and its story seemed to become for myself a semi-investigated, almost mythological thing.

When this single was released it was prior to the ease of access to information that the internet has brought about.

Back then finding much information about the musicians you liked was very hit and miss; you might pick up snippets of information via the weekly music press or in a passed around, Chinese Whispered, golden nuggets manner amongst friends and acquaintances but it was all often fairly patchwork or threadbare.

A Book of Dreams was the biographical story of Peter Reich growing up amongst the world and work of his father, the non-conventional and controversial scientist and psychologist Wilhelm Reich.

Wilhelm Reich amongst other activities did build actual cloudbusting-style devices and at points used them to attempt to break droughts in the US.

At the time of the single being released the book was rare; as just mentioned the song and album were released prior to internet ubiquitous ease of access to knowledge and/or purchasing books and other cultural artifacts, although looking back it had not been reprinted after 1974.

In fact, it was reprinted in US in 1989 after Cloudbusting was released but presumably its status as an out of print Kate Bush-connected book kept its price high and out of my reach for a fair while even once online, international e-commerce became more accessible in the early 2000s.

In 2005 the book was republished with a new cover design but the appeal remains with the original, the one Kate Bush's character pulled from her fictional father's pocket and the associated sense of layering and stories within stories that it induced. And although now more easily available, there is a sense that it possibly should be left alone to continue to work its magic unimpeded.

1. This single is also discussed in Chapter 13.

40

The Stone Tape, Quatermass, The Road and *The Twilight Language of Nigel Kneale*: Unearthing Tales from Buried Ancient Pasts

WRITER NIGEL KNEALE'S work has been something of an ongoing touchstone, point of reference and inspiration for those interested in or creating work that takes in a sense of the uncanny or unsettled in the landscape and the spectral concerns of hauntology.[1]

The Stone Tape is a 1972 television drama written by him which features a team of British scientists holed up in a country mansion while they attempt to create a new recording technique (and presciently to compete with the Japanese at such things).

They discover a form of historic, spectral recording which exists within the substance or literally the stone of the house itself and attempt to study, initiate and possibly capture it as part of their research and development process.

The programme mixes and layers scientific techniques along with an interest in preternatural or supernatural occurrences and while it is set in a country mansion it is not overtly concerned with depicting a rural setting but has nonetheless come to be connected with an interest in folk horror.

This is commented on in reference to The Stone Tape by Andy Paciorek in his article "From the Forests, Fields and Furrows", which acts as an introductory essay to the loose genre of folk horror at the *Folk Horror Revival* website:

> "Some consider that the setting should be rural for the film to be 'folk', but I think a broader view may be considered. The tradition of the horror may indeed have rustic roots and pastoral locations may provide the setting for many of the stronger examples, but people carry their lore and fears with them on their travels and sometimes into a built-up environment. Also, below the foundations of every town is earth with a more ancient past."

The premise behind the programme comes from the Stone Tape theory, which speculates that ghosts and hauntings are analogous to tape recordings and that electrical mental impressions released during emotional or traumatic events can somehow be "stored" in moist rocks and other items and "replayed" under certain conditions.

This was an idea which was first proposed by British archaeologist-turned parapsychologist Thomas Charles Lethbridge in 1961 (philosopher H. H. Price also formed a similar concept in 1940). Lethbridge believed that ghosts were not spirits of the deceased but were simply non-interactive recordings similar to a movie.

The Stone Tape television drama popularised the idea and the phrase and as with the recordings in the walls of the mansion featured in it, has continued to echo down the years.

This is particularly so in terms of its title that has been used as the name of record label Stone Tape Recordings, which was founded by Steven Collins who was also the founder member of folk rock band The Owl Service, as the title of an album of site specific spoken word recordings by Iain Sinclair called *Stone Tape Shuffle* released by Test Centre in 2012 and the name of hauntological otherly folkloric explorers duo The Stone Tapes.

In 2015 there was also a radio play version of The Stone Tape which was broadcast on BBC Radio 4 as part of their Halloween *Fright Night* season. This added extra layers of cultural intertwinings with hauntological related culture:

It was directed by Peter Strickland who wrote and directed the 2012 film *Berberian Sound Studio*, which in itself has a number of hauntological intertwinings, not least its depiction of an imagined folk horror-esque giallo film and sound recording studio and the inclusion of film and design work by Julian House of Ghost Box Records.[2]

The radio play also featured music by James Cargill of Broadcast (who also created music for Berberian Sound Studio[3]).

The soundscape was by Andrew Liles, who has worked with a number of musicians/performers that through the title of a 2003 book by David Keenan which explored such areas of at times culturally subterranean music, have become known as *England's Hidden Reverse*, including Current 93 and Nurse With Wound.

Further connections to hauntological points of interest include that the script was by Matthew Graham who was also the writer and/or co-creator of mainstream hauntological-esque timeslip series *Life on Mars* (2006-2007) and *Ashes to Ashes* (2008-2010), alongside post-apocalyptic accidental cryogenic time travel science fiction series *The Last Train* (1999).

Andy Paciorek's mention of an "ancient past" below the earth in relation to Nigel Kneale's work connects with one of the recurring themes in his writing; that of the existence of echoes or artifacts from far distant times that may be hidden from view, or literally buried beneath the ground.

In The Stone Tape this takes the form of the spectral recordings in the material of the house, while in the television series and film *Quatermass and the Pit* (1958-1959 and 1967 respectively) it is depicted via the discovery of an ancient alien spacecraft under London which is found to have a malign influence and be part of an alien experiment in genetic modification and manipulation of humans over hundreds or thousands of years, which has been responsible for much of the war and conflict in the world.

As an aside and returning to a sense of echoing down over the years, the main location in Quatermass and the Pit is used in the 2001 album title *The Séance at Hobs Lane* by Mount Vernon Arts Lab. This album was created by Drew Mulholland and is in itself an exploration of the echoes of society and culture, being a psychogeographic exploration of London's hidden and underground spaces, eighteenth century secret societies and Quatermass itself. It is seen as a forebear of hauntological work and in what could be seen as an acknowledgement of the pathways it helped to pioneer was reissued by Ghost Box Records in 2007.

A sense of the buried "ancient past" can also be found in the final series of Quatermass from 1979, where in the near future large numbers of young people who call themselves "The Planet People" are being drawn to travel across the countryside to gather at ancient prehistoric sites such as stone circles, believing that they will be transported to a better life on another planet.

However the ancient sites are essentially markers put in place thousands or more years ago to enable the gathering and harvesting of humans by an extra terrestrial force, harvesting that may have already occurred at these sites at least once before.

In this manner the final series creates a sense of the landscape and fields being places where ancient stories are told and retold, where the patterns beneath the plough are deeply sewn from elsewhere in the cosmos and stretch way back through our history, possibly to a previous (almost) final harvest.

I first came across the series in the early 1980s via its novelisation written by Nigel Kneale which I bought from the bargain bookshelves of one of my local newsagents.

Such places were something of an exciting cultural node for a young chap: many an hour could be spent wandering their shelves of comics and books, which often seemed to contain a mixture of superhero fantasy and exploitational fare intertwined with at times slipstream, more exploratory science fiction.

This particular book contains a large number of interlinked and intriguing elements and images: the aforementioned representation of ancient stone circles as markers for where the human race was once reaped by an alien intelligence, of that intelligence possibly taking just a trace of the people it destroys/harvests, which is compared with the way that humans take just a trace of the musk deer to make perfume, the prime minister's home having a tank outside to guard it (though it was said to not be mobile and to have a family of cats living in it) and the new age-esque Planet People wanderers seeking to be taken to the "planet".

The series also features an imaginary television show called *Tittupy-Bumpity* that is said to be the only programme that people watch any more and which is an audience-pandering erotic dance programme, the depiction of which appears to be Nigel Kneale commenting on and extrapolation of where lowest common denominator, highly sexualised television programming could lead.

The Year of the Sex Olympics television drama from 1968, written by Nigel Kneale, can also be seen as a comment on such topics in its depiction of a future where the lower classes are kept docile by a small elite which feeds them not dissimilar television.

Nigel Kneale initially began writing the final Quatermass script in 1972 but after a number of production difficulties and it passing from the BBC to the independent Euston Films company, filming took place in 1978 and the series was broadcast in 1979, with a condensed film version also being released that year.

During this extended period of development and production of the series, Britain underwent a period of considerable societal, political and economic conflict[4] and the Quatermass book and series capture the spirit of and extrapolate from those troubles and presents an evocative depiction of Britain gone to seed and a crumbled, dysfunctional society.

Alongside which the Planet People seem to be an evolution of and possibly a comment on the more extreme aspects of 1960s hippie or counter-cultural ideals and ways of living when taken to an extreme (something which is also present in the permissive aspects of society that are shown in The Year of the Sex Olympics), accompanying which part of the depiction of social dysfunction is the breakdown of social norms in youth through its depiction of gang culture and related conflict.

In these aspects it connects with 1979 television series *Noah's Castle*, which also extrapolates from social strife and youth unrest of the time.[5]

One striking element of Quatermass is just how genuinely watchable and gripping it is; it stands up well with the pace and entertainment qualities of modern-day broadcasts. This seems in contrast to some other hauntological-related television programmes from the 1960s and 1970s, which you may need to recalibrate yourself to a previous era's rhythms of storytelling to fully appreciate in a conventional entertainment manner rather than as cultural points of interest.[6]

Nigel Kneale's own work also has its own spectral, buried history as some of his work has been lost due to broadcasts being transmitted as live performances, recordings being wiped in order that the tapes could be reused or only black and white versions of the colour recordings remaining as is the case with The Year of the Sex Olympics.

One of his lost television plays is *The Road* from 1963. This was set in 1770 and involves a country squire and "natural philosopher" Sir Timothy Hassell investigating a haunted wood where men pass away screaming after hearing strange cries "as if all the dead people was risin' out o' Hell".

This is a phenomenon that occurs just once a year, on Michaelmas Eve. Sir Timothy decides to investigate, thinking it is a past echo of a retreating Roman army but it is actually the cries of those suffering in a future apocalyptic attack.

The script is included as a PDF on the out of print BFI DVD of The Stone Tape released in 2001 and it was also published in book form in 1976 as part of *The Year of the Sex Olympics and Other TV Plays by Nigel Kneale*, which also includes the script for The Stone Tape, although that is also now long out of print; used copies are often priced in the hundreds of pounds.

There have been other fleeting glances of The Road: for a while there was a live amateur production of it available to watch online but that has since disappeared and transgressive horror research project *The Miskatonic Institute* presented a live reading of it at The Horse Hospital venue in London in 2015. That reading was to mark the launch of a book of essays about Nigel Kneale called *We Are The Martians: The Legacy of Nigel Kneale* edited by Neil Snowdon, the release of which was delayed until 2017, that features writing by and conversations with writers and critics including Mark Gatiss, Kim Newman and Tim Lucas, with cover art by David Chatton Barker of Folklore Tapes.[7]

There have been a number of other books published which have focused on Nigel Kneale's life and work, including:

The biographical *Into the Unknown: The Fantastic Life of Nigel Kneale* by Andy Murray and published by Headpress (originally released in 2006 and revised and republished 2017), film critic and author Kim Newman's *Quatermass and the Pit* published by the BFI in 2014 which focuses on the film and its origins and the beautifully produced, Risograph-printed collection of essays *The Twilight Language of Nigel Kneale*, which was edited by Sukhdev Sandhu, published by Strange Attractor and Texte und Töne and designed by Seen Studios.

The Twilight Language of Nigel Kneale was published to accompany a one day 2012 event in New York called A *Cathode Ray Seance: The Haunted Worlds of Nigel Kneale* which featured screenings and discussions of his work and in a further echoes of lost work manner also featured a reading and live soundtrack performance of The Road.

It contains a set of essays, conversations etc. produced in response to Nigel Kneale's work and features work by Sophia Al-Maria, Bilge Ebiri, Mark Fisher, William Fowler, Ken Hollings, Paolo Javier, Roger Luckhurst, China Miéville, Drew Mulholland, David Pike, Mark Pilkington, Joanna Ruocco, Sukhdev Sandhu, Dave Tompkins, Michael Vazquez and Evan Calder Williams.

The book also came with a cassette tape called *Restligests*, featuring specially-composed work by The Asterism, Emma Hammond, Hong Kong In The 60s, Listening Center, The Real Tuesday Weld, Robin The Fog of Howlround and Mordant Music.

As a package and cultural event it positions Nigel Kneale firmly within the cultural setting of hauntology while also maintaining his own particular space and created worlds.

The book was printed by Circadian Press using the Risograph printing technique which gives it a distinctive tactile and matt finish.

Risograph are a brand of digital duplicators which use a printing process that is essentially like a digital, photocopier version of screen printing, which can be used in the place of traditional lithograph printing or toner based digital printing and copying.

This process of duplication has its own unique character and a very human feel that can have variations from print to print, with the resulting printing seeming less clinical and nearer to artistic techniques than most printing mass reproduction technologies.

The printing process combines and complements the design work by Rob Carmichael of Seen Studios, which reflects the spirit of Nigel Kneale's work in a contemporary hauntological/spectral design manner.

Although it has its own character, if you should think of the half-toned, otherly geometrical forms, layering and collaging of Julian House of Ghost Box Records or David Chatton Barker of Folklore Tapes (who as mentioned earlier also created the artwork for We Are The Martians) then you may well be heading the right direction.

The book was released in a limited edition and as seems to be the way with a number of Nigel Kneale-related releases (and quite possibly reflecting the ongoing popularity of his work) is now out of print.

It is an elusive book to find but is well worth seeking out both as a handsomely and evocatively produced and designed cultural artifact and as an intriguing and inspiring appreciation and exploration of Nigel Kneale's work and the worlds he created.

1. Hauntology is discussed and defined in Chapter 3.
2. Peter Strickland's work is discussed in Chapter 26.
3. And whose work is discussed in Chapter 8.
4. Discussed in Chapter 7.
5. Considered further in Chapter 44.
6. Also discussed in Chapter 8.
7. Whose work is discussed in Chapter 41.

41

Folklore Tapes and the *Wyrd Britannia* Festival: Journeying to Hidden Corners of the Land/the Ferrous Reels and Explorations of an Arcane Research Project

FOLKLORE TAPES BEGAN in 2011 and is described on its website as being:

> "...an open-ended research project exploring the vernacular arcana of Great Britain and beyond; traversing the myths, mysteries, magic and strange phenomena of the old counties via abstracted musical reinterpretation and experimental visuals. The driving principle of the project is to bring the nation's folk record to life, to rekindle interest in the treasure trove of traditional culture by finding new forms for its expression."

The core of the project's activities is a series of generally themed music releases that have been split into often geographical groupings such as Devon Folklore Tapes, Lancashire Folklore Tapes, Cheshire Folklore-Tapes and the more seasonally based Calendar Customs.

The themes of these releases have included "Mid-Winter Rites & Revelries", "Inland Water", "Ornithology", "Memories of Hurstwood", "Stanton Drew Stone Circle" etc.

The packaging is an inherent part of the releases and will often include booklets, essays, film work and accompanying ephemera such as seed envelopes that act as a further space or accompaniment for the exploration and expression of the themes.

David Chatton Barker is the instigator of the project and has created much of the Folklore Tapes visual imagery and presentation which, as referred to in the website text above, delves in amongst folkloric and pastoral layers and signifiers of culture from other eras and related overlooked esoteric corners and artifacts, retaining their spirit but also reinterprets them to create thoroughly modern visual work.

The music/audio collaborators and contributors to the series have included Rob St John, Children Of Alice (members of Broadcast and Julian House of Ghost Box Records), Magpahi, Sam McLoughlin, Ian Humberstone, Anworth Kirk and David Orphan (an alias of David Chatton Barker).

Initial releases came packaged as cassettes housed in hollowed-out vintage hardback books and hand-stamped envelopes, which has progressed to vinyl releases, box sets and so forth, generally in larger editions while the project has continued to explore similar and interrelated themes.

In the earlier days of the project the very limited releases and the associated feeding frenzy induced a sense of "whoosh, blink and they're gone". Although this could be frustrating and limited the number of people who could actually listen to and explore the work, in some ways the scarcity seemed to reflect the character of Folklore Tapes at the time and the sense of it being an arcane research project that explored the hidden corners of culture and the land.

Of these earlier releases, a particular favourite is *Devon Folklore Tape Vol. IV - Rituals and Practices*, which was released in 2012 and features Magpahi and Paper Dollhouse.

The Magpahi side contains haunting folkloric vocals and a certain left-of-centre almost at times pop sensibility would be a starting point of reference, while Paper Dollhouse wanders off into early morning free floating word association.[1]

Online record shop Boomkat described Rituals and Practices rather well and concisely:

"Volume IV in this enchanted series surveys is 'Rituals and Practices', connected to the folklore of Devon in the south west of England. Research was carried out by Magpahi and Paper Dollhouse into the myths, legends and strange phenomena of the old county, resulting in a creaking combination of wyrdly symbolic sonic energies and spirits that manifest as haunted ambient pop and folk song. At risk of breaking the spell, we won't go any further, other than to tell you this is our favourite in the series so far and comes recommended to fans of Broadcast, Nico, stone circles and fine storytelling."

Folklore Tapes have also been involved in a number of live events, one of which was the *Wyrd Britannia*[2] festival of 2012 that took place in Halifax and Hebden Bridge.

The event seemed like one of those times and events where somebody who works for the council/public services was given the go ahead to put something culturally rather leftfield that they were genuinely passionate about into the world.

Organised by James Glossop, the festival was to mark the relaunch of the Calderdale libraries Wyrd Britannia collection of films, books and music. The collection and the festival explore and reflect not dissimilar territory to Folklore Tapes itself, which is reflected by the following quote from the council's site which says that the collection:

"...reflect(s) the dark and complex underbelly of English rural tradition and beliefs."

The festival featured screenings of some of the core films and television of what could be called British hauntological folklore or folk horror: *The Wicker Man* (1973), *Robin Redbreast* (1970) and the at the time pre its DVD/Blu-ray release by the BFI the then rather rare *Penda's Fen* (1974).[3]

Also featured in the festival were readings and performances by Alison Cooper (Magpahi) collaborating with David Chatton Barker and Sam-

McLoughlin of Folklore Tapes, Chris Lambert who is the author of the hauntological folkloric *Tales from the Black Meadow* collection of stories published in 2013 and Andy Roberts on his *Albion Dreaming* book from 2012 which focuses on the history of LSD in Britain.

At the time of the festival I seemed to travel to visit libraries in the same way that I used to track down record shops and so I took myself off to a night of these explorations of the semi-hidden corners of the landscape.

After sitting on the train in the dark with Saturday night revellers, I stumbled blinking into the night of a strange town, accompanied by other travellers headed for the same event who I had bumped into on the train.

With scarcely a moment to take in the town we were at a rather lovely old library building where the event was taking place.

First up was Chris Lambert, reading from his book Tales from the Black Meadow and informing us about this multi-faceted project which takes as its starting point the imagined history of Professor R. Mullins who was alleged to have gone missing in The Black Meadow atop the Yorkshire Moors in 1972.[4]

As a project Tales from the Black Meadow incorporates elements of folklore, Radiophonic-esque scores, imagined semi-lost documentaries and the flickering cathode ray transmissions of a previous era; a creaking rural cabinet stuffed full of hidden and rediscovered government unsanctioned reports.

It has been sent out into the world in various forms: the aforementioned book of folkloric tales, an album, a documentary and archival material etc. Be careful on the moors.

Next in front of this very polite, appreciative and well-behaved audience was *Echo of Light*, presented by Folklore Tapes and featuring Alison Cooper, Sam McLouglin (who also performs as Samandtheplants and co-oversees the record label Hood Faire) and David Chatton Barker.

It has been described as incorporating the projectionist as puppeteer and having watched it, that is an apt description.

To an electronic and acoustic soundtrack of largely improvised music, two of the collaborators were hidden behind a screen as they essentially live-mixed/live-created a series of projections onto the screen using various physical props, found natural materials and artwork, which in turn were also used to create some of the soundtrack.

At one point, an old birdcage was placed on a wind-up gramophone turntable and then as it span it struck a series of prongs to create music in a manner that was not dissimilar in its own way to the workings of a traditional music box but on a larger and more arcane scale.

Accompanying this was a traditional spinning wheel, which also appeared to be creating music and Alison Cooper playing keyboards/synthesizer and who at times read text from what appeared to be books from earlier eras or possibly even centuries.

Alongside such things, there were also projections created which borrowed from the tropes and imagery of Folklore Tapes releases and the project as a whole.

As a set of work, as with Folklore Tapes itself, it appeared to be an exploration of the hidden in nature and folklore which surrounds it (or the pattern under the plough).

All in all, quite entrancing, and there was something about the street light glow from the grand old library windows that seemed to fit with the performance.

Libraries seem like centres of calm, civility and culture in a rapacious landscape and there is often a sense that whoever is picking the stock for them has a good eye and ear for intriguing and left-of-centre culture.

This was one such time and on display that night were book, CD and DVD selections from the Wyrd Britannia collection.

These included a number of *Quatermass* films, *The Miners Hymn* (2010), albums by 1960s/1970s acid folk band Forest, The Owl Service's fine folk revisiting album *The View from a Hill* (2010), a 3 disc DVD reissue of *The Wicker Man, The Stone Tape* (1972), Trembling Bells *Abandoned Love* (2010), *Broadcast and the Focus Group Investigate Witch Cults of the Radio Age* (2009) and the *Gather in the Mushrooms* compilation of underground 1960s/early 1970s acid folk released in 2004.[5]

Alongside such videos and CDs, it seemed that those involved had been delving in the library's dusty storage rooms to find all kinds of long neglected tomes.

On display were Bob Pegg's (of the early 1970s the-darker-shade-of-folk band Mr Fox) *Rites and Riots* (1981), a whole slew of books on folklore and song, various selections of witchery, George Stewart Evan's *The Pattern Under the Plough* (1966), *The Owl Service* author Alan Garner once or twice and a particularly intriguing looking *The Cylinder Musical-Box Handbook* (1968) by Graham Webb.

(Looking inside the Bob Pegg book, it was taken out in 1989 and then once in 2012. There was something about the passage and lost-in-time-ness of that which quite appealed.)

As a final note, attendees went away bearing what can only be described as a Folklore Tapes artifact goodie bag which was hand stamped and containing dried fauna, alongside a Tales from the Black Meadow bookmark, that they were given as they left and which was a fine end note to an intriguing and multi-layered event.

1. This release is also discussed in Chapter 35.
2. The word "wyrd" is ancestral to weird and in such a context is generally used to imply a certain kind or spirit of an alternative Albion and the further flung, more esoteric, hidden or underlying areas of folklore.
3. These are discussed further in Chapter 11.
4. The project is discussed further in Chapter 9.
5. Some of these are discussed in Chapter 40.

42

Skeletons: Pastoral Preternatural Fiction and a World, Time and Place of its Own Imagining

Skeletons is a 2010 film by Nick Whitfield. It is something of a gem in amongst British film, one which in part deals with the sense of loss associated with unrecapturable moments and people in our lives and the way in which we may wish to try and revisit the gossamer strands of those now gone times.

However, it is not a heavy or dark view, but rather it is humorous, touching, fantastical and intriguing.

The plot involves two suited, slightly shabby (or even seedy in one case), privately-contracted investigators who walk through the British countryside to visit couples and others who want to exhume and clear out the secrets and skeletons in one another's closets before for example getting married.

This is done via visiting a form of portals to the couples' histories, that are accessed through the cupboards in their houses and which allow the investigators to view and experience the hidden parts of their customers lives.

Things are complicated though because one of the investigators is what is known as a glow chaser – he is hooked on visiting scenes of his own childhood and such behaviour can corrupt their official contracted viewings. They are asked to help locate the lost husband of a wife whose daughter will no longer speak. However, the rural home where she lives is situated on a ley line like path which misdirects the readings they need to take.

It is a curious item amongst British film; one which at first glance has some visual similarities with realist film but which is actually a journey through a fantastical world, one that is set alongside but slightly apart from the real world.

This separateness is done in a subtle, not fully explained way, with the science, methods, organisation they work for etc. of the investigators being just taken as is rather than accounted for logically; people contract them to do their work, what they do works.

In this sense it could be linked to a film such as 2012's *The Wall/ Die Wand* where a lone inhabitant is trapped by an invisible barrier in a rural location, while all of the outside world has been frozen in time; both that film and Skeletons are pastoral science fiction as a genre, set in a landscape where the fantastic happens/has happened but where the reasons, whys and wherefores are not fully explained.

It has also been described as a very British *Ghostbusters* (1984), which is rather apt; if you were to put the comedic paranormal investigators story of Ghostbusters through a British pastoral and independent film filter, it might just come out a little like this.

Also the infrastructure practicalities of the investigators' work are not explained.

For example how much are they paid for their services? Is it a reasonably well-recompensed thing to do? Are they paid in monetary form? Are the people they visit invoiced by a central organisation? We never see the exchange of money or any related activities during the film.

In Skeletons the investigators' working methods seem curiously lo-fi and understated for what is actually quite a fantastical activity; the ability to step into and view the lives of others at different times and places.

Their work is not shown in a big budget high-end effects manner, which seems to connect with and compliment the lo-fi techniques of the investigators.

Provisionally Skeletons appears to be set in contemporary times but there are a number of pointers and signifiers which also set it aside from today: the instruments the investigators use could be post war, the suits they wear are contemporary-ish, while the aprons and goggles they don for protection when carrying out their viewing seem to hark back to some earlier possibly mid-twentieth century industrial Britain.

Further reflecting this mixing of the styles and artifacts of different time periods their boss could have tumbled from the parade ground of a 1960s comedy (and is a standout turn with his clipped parade ground manner) but there are no mobile phones or computers and we hardly see a car. It is now, but not.

One of the only references to modernity are the power station cooling towers that background one of the investigator's homes but even then what decade are we in?

Although still in use, such modern-day structures, their design and utilitarian stance tend to suggest a scene from previous decades, possibly nearer to the 1970s than today.

Skeletons shares some common ground with the 1979-1982 British television series *Sapphire & Steel.*[1] This does not appear to be a deliberate connection or point of reference and when director Nick Whitfield was asked about it at a post screening Q&A he said that he was aware of the series but could not remember it particularly.

Both Sapphire & Steel and Skeletons deal with a pairing of investigators who in some ways could be said to be working with problems based around a modern updating of supernatural concerns and stories: areas of activity where science and the preternatural combine and co-exist, where a domestic freezer can be reconfigured to freeze malevolent spirit creatures from the beginning of time or valve like instruments are used to measure the readings required for viewing and portal like visitings of previous events and periods in people's lives.

As well as some similarities in terms of the main protagonists, their work and methods, as just mentioned about Skeletons, in Sapphire &

Steel the beyond the realms of normality events and activities are represented without the use of higher end effects; both seem more to be about the creation of an impressionistic atmosphere of fantasy rather than its visually spectacular portrayal.

Also both seem to exist in relatively isolated worlds of their own imagining, ones where the outside or wider world rarely intrudes. Connected to this, geographically Sapphire & Steel and Skeletons tend to take place in isolated spaces or those that are removed from the wider world.

The setting of a particular story from Sapphire & Steel may for example be the interior of one rural cottage or one particular flat and its immediate surroundings.

Skeletons shows a wider view of the landscape, with almost all of the film taking place in the countryside and the investigators seeming to mostly walk to wherever their next job is over stiles and down railway tracks (which are curiously free of their rolling stock).

However, there is still a sense of viewing a largely self-contained existence, with the investigators living and working parallel but removed from the day-to-day world and only briefly connecting with it when their work requires.

1. Discussed in Chapter 15.

43

Field Trip-England: Jean Ritchie, George Pickow and Recordings from the End of an Era

Field Trip-England is a 1960 album released by Folkways where Jean Ritchie and George Pickow travelled around England recording literally the music of the folk of the land: from the peels of church bells to children's rhymes via sailors' laments and folk songs passed down through generations of families. It includes stories of seafarers who squander their money and life wandering with "flesh-girls" (ladies of the night) and a grand old gardener singing crackedly of riding up to Widdecombe Fair with "Phil Lewer, Jan Brewer, Harry Hawkins, Hugh Davy, Philly Whitpot, George Pausley, Dick Wilson, Tom Cobley and all".

Alongside this are children's rhymes with instructions for chopping off of heads in "Oranges and Lemons", tabloid scandal mongering and sensationalism from days gone by via folk song in "Death of Queen Jane", a paper costume adorned Mummers Play and a particularly boozy version of "John Barleycorn" from the Haxey Hood games:

"He'll make a maid dance around this room
Stark naked as ever she was born;
He'll make a parson hold his boots
With a little John Barleycorn
He'll turn your gold into silver
Your silver into brass;

He'll make a man become a foll
And a foll become an ass"

This is an album which feels as though it could be a long lost project that has been sent out into the world by a modern day cultural rarities curator such as Jonny Trunk: it almost feels too authentic, too real.

The Folkways records releases from that time had lovely packaging and a very solid physical presence; all matt printing on textured stock and they feel built to stand the tests of time. The copy of the album I bought has indeed stood the test of time; it is one of the original 1960 issues, as far as I know it has not been reissued on vinyl and it was one of those rare occasions where even via the ease of access and seeking out of secondhand records afforded by the internet, it was actually quite hard to find a copy.

Although it is available as a print on demand CD, to do it justice I wanted to hear and feel how it looked and sounded at the time when it was first sent out into the world, crackles and all.

Jean Ritchie grew up in the Cumberland Mountains in Viper, Kentucky, one of 14 children, part of a generation in that area where traditional living finally began to succumb to technological advances, travel etc., long after much of the rest of the US had already done so.

She grew up singing traditional and more recent folk songs with her family, which in part lead her to travel the British Isles in order to trace the sources of her family songs.

These recordings seem to document a sense of an end of an era, which possibly parallels her own family/cultural history, with them capturing some kind of final golden age of pre-technological transmission of songs and stories. This is not done in a clinical capturing and preserving things just so way but rather the recordings feel like living, breathing documents and contain a very human spirit.The album is allowed to retain its raw field recordings air; you can hear laughter at the end of songs and possibly the reels of the tapes going round.

44

Noah's Castle: A Slightly Overlooked Artifact and Teatime Dystopias

There is an almost canon of late 1960s and 1970s British television dramas and series that have come to be seen as hauntological touchstones and which have resonated through the years and come to represent an otherly spectral folklore.

That grouping includes *The Owl Service* (1968), *Children of the Stones* (1978), *The Changes* (1975), *Sky* (1975) and *The Stone Tape* (1972), some of which are discussed in Chapter 11: "...Wanderings Through Spectral Television Landscapes". One series which often seems to be slightly overlooked amongst such things is 1979's *Noah's Castle*, based on John Rowe's 1975 novel.

Many of the above series were intended as children's/younger persons entertainment; their oddness and possibly advanced or unsettling themes for their target audience is now part of their appeal.

However, the ideas and plot of Noah's Castle quite possibly trumps them all in such terms; it is a series that has at its core hyperinflation, food shortages, societal collapse and a patriarch's attempt to hole up and bunker away with his family in their middle class home (the "Castle" of the title). Cue troops on the streets, food riots and looting.

As mentioned in Chapter 28: "*No Blade of Grass* and *Z.P.G.*: A Curious Dystopian Mini-Genre", Noah's Castle could also be linked to a mini-genre of 1970s largely cinematic science fiction that dealt with societal, ecological and resource collapse, overpopulation and the resulting attempts at control, a mini-genre which includes *Z.P.G.* (1972), *Soylent Green* (1973), *Logan's Run* (1976), *Silent Running* (1972) and *No Blade of Grass* (1970).

As can be the way with fragmented or misremembered series from previous eras, when I revisited the series it did not necessarily seem as though I was rewatching the same programme,[1] the images on the screen seemed in some ways quite removed and separate from the stories I had created in my mind though they still had a surprisingly adult and possibly bleakly prescient air.

The end titles are particularly striking: as the sun sets on a hill overlooking a classic British industrial town or cityscape, armed and riot helmeted soldiers stand watch and gather around their vehicle.

They are framed by the sunset and there is something decidedly Eden-askew about the juxtaposition of them and a bare branched tree that appears to be almost growing from their transport.

As a synthesised soundtrack by Jugg plays in the background, a news reporter tells of the looting of food trains, the collapse of British society, its economy and currency, silent protests by the nation's youth, international resource restrictions and political game playing.

The end titles on the final episode have no voiceover. Watching them causes a longing for them to start, partly to hear what wonderfully inappropriate political events for tea time viewing they would cover, partly because them not being there sends the mind wandering and invokes a sense that it is all over, that the societal collapse and unrest has come to some kind of final conclusion.

You could say that tales of economic division, social unrest, shortages and repression have become mainstream fodder in more recent times for a younger audience via the likes of the film and book series *The Hunger-Games* (2012-2015 and 2008-2010 respectively). However, that series is all flash and fantasy.

As discussed Chapter 13: "...The Ascendancy of Apocalyptic Popular Culture", The Hunger Games presents a story and world that are a safe remove from the one in which its viewers live.

While the strifes of Noah's Castle are set today, possibly tomorrow but on recognisable streets; yours, mine, the street next door and the conflicts shown in it were a direct product, reflection of and extrapolation from societal strife and conflict around the time it was made.

In this sense, Noah's Castle could be seen as the lower budget, more youth-orientated flipside to the final series of *Quatermass* (1979) and its consideration of societal collapse and norms.[2]

Although in terms of subcultures the restless youth in Quatermass are more new age traveller-ish in their actions and style, whereas those in Noah's Castle are nearer to unruly urban youth that might have set tabloid opinions a-twitch and worrying at the state of the nation, with their clothing being nearer to street-level punk or late teen/early twenties, adolescent day-to-day casual.

These "punks" and "youth" are particularly highlighted in the opening sequence which opens with an image of the "Castle", which is a classic British larger-sized middle-class home, standing amongst the trees and enclave of its garden, which fades into street scenes of rioting youth running towards the camera, one in then contemporary zipped punk or new wave fashion, one wearing a balaclava mask, some carrying sticks and pipes as weapons.

They are then shown engaging and grappling with uniformed armed soldiers, with some of the youthful civilians carrying bags of what we assume is looted food.

In a further connection to and extrapolation from the time in which the series was made, these scenes seem to be reminiscent of or could almost be actual footage from the conflict in Northern Ireland at the time.

1. A phenomenon discussed further in Chapter 8.
2. Also discussed in Chapter 40.

45

Jane Weaver Septième Soeur and *The Fallen by Watch Bird*: Non-Populist Pop and Cosmic Aquatic Folklore

The Fallen by Watch Bird is a conceptual pop album/project by Jane-Weaver released on her own label Bird Records in conjunction with Finders Keepers Records, the theme of which is:

> "...a floating storyline based around missing seamen, telekinesis, avian messengers, white witchkraft and death & re-birth..."

The project includes the main album The Fallen by Watch Bird, a sort of sequel or companion record called *The Watchbird Alluminate* that revisits and reinterprets the main album, an illustrated fictional book, video work, poster and an accompanying compilation mix called *Europium Alluminate.*

It is not a project or album which is easily definable within any particular genre or culture and it weaves and creates a unique and multi-layered world unto itself.

The project takes inspiration from a number of areas of inspiration including Eastern European children's cinema, Germanic kunstmärchen (fairy tales or one online service literally translated it as "art fairy"), 70s television music and traces of 80s synth pop to create what is described as cosmic aquatic folklore; the resulting work creates a fable like atmosphere that creates a sense of it connecting or belonging to some of its source material but is far from homage, with any such aspects being via a reimagined dreamscape.

The Fallen by Watch Bird is credited to Jane Weaver Septième Soeur and features seven other female musicians alongside Jane Weaver, including Susan Christie whose lost 1960s acoustic pop recordings were released by Finders Keepers, 1960s soft psych pop rock musicians Wendy & Bonnie, Lisa Jen who is a member of Welsh language folk band 9Bach and members of Jane Weaver's former band Misty Dixon.

At points the 1960s roots of some of the collaborators makes it presence felt in a certain almost Californian, hazy sunshine pop, psych and folk aspect to The Fallen by Watch Bird album, albeit through a distantly and very refracted filter.

The Watchbird Alluminate adds to that cast and includes collaborations, extensions, revisitings and reinterpretations of the The Fallen By Watch Bird also by Jane Weaver Septième Soeur, alongside Demdike Stare, The Focus Group, Emma Tricca, Wendy Flower, Anworth Kirk, Magpahi, Samandtheplants and Susan Christie.

This album adds to the loose conceptual theme and is said to be about "telepathy, technology, lost-love, wiccan, war and watchbirds".

It is more overtly experimental than purely conceptual pop-orientated and adds a certain spectral, hauntological aspect via the likes of the unsettled soundscaping of Demdike Stare and the woozily cutup chimes and tinkling of Ghost Box Records artist The Focus Group, alongside tremulous, enchanting folkstress revisitings by Emma Tricca and Magpahi.

The Europium Alluminate mix CD was compiled by Jane Weaver alongside Finders Keepers Records co-founder Andy Votel and it is described as:

> "A 70 minute transmission of cosmic aquatic folklore, flickering luminescent lullabies & hand-plucked pop."

It is an explorative and intriguing musical journey which serves as an accompaniment and musical backgrounding for The Fallen by Watch Bird, one that hints at some of the possible influences and inspirations for the project but leaves these as hints as there is no tracklisting.

The project's influences led me down a path to discover or rediscover a strand of cinematic history known as the Czech New Wave.

This was a loose grouping of 1960s films by Czech directors who were disgruntled with the communist regime that had taken over Czechoslovakia in 1984, with their films at times containing expressions or symbolism that was part of a form of creative dissent and comment on or against the ruling regime.

The genre was also known as the Czechoslovak film miracle, which considering the otherworldly nature of some of the films seems quite appropriate, in particular the variously playful, surreal, fairy tale-esque and sometimes anarchic or darker hued likes of *Daisies* (1966), *Valerie and her Week of Wonders* (1970) and *Malá Morská Víla* (1976).

Jane Weaver quotes an unsubtitled copy of Malá Morská Víla (also known as *The Little Mermaid* but something of a world away from the more well known mainstream 1989 Disney film) as having been the starting point for this album and some of the stylings from it have found their way into photography associated with The Fallen by Watch Bird and the title track's accompanying video by klunklick.

That video brings together many of the elements of The Fallen by Watch Bird project and concept.

It mixes photography of Jane Weaver dressed as a fallen-through-a-portal sister of one of the characters of Malá Morská Víla, found illustrations from children's fairy stories (which also accompany the albums' artwork), live action mixed with animation, cosmic symbolism, fantasia like pastoral and at sea scenes, the appearance and reappearance of black feathered birds and documentary war photography all of which interweave with the left-of-centre pop of the song to create a phantasmagorical, darkly hued and yet also whimsically entrancing fairy tale fable.

The layering present in the video and song expresses one of the defining characteristics of The Fallen by Watch Bird project which is its culturally multi-layered nature.

Part of that layering includes avant-garde elements in terms of its concept, influences and at times presentation.

However, it also works as left-of-centre pop culture and music, having tunes you may well find yourself humming as you walk down the street and a distinct visual accessibility.

In that sense if could also be aligned with the Finders Keepers released 2012 conceptual album *1612 Underture* by The Eccentronic Research Council[1] in that it is a form of non-populist pop; work which utilises some of the tropes and accessibility of pop music while retaining an exploratory nature.

1. Discussed further in Chapter 35.

46

Detectorists, *Bagpuss*, *The Wombles* and *The Good Life*: Views from a Gentler Landscape

THERE IS AN interconnected strand of often comic, gentle and uncynical work within British television which variously revolves around the landscape, self-sufficiency and recycling.

The Good Life is one thread of such things.

This was a BBC sitcom broadcast from 1975-1978; a chap who lives in suburbia decides he has had enough of the rat race, quits his job and along with his wife tries to live self-sufficiently via growing their own food, keeping livestock etc.

However this is not self-sufficiency on a smallholding out in the countryside.

Rather this is self-sufficiency attempted in a normal house in middle class suburbia, next to their more conventional affluent neighbours.

It is enjoyable lightweight comedy that has aged reasonably well, not quite *Fawlty Towers* (1975-1979) or *Rising Damp* (1974-1978) but still rather watchable.

What is curious about it is the theme of self-sufficiency and how it involves a middle-class back-to-the-land suburban utopianism that at the time probably seemed rather out there.

In the 1970s, as is mentioned in Chapter 10: "…Notes on a Cultural Behemoth", there was a movement or urge within society to look towards the land, folk culture and music and an attempt to find a more authentic meaning to life often via non-conventional or new avenues and The Good Life can be seen as part of this.

With the passing of the years, many of the ways that the main characters Tom and Barbara use to get by and adopt have become quite mainstream; recycling and avoiding waste, eating what are essentially organic foods that they grow and harvest themselves and so on.

Generally the taking up of such things has more been incorporated into mainstream modern life and often organised or offered by councils, supermarkets, health food shops and the like rather than being undertaken via the self-sufficient dropping out that is shown in The Good Life.

Although some of the ideas presented within the series are quite radical and much of the comedy is derived from the conflict between the self-sufficient lifestyles of Tom and Barbara and their attempts at this way of life next door to conventional ways of life, this is still gentle uncynical comedy – a form of bucolia in suburbia.

Initially slightly preceding The Good Life, an interconnected strand of television is *The Wombles*, an animated series originally broadcast in the UK in 1973-1975.

The series features fictional pointy-nosed furry creatures that were created by author Elisabeth Beresford and appeared in a series of children's novels by her which began to be published in 1968.

The Wombles lived in burrows and could be found internationally, although the series focuses on those who live below Wimbledon Common in London.

As with The Good Life it was ahead of its time in the way that it dealt with themes of recycling, waste and helping the environment, which were the main activities of The Wombles.

There were also a number of hit records by The Wombles, which were sung, written and produced by Mike Batt, who in 1975 would go on to produce folk rock band Steeleye Span's top 5 single "All Around My Hat".[1]

1970s British television seemed to be notably populated by such gentle, whimsical programmes with one particular highlight being the also animated series *Bagpuss*, first broadcast on the BBC in 1974.

Set around the end of the 19th century in the Victorian era, it featured the goings on of a set of normally inanimate toy creatures in a shop for found things. They come to life when the shop's owner, a young girl called Emily, brings in a new object and they debate and explore what the new thing can possibly be.

Made by Peter Firmin and Oliver Postgate through their company Smallfilms it contains a sweetness, a uniqueness and gentle melancholia that arguably has never been repeated or equalled.

Firmin and Postgate also created such other exemplary and distinctive work as the softly psychedelic and just a touch pop-art space age animation the *Clangers* (1969-74) and *Ivor the Engine* (1975-77), which followed the adventures of a steam engine and his companions in the "top left-hand corner of Wales" and memorably at one-point features dragons who instigate a search for the pre-decimalisation coinage that they need for the gas meter in the dormant volcano where they live.

Theirs was work that did not feel that it had been created as part of an assembly line and targeted at a well defined cultural demographic and marketplace. It was more personal and precious feeling and seems nearer to examples of a form of folk art.

Which makes it somewhat appropriate that Trunk Records archival record label head Jonny Trunk was responsible for the retrospective *The Art of Smallfilms* book published in 2014 and via his label he has released the soundtrack albums to the Clangers and Ivor the Engine.

Julian House of Ghost Box Records has said that rather than being an archivist record label proprietor that "Jonny's more like a folk art scholar."

He goes on to say:

> "That vision of a lost Britain that Ghost Box draws its energy from is hugely influenced by Trunk's commitment to the neglected artists of post war UK culture."[2]

* * *

That sense of a lost Britain is something that could be linked to Bagpuss as in many way it is *the* lost, arcadian, edenic, idyllic and idealised vision of a golden age of Britain (or possibly more specifically England) made incarnate.

It represents a sleepy sepia and vintage vignette-tinged village world full of shops brimming with discarded nick-nacks, eccentrics, a sense of never-ending lazy afternoons, gentle exploration and quiet industriousness.

The world it creates and presents is curiously unsullied by what could be considered the sometimes dirt, grime and grasping of commerce; the shop where Bagpuss and his compatriots live does not sell anything, everything in the window is just a collection of things that people had lost.

Some of the voices and all the music in Bagpuss were played and in part written by Sandra Kerr and John Faulkner who, according to Rob Young's *Electric Eden* book from 2011, had been former alumni and apprentices with Ewan MacColl and Peggy Seeger's The Critics Group.

This was a kind of master class for young singers performing traditional songs or who were writing songs using traditional and folk music structures.

Ewan MacColl was a left-wing folk musician, activist and poet who was married to fellow folk singer and activist Peggy Seeger.

Peggy Seeger was once-upon-a-time blacklisted by the American government for what they considered politically unsafe travel to various communist countries, while MacColl was also barred from travelling to the US with his wife due to his political views.

While Sandra Kerr went on to lecture in folk music and taught future generations of folk musicians including The Unthanks and Emily Portman.

The soundtrack for Bagpuss is rather lovely, taking in various strands of folk and traditional music and is able to stand on its own merits aside from the connections to the series.

A favourite is still "The Miller's Song", which is a lilting, life affirming and yet also curiously quietly melancholic song about the cyclical nature of farming and rural life, the growing of crops and the passage of those crops to the mill and eventually via the baker to become loaves of bread.

The section in the series it accompanies features a number of illustrations which fade into one another and reflect this cycle and the sequence seems to not be rooted in any particular era while also harking back to previous times.

It opens with a view of an evocatively archetypal British rurally set building with a water wheel on its side.

The sequence goes on to include what seems like a curiously out-of-place and anachronistic modern combine harvester alongside a combustion engine tractor and delivery truck, while also showing more traditional milling methods.

The baker's shop where the harvested and milled flower is delivered to could be a contemporary small-scale local establishment but via the style of its staff and customer also more than hints at a previous era.

As with the series in general the song and its illustrated sequence seem intrinsically imbued with a yearning for some hazily, goldenly remembered or imagined simpler, purer way of life; an expression of what Rob Young has called a form of imaginative time travel, which seemed prevalent at the time of its first broadcast.[3]

A more recent series which could be placed amongst these strands of gentle uncynical television is *Detectorists.*

First broadcast in 2014 by the BBC it revolves around the lives of a pair of metal detectorists and their passion for their hobby of exploring the landscape with metal detectors and hoping to find lost artifacts.

The series is written and directed by Mackenzie Crook, who also appears as one of the main detectorists, alongside sometime *By Our Selves* straw bear companion and *Berberian Sound Studio* engineer Toby Jones.[4]

Detectorists is part of a lineage, which stretches back to the likes of Fawlty Towers; one of those times when mainstream entertainment and comedy somehow manages to escape into the world without being neutered. It undertakes astute observations of the ways and wiles of people, a love of the land and country and there is a sadness portrayed in its characters' lives.

This is not expressed in a maudlin or the sometimes grim and gritty default setting of some of modern television; the characters in the series are shown with great love and affection – a portrait of people just trying to make the most of things while hopefully adding some magic to their lives.

In this instance that involves quietly and contemplatively walking the land, hoping that with their modern-day divination rods they will discover treasures buried beneath the earth, findings from (to quote the title song) "the ghosts of men who can never sing again".

That main title song, also called "Detectorists", is by Johnny Flynn and in its lyrics and modern-day take on traditional folk music reflects the gentle roaming of the series somewhat perfectly.

As with "The Miller's Song" from Bagpuss, lilting would seem to be a somewhat apposite word and it also contains within it a sense of yearning and loss, themes which seem to recur throughout much of these particular strands of television.

1. Discussed in Chapter 1.
2. Jonny Trunk's work is discussed further in Chapter 38.
3. A topic also discussed in Chapter 1.
4. Films from 2015 and 2012 respectively, discussed in Chapters 27 and 26.

47

Weirdlore, Folk Police Recordings, Sproatly Smith and *Seasons They Change*: Notes from the Folk Underground, Legendary Lost Focal Points and Privately Pressed Folk

ONCE UPON A TIME in 2012 there was an event called *Weirdlore*, which could well in future years have come to be known and referred to as a focal point for a new wave of what has variously been called acid, psych, underground or wyrd folk.

The phrase weirdlore was coined by Ian Anderson of *fRoots* magazine, who organised this event, as a name for the one-day gathering and also as a possible genre title for such things.

There have been quite a few different genre titles attached to this area of music but none has ever really fully stuck or come to fully define or delineate a loose grouping of music that draws from various strands of folk music, culture and traditions, while also often being exploratory and/or underground in nature and audience.

Unfortunately said event was cancelled. Apparently there was a lot of enthusiasm for it but this did not translate into actual ticket sales.

However, an accompanying compilation album called Weirdlore was still released in 2012 by the no longer-operating Folk Police Recordings.

Folk Police Recordings was a Manchester-based record label that was active from 2010-2013 and was a home for work that took folk music as its starting point but which wandered off down its own paths (while still generally keeping an eye cast towards its roots).

To quote the label:

> "We are purveyors of folk brut and other rough music. We like our folk skewed, raw and otherworldly. We're basically traddies at heart but we also like stuff that can trace its ancestry back to the Incredible String Band and the first psych-folk explosion. We like a bit of folk rock too, but not when it's cunningly disguised pub rock, and we even like some singer songwriters, especially if they're a little deranged. And we are always on the look out for the new Bert Jansch – all self respecting labels should have this as one of their goals."

In keeping with the above, this was a label that seemed to sidestep the more strict gate-keeping of tradition aspects of folk music and put out work that while it could be experimental, was also particularly listenable to/accessible. That is not always an easy fence to stay standing upon but they seemed to have a good ear for such things.

Their releases included work by amongst others Sproatly Smith, The-Woodbine & Ivy Band, The Owl Service, Harp and a Monkey and Lisa-Knapp as well as an album by Frugal Puritan which was alleged to have been a recording of lost Christian acid folk (please note the "allegedly" as this may in fact have been a project created and imagined in contemporary times).

Folk Police Records could be seen to be one of a number of record labels and music orientated projects which to various degrees have worked in and released left-of-centre, exploratory folk and related work and/or work related to the flipsides and undercurrents of pastoralism and the land.

Along which lines are included amongst others Deserted Village, Was Ist Das?, Hood Faire, Patterned Air Recordings, Front & Follow, Caught By The River's Rivertones, Stone Tape Records, Clay Pipe Music, The Geography Trip, Folklore Tapes, Rif Mountain and *A Year In The Country* itself.

The Weirdlore album is, as was the intended event, a snapshot of things musically weirdloric and includes tracks by performers whose work was released separately by Folk Police Recordings and others and included songs by Telling The Bees, Emily Portman, Rapunzel & Sedayne, Nancy Wallace, Pamela Wyn Shannon, Katie Rose, The False Beards, Foxpockets, Boxcar Aldous Huxley, The Straw Bear Band, Starless & Bible Black, Alasdair Roberts, Corncrow, Rosalind Brady, The Witches with Kate Denny, Harp and a Monkey and Wyrdstone.

Aside from the music the album is also well worth a peruse in part for the accompanying text by Ian Anderson, written with Weirdlore still a month away and not yet cancelled. In it he rather presciently describes the album as "celebrating a day which has yet to happen and a genre that quite conceivably doesn't exist."

A particular standout track is Sproatly Smith's version of traditional folk song "Rosebud in June", which was described by website *The Gaping Silence* as being:

> "...like something from *The Wicker Man*, if The Wicker Man had been a 1960s children's TV series about time travel."

Which sums up the song and the atmosphere it creates rather well; otherworldly, transportative, dreamscape acid or psych folk.

Sproatly Smith were described by fRoots magazine as "the mystery flagship band of the new wave of weirdlore" and in keeping with that sense of mystery, for a while there did not seem to be any photographs of them online.

On the Folk Police Recordings released *Minstrels Grave* album from 2012 by Sproatly Smith two songs in particular stand out: "Blackthorn Winter" which manages to be shimmeringly stark, dark and beautiful all at once and "The Blue Flame", which while gentler conjures visions of a land rolling away just out of sight of the mind's eye.

Another recording of Sproatly Smith's which is particularly appealing is a split seven-inch single with fellow Folk Police Recordings released performers The Woodbine & Ivy Band on Static Caravan, released in 2012.

On this release they both covered the traditional and evocatively erotic and unblushing song "Gently Johnny" which was reinterpreted by Paul Giovanni for *The Wicker Man*'s soundtrack in 1973. Static Caravan said of this:

> "In his 1958 exploration of the more ribald aspects of English folk-song, *The Idiom of the People*, James Reeves suggests that "Gently Johnny" has its roots in medieval minstrelsy. However, it is better known as the slightly sinister song of seduction sung by the regulars in the Green Man pub in the cult British horror film The Wicker Man. The song has continued to exert an influence over musicians, but many of the recordings that have been made of it are a little reverent and bloodless – either too faithful to the film version or treating the song as a precious and fragile faux-pagan remnant, maybe these two versions will go some way to redress the balance."

Sproatly Smith's version has a lilting gentleness to it that does not belie its salaciousness, while The Woodbine & Ivy Band's has a graceful delicateness that is all English Rose and soft wantonness with just a hint and twang of dustbowls across the sea here and there.

Music such as this builds visions of pastoral otherliness, taking the roots of folk and late 1960s and early 1970s acid or psych folk music and quietly wandering somewhere new.

Within Weirdlore's album packaging there is an extended piece of writing by Jeanette Leech who is the author of the book *Seasons They Change: The Story of Acid and Psychedelic Folk* (2010), which to quote the back cover "tells the story of the birth, death, and resurrection of acid and psychedelic folk". Which it does indeed do, dropping a trail of breadcrumbs largely chronologically through that particular story.

(Acid and psychedelic/psych folk is a parallel offshoot of folk rock that originated in the later 1960s and 1970s and which reinterpreted traditional folk music and its themes, adding and combining psychedelic, exploratory elements with folk and folk rock.)

Seasons They Change is one of only a small handful of books that focus on such or interconnected areas, which includes Rob Young's *Electric Eden* (2011), Shindig magazine's *Witches Hats and Painted Chariots* (2013), *The Electric Muse: The Story of Folk into Rock* (1975) and Dave Thompson's *Seance at Syd's* (2015) which loosely groups contemporary acid folk with, amongst other areas of music, psych and space rock.

Seasons They Change draws connecting lines of history between everything from 1960s psychedelic folk to the 2000s arrival of freak folk such as Devendra Banhart and Joanna Newsom via the apocalyptic underground folk of Current 93 and the world of privately pressed folk music.

Today when it can be a relatively easy task to record and put music out into the world via home recording, digital distribution and sites such as *Bandcamp* and *Soundcloud* it is almost hard to imagine the dedication and commitment that was once required to do such things.

Without the support of a record company, the money, expertise and access to equipment needed to record and press vinyl records in the 1960s and 1970s proved a heavy-handed filtering system.

However, some records made it through that system and a handful of the privately-pressed (ie. without the support of a record label) results in the area of acid or psych folk have become rarefied, treasured artifacts, totems and tokens of semi-hidden and once almost lost culture, a selection of which are mentioned below.[1]

Some of those featured appear on the compilation *Early Morning Hush: Notes From the Folk Underground 1969-76*, released in 2006 and compiled by musician and writer Bob Stanley, which included privately pressed folk amongst its tracks.

Along with its companion album *Gather in the Mushrooms* from 2004[2] it presented folk music that was a far sweeter and stranger set of concoctions than anything that springs to mind under the label of folk before, which is a description that could well be applied to much of privately pressed folk from the later 1960s and 1970s.

The Early Morning Hush album features songs that were originally released via private pressing by Stone Angel on their eponymous album from 1975 and Shide & Acorn from their 1971 album *Under the Tree*, of which just 99 copies were pressed.

The album also includes a track by Midwinter (who later evolved into Stone Angel) that was part of a set of recordings from 1973 that were not released until 1994.

Other privately pressed folk from the time includes the eponymously titled Caedmon album from 1978 and the album *A Midsummer Night's Dream* from 1971 by Oberon, which as with Under the Tree was originally pressed in an edition of just 99 copies.

Oberon's version of the traditional song "Nottanum Town" opens the album and can be filed alongside other privately pressed psych folk from that period such as Stone Angel and Midwinter, in the way that it features transportive female vocals and conjures and captures a very particular otherly spirit of Albion atmosphere that seemed to prevail around the time of its release.

There is a mixture of the lost and found, the strange and familiar to such music which is possibly a result of it springing from earlier traditional music while progressing and exploring elsewhere.

When John Coulthart was discussing at his Feuilleton website the *A Year In The Country*-released themed compilation album *The Forest/The Wald* from 2016, which in part contained music that could be seen as a continuum of the experimentations of the acid or psych folk found on such private pressings, he said that it is:

> "...a response to British folk traditions that acknowledges the history without seeming beholden to it."

Which could also be a way to describe both the likes of Midwinter and Shide & Acorn or the contemporary visitings and revisitings of traditional folksongs and acid or psych folk by Sproatly Smith (whose work is featured on The Forest/The Wald).

Similarly to some of those privately pressed records, quite a number of Sproatly Smith's records have been released by independent limited edition CD-R based record label Reverb Worship; it can now be hard to find the CDs as the relatively short runs they are released in tend to sell out.

Although from different times, in spirit this could be seen as nearer to privately pressed records from years gone by than a more mainstream or conventional form of release.

1. Chapter 47 focuses on privately-pressed folk records that were generally released in small numbers and well away from the lights of mainstream media or record buyer's attention.
2. Discussed in chapter 2.

48

The Moon and the Sledgehammer and *Sleep Furiously*: Visions Of Parallel and Fading Lives

The Moon and the Sledgehammer is a 1971 documentary film directed by Philip Trevelayn that shows a snapshot of a family (a father, two sons and two daughters) who live in an isolated woodland English house.

Their lives and ways of living have a sense of drawing from the past while living in the present; water is drawn by bucket from a well, if there is any mains electricity it is not to be seen, they run and hand build old steam engines, the men dress like working class labourers from earlier in the 20th century (all suit jackets and hats for hard manual and engineering work) and the family play hand-pumped organs and pianos out in the open.

This way of life does not appear to have come about in any modern dropping off the grid, overly conscious manner but rather to have happened or continued to happen naturally over the years.

The only time the film shows them leaving their own land and home is during a police-escorted trip down country lanes on a black-smoke puffing steam engine amongst the Morris Minor etc. cars of the period.

In part, it is a fitting travelling companion with the 1974 film *Akenfield*, which is more a recreated/partially dramatised but based on the stories of rural living example of filmmaking (it draws from Ronald Blythe's oral history 1969 book *Akenfield: Portrait of an English Village*) than documentary representation but which also seems to represent some kind of earlier 1970s interest in, and attempt to, capture or recapture a disappearing world and pastoral idyll.

Both can be seen to be films that capture a nation's then, possibly ongoing, yearning for an imagined idyll away from the pressures and social unrest of the time.[1]

However, The Moon and the Sledgehammer is possibly nearer to Ben Rivers' *Two Years at Sea* film from 2011, which focuses on the life of a man who lives alone in an isolated rural environment, in that it is a picturesque but also unadorned document of lives that have stepped to one side of normal life, with both being filmmaking which records and presents its subjects lives largely without narration.

As with that film, The Moon and the Sledgehammer is a fascinating snapshot of these very particular ways of life, in spirit not a million miles from an anthropological study of a group of people in some far flung tropical forest who have been left alone and apart from the advances of civilisation.

It is not quite the case though that modern life has completely passed them by as there are glimpses here and there of modern day consumables, even if only glimpses; there is a bottle of washing up liquid that is used at the kitchen sink and a bag of large-scale commercially produced Mother's Pride bread is also shown (in a waxed bag as were once used for packaging loaves and which now seem so evocative of another time and place).

Automotive and combustion power is present in that their land seems to be littered with collapsed and foraged automobiles, from buses to cars, which curiously are rarely mentioned or focused on in the film, although an intriguing looking wheeled "dirty diesel" stand-alone engine is used at one time to power their equipment.

However, these are only glimpses and there seems to have been a selective choice by the family to have largely stopped moving with technological advances at some not quite definable time somewhere between the earlier twentieth century and possibly the early 1960s.

Apart from the diesel engine, the only still-functioning mechanical equipment they are shown as using are small scale industrial equipment of a particular type and vintage that today you may only see as part of historically preserved quarry workings and the like.

Watching the film creates a certain curiosity about how the family actually funded the way they lived and how they came to live as they did. Nobody is shown as having any kind of gainful employment in a traditional money-earning sense.

There is the occasional brief reference to the sons doing mechanical and electrical work away from the family home but very little mention of the history of the family.

Also, what happened to the family after it was made: did they continue to live in a similar manner?

Connected to which there is a reasonable amount of conflict and even dysfunction shown, a yearning in some family members to break free from their immediate orbit.

Having said all of which, there is an accompanying film called *Behind the Moon and the Sledgehammer*, which takes as its basis a reunion of and Q&A with the cast and crew 38 years after the film was shot that is said to "answer many questions about the film and the Page family" which may explain further but contrarily, do we need to know much more about the film or how it was made?

Or should it exist just as a pocket of time, place and way of being all unto itself?

As a documentary filmmaker (or film watcher) it may well be good to be wary of purely being a voyeuristic observer of the differing lifestyles of others.

The Moon and the Sledgehammer walks that tightrope in what seems to be an at least reasonably respectful manner; the family play up/mug for the camera here and there but there is a sense that generally they want to and are overall enjoying the attention (at least in four-fifths of the family) and this is an entertaining, playful piece of film making: a stepping into another world for just a moment or two.

The Moon and the Sledgehammer, along with Two Years at Sea is connected to a small genre of British filmmaking that is in part landscape/ pastoral based documentary but which to varying degrees is non-conventional and/or may include elements of art or expressive film.

Along with which, we could include Gideon Koppel's 2008 film *Sleep Furiously*.

This film is a view of a small village community that is slowly fading away as the population and local amenities decline. Parts of it are nearer to stills than film; contemplative views of the landscape, sometimes time-lapsed, sometimes with just one tiny figure or vehicle traversing the land.

It shares a sense of an almost painterly or photographer's eye for such things with the 2009 film *General Orders No. 9*[2] and reminds me of art-photography views of the landscape such as Paul Hill's *Dark Peak, White Peak* photography book from 1990; work which combines that just-mentioned expressive view alongside a documentary recording of the landscape.

In contrast to General Orders No. 9, Sleep Furiously is not an overtly otherly view of the countryside and pastoralism but it is more than just a straight documentary in some manner which is hard to define; there is an understated gentle magic to it.

And gentle is an apposite word as in many ways this is a gentle film; gently soporific and largely gently soundtracked, a gentle possibly muted visual colour palette and gently visualised.

The soundtrack is in large part by Aphex Twin and apart from one brief venture into more intense music comprises mostly of subtle, quiet keyboard refrains and motifs, nearer to classical sketches than those with a casual knowledge of his more electronic work might expect.

The film, indeed possibly the village itself, is threaded and woven together by the visits, journeys and returns of the mobile library van.

This is a service that feels like its public service intentions belong to a previous, more municipally caring era and watching it wend its way amongst these few villagers, there is a definite pang for the time when it would do so no more.

1. A theme explored in Chapters 7 and 25.
2. Discussed in Chapter 27.

49

From Gardens Where We Feel Secure, Wintersongs, Pilgrim Chants & Pastoral Trails: Lullabies for the Land and Gently Darkened Undercurrents

Virginia Astley's 1983 album *From Gardens Where We Feel Secure* is the very definition of bucolic and is an album which summates England's pastoral, Edenic dreams, albeit with subtly melancholic and unsettled undercurrents.

It is a largely piano and woodwind-led melodic record, which is accompanied throughout by the sounds of the countryside and blissful repose: birdsong, lambs, church bells and rowing on the river.

I first heard songs from it late one hot, hazy, summer night and appropriately I think one of the initial tracks I listened to was "It's Too Hot to Sleep", in which the recurring refrain of the soft hoots of owls accompany a gentle, lilting lullaby of a song.

That could well be a description of much of the album, while the title could be considered a concise capturing of some of English needs and wants; the small spot of greenery contained within the grounds of domestic castles in which its inhabitants can hopefully feel secure.

It features in Rob Young's *Electric Eden,*[1] the final "Poly Albion" section, in the chapter "Towards the Unknown Region", where he considers the more outerlying areas of the music and culture which has sprung forth from the likes of hauntology and an otherly, spectral take on pastoralism.[2]

In this section when describing From Gardens Where We Feel Secure he begins by saying that it "does not go anywhere", in presumably an attempt to show the album's ambient, non-formal song structure.

It is an interesting choice of phrase as it also suggests how the English can sometimes hanker after unchanged, unending idylls where the gates can be locked, allowing rest, slumber and dreaming, with the rambunctious march of progress safely held at bay even if just for a moment.

Although the album is largely a suite of music which invokes such an Albionic Arcadia, conjuring up lives spent in timeless English villages, it is not merely a chocolate box or twee reverie, as it also contains a sense that there is a flipside to those dreams: that the nightmare may well intrude on the secure Eden.

This is reflected on the album as the cries of lambs, the sound of a swing gate and the reverie of "The Summer of Our Dreams" gives way to "When the Fields Were on Fire".

This is a more fractured, staccato piece of quietly unsettling pastoralism, where the birds still sing, the piano still plays and the church bells still ring off in the distance but the atmosphere is no longer quite one of rest and repose but is now rather a harbinger of darkened times.

The record distantly wanders some of the same fields as the outer regions of an alternative landscape which can be found in say the film *The Wicker Man* (1973) or some psych/acid folk music but here while the sense of an idyllic rural Eden has an otherly quality it is not overt: more it is a form of wistful nostalgia or reverie, even where such aspects are most present on When the Fields Were on Fire.

Such views of the landscape which are both bucolic but also quietly, subtly travel through its flipside can be found on the 1999 album *Wintersongs* by Plinth, which was made by Michael Tanner with Steven Dacosta, accompanied by Nicholas Palmer and Julian Poidevin.

This is an album to drift off into, one which musically could be loosely described as a form of folkloric or pastorally themed ambient or possibly soundscaping but it is not an easy piece of work to pigeonhole in such a way.

In a similar manner to From Gardens Where We Feel Secure it creates a soundtrack for the landscape: one that is in parts gently melancholic but also gently magical and on a track like "Bracken" it almost feels like a walking companion for Virginia Astley's album in its melodic, looping and minimal exploration of a bucolic atmosphere.

However, as with From Gardens Where We Feel Secure this is not a twee trip through the land; while at times it may be a journey amongst a certain kind of pastoral reverie there is also something else going on amongst the hills and trees.

There is heartbreak in the pathways of its songs at points and the quiet melody and refrain of "Hearth" makes the mind wander towards losses along the byways of life.

The album has gone through various incarnations over the years since it was first released: as a cassette in 1999, CD-Rs in 2002 and 2006 by Dorset Paeans and then Rusted Rail and on vinyl in 2014 and 2016 by Kit Records, housed in a rather lovely and lovingly produced linocut sleeve.

The instruments listed in its making include glockenspiel, trumpet, clarinet, guitar, clocks, fireplace, ring modulator, birds, teapot, train, voices, piano, garden, sleigh bells, cymbals and melodica.

When I first listened to it a few layers and instruments were added to that mix; I was sitting outside letting my mind wander over the valley in front of me as the album played.

The birds in the trees around me were singing and chirruping, local dogs would break into barking, cars would pass, the neighbours were nattering and the wind was gently rustling.

At points, I could not quite tell which sounds were on the album and which in the world around me.

As the recording of somebody's footsteps played I found myself turning round thinking I had a visitor coming up the steps to my side and the album became almost like a live field re-recording, which seemed fitting in a way as the first time to appreciate and travel with the album.

Walking and exploring amongst similar territories is Sharron Kraus' 2013 album *Pilgrim Chants & Pastoral Trails.*

In the text that she wrote to accompany it there is a sense of her discovering and rediscovering the land as she had begun to live in or visit the Welsh countryside, exploring her surroundings and unlocking some kind of underlying magic or enchantment to the landscape.

Her text for the album also infers a sense that she was initially creating something which was for herself, which could be a soundtrack to her own experiences, early cultural pathways which had pointed to the land and making work which could try to interpret and/or represent the secrets in the valleys, streams and pathways through which she wandered.

A phrase which springs to mind when listening to Pilgrim Chants & Pastoral Tales and its bonus disc *Night Mare* was "these are lullabies for the land" and in many ways they do literally feel similar to or have a lullaby-like effect, as they contain a dreamlike quality that is rooted in the land but is also a journey through its hidden undercurrents and tales.

This is music which also literally soundtracks the landscape where it was made, utilising field recordings captured along the way; the sound of birds, streams, waterfalls, animals, the wind and jet planes which were recorded on Sharron Kraus' explorations.

A sense of wandering the land is brought to life through these found sounds and at points you can hear the journey being taken as leaves crunch underfoot.

Musically the two albums are largely instrumental or wordlessly-vocalled pieces, which while creating and reflecting a pastoral atmosphere and explorations are not all bucolic countryside pleasantness.

As with From Gardens Where We Feel Secure there is also a sense of dread to some of the songs, a quiet unsettledness.

This is particularly so on the likes of tracks "Dark Pool", "Nightmare" and "Sleepless", whilst "An Army Of Woes" takes a step or two towards hauntological reinterpretations of library music from another era. Along which lines, in part they seem as though they could be rediscovered artifacts from some other time.

Another reference point might also be some of the Czech New Wave films, in particular *Valerie and her Week of Wonders* from 1970[3] as the album at points contains a sense of conjuring an indefinable point in history, one steeped in folklore and fables which would not be out of place in the hinterland fantasia of that film.

Pilgrim Chants & Pastoral Trails is beautifully packaged; it was released in a very limited edition by Second Language Music and designed by Martin Masai Andersen/Andersen M Studio and it feels like a precious artifact: one which you want to pick up carefully and gently.

The album was presented as a small book-sized gatefold, with the packaging and the gently transformed nature and landscape photography (which in its textural qualities recalls the 23 Envelope work of Vaughan Oliver and Nigel Grierson for 4AD records[4]), capturing the beauty and grace of the land through which Sharron Kraus travelled and in which she worked.

1. The book is discussed further in the Chapter 1.
2. Themes in relation to the book that are considered in Chapter 14.
3. Discussed in Chapter 45.
4. Discussed in Chapter 37.

50

Strawberry Fields and *Wreckers*: The Countryside and Coastal Hinterland as Emotional Edgeland

THE PLOT OF Frances Lea's 2012 film *Strawberry Fields* involves a youngish postwoman who is possibly running away from the loss of her mother and her over demanding, somewhat unsettled sister. She seeks escape in seasonal strawberry picking work in a rural coastal area and within this temporary community the film becomes a compressed microcosm of lives, loves, family and friendships, all of which seem to fracture, stumble and tumble in a brief moment of time.

The setting feels like an isolated, separate world unto itself; it comprises mostly of just the picking fields, ramshackle semi-derelict buildings, temporary accommodation, deserted beaches, neglected barns and equipment, the concrete brutalism and shabby infrastructure of the local railway station and monolithic overhead roadways (a spaghetti junction relocated amongst the fields and flatlands).

Everything apart from the roadway looks cobbled together, patched up, built from whatever could be found, while the colours in the fields are often ever so slightly over-vivid, adding just a touch of unrealness to the film.

Accompanying this the image of a short-lived community that is created by the youthful seasonal workers living in the provided rough and ready, basic accommodation gives an impression of this being an almost frontier like, unregulated place.

This is a world curiously free of controlling older adult influences and there is possibly only one such person whose face is seen.

The result of these circumstances seems to have created an unregulated temporary autonomous zone, one that allows for unfettered and sometimes-destructive human actions, behaviour and responses; the inhabitants are adults but their behaviour appears nearer to that of rampaging unsupervised children.

As an aside, there is a lovely soundtrack to Strawberry Fields, largely by Bryony Afferson and her band Troubadour Rose, which is all slightly dusty Americana tinged folk songs, drones and snatches of ghostly vocals that lodge in the mind for days.

Wreckers (2011), directed by D. R. Hood, focuses on a young couple who have moved from the city to a small rural community.

Their lives are unsettled when one of their siblings, who is a combat veteran on whom his experiences in conflict have taken a considerable toll, unexpectedly arrives and brings with him an unearthing of hidden, painful secrets from the family's past.

In contrast to times when the British village is depicted in cinema as an orderly country idyll, here this is gently flipped on its side; at one point in the film a tour around the locale leads not to "Oh, that's a pretty church" comments and the like but rather to a cataloguing of who did what traumatic thing where and the emotional relationships and rules depicted in the film feel like they have reverted back to some earlier unregulated medieval time.

As in Strawberry Fields, the physical structures are not neatly polished chocolate box visions of the countryside; the cottage that should have roses running up the outside and be full of quaint comforting knick-knacks is in the process of being renovated.

However, it does not feel as though it is being spruced up, rather that it has had its niceties stripped away and been left raw, while the other buildings shown are generally tumbledown throwbacks and bodged together barns and as with some of the emotional relationships portrayed there is a sense of undernourishment or even neglect.

The above descriptions of these two films may appear to depict them as grim, gritty realist drama. However, in part Strawberry Fields is in many ways a gentle, touching film.

Not too dissimilar could also be said about Wreckers, although that is possibly a touch more emotionally harsh. As with Strawberry Fields, Wreckers is a brief view of the British countryside, that as previously mentioned is sometimes a place of idyll and escape, where normality and the subtle veneers of civility and civilisation have quietly stepped back for a moment and come unfrayed around the edges.

These are visions of the countryside and rural coastal hinterland as a form of literal and emotional edgeland, with their structures, physical and personal, being thrown together, tumbledown, temporary and in a state of unsettled flux.

51

Zardoz, *Phase IV* and *Beyond the Black Rainbow*: Seeking the Future in Secret Rooms from the Past and Psychedelic Cinematic Corners

Zardoz (1974), *Phase IV* (1974) and *Beyond the Black Rainbow* (2010) could be gathered in a left-of-centre, science fiction and fantasy orientated corner of more exploratory cinematic culture that to varying degrees incorporates and/or draws from psychedelic culture and imagery and associated dreamlike or altered reality states, often in pastoral or nature orientated/connected settings.

Zardoz was written, produced and directed by John Boorman.

The plot involves a future Earth ruled by immortal Eternals, an advanced sect of humans who live a luxurious but aimless life in an area known as the Vortex, protected by an invisible barrier from the wasteland of the outside world which is inhabited by Brutals who carry out forced labour farming.

The Eternals have created a false god known as Zardoz, which is represented by a huge flying stone head and is used to control and intimidate the Exterminators, who in turn control the Brutals through the use of force.

The Zardoz head travels around the world collecting crops and other resources, while also dispensing weapons to the Exterminators. An Exterminator called Zed breaks with the accepted order of this world and boards this head icon, enabling him to enter and subsequently disrupt and bring chaos to the Eternals' world when it returns there.

The Eternals' idyll that he enters is degenerating and many of those who have been dancing its slow, indolent, self-regarding waltz for hundreds of years are slipping into a literally catatonic state of apathy or have to come to just wish to be able to end their unending lives.

The secluded paradise of the Eternals is a curious mix of advanced technology, new age-isms and a kind of indulgently folkloric ritualised way of life set in what appears to be an almost village like insular idyll; the Eternals partake in a liberal, democratically decided and also underlyingly conformistly oppressive way of life, with its functioning and continuation only enabled because of the forced labour farming carried out by the Brutals.

Zardoz is one of the stranger larger scale, generously budgeted films to have escaped into cinemas, something which is particularly highlighted as it starred Sean Connery as Zed who at that time due to him playing James Bond in the popular and commercially successful film franchise was an international star.

Watching Zardoz is a dreamlike, at points hallucinatory or psychedelic, stepping through the looking-glass experience, notably so when Zed crosses over into the crystal based Tabernacle which controls the Vortex and when he is absorbing all the Eternals' knowledge outside of time and the real world.

In both he finds himself in a blackened featureless dreamscape, which in the Tabernacle is full of endlessly repeated, mirrored and distorted visions of himself and the Eternals.

Later while undergoing the absorption of knowledge process a projected lightshow of collaged and drifting images representing this knowledge plays over and completely covers his and the Eternals' faces and unclothed bodies as they float disembodiedly across the frame in what becomes a swirling, speeding up carousel of faces.

Visually it is a film full of beauty and brutality with the lithesome and effete, youthful in body but ancient in years Eternals wandering the bountiful pastoral enclave of the Vortex, dressed in flowing semi-transparent garments as they drift through their cosseted, indulged, sheltered and largely unchanging immortal lives.

This is starkly contrasted and threatened by Zed as the hirsute interloper from the wastelands, who when he breaks into their world brings with him his violent memories of the outside world, which are viewed by the Eternals when his mind is probed and also a sense of action, virulent fertility and the threat of violent change.

It is an exploratory, dissonant, challenging blockbuster or spectacle film, one which questions society's actions, accompanied by references to 20th century cinematic fantastical fairy tales and philosophy, while also being full of "I can't actually believe that this was allowed to come to the big screen" moments.

All of which is complemented by a former James Bond wearing what can only be described as revealing futuristic Mexican fetish-bandit wear.

To use a phrase from the film itself, this is one of those times when popular culture goes "renegade".

Apparently, the film studios had given John Boorman a free pass and creative freedom after the success of his "city slickers up against the folk from the woods and swamps" film *Deliverance* (1972), which was the film he made prior to Zardoz.

Reading John Boorman talking about the making of Zardoz, there was possibly a literally psychedelic element to its production:

> "It was the 70s, and I was doing a lot of drugs. Frankly, even I'm not entirely sure what parts of the movie are about."

In part it seems to be almost a critique or comment on some of the late 1960s to mid-1970s hedonistic, self-indulgent hippie tendencies when they were underpinned by material wealth and where that can lead.

PHASE IV IS THE only film made by renowned designer Saul Bass and as with Zardoz it is a cultural oddity, and Paramount Pictures were probably more than a little surprised when they saw what they had financed.

In the film two scientists and one younger woman they rescue are held hostage in a desert research facility by ants which they are meant to be studying but who seem to have gained some form of collective consciousness and higher intelligence due to some unknown cosmic event.

In some ways it could be seen as an alternative mirror view of the rising of the beasts in the original *Planet of the Apes* series of films released between 1968 and 1973 or to be a relatively straightforward man vs. beast horror exploitation film (and some of the posters attempt to show it as that).

However, this is far removed from standard cinematic fare and genre tropes. It is a much stiller, more contemplative film which although in many ways fantastical in premise, as a cinematic piece of work and in its officially released form is actually quite a low key, almost downbeat, piece of near realism (well, as near to realism as you can get with its premise).

Having said which it literally explodes in a psychedelic coming of a new age and order collage of imagery sequence at the end. Well, sort of...

There was full-length journey into and through the new world fantasy sequence filmed as an ending but it was not used for the general release.

The film that most people have seen ends with a glimpse of this new world but it is merely a brief view.

The full sequence had a limited public cinematic outing when a version of it was found in 2012 at the Academy Film Archive in Hollywood, USA but it has never been included as part of an official release for home viewing.

The cutting of this ending may have been due to film studio executives thinking they wanted to try and salvage something a little more conventional from the film they had been presented with, but it was too late for that due to the intrinsic nature of the film and its intelligent, layered cinematic view and explorations. Fortunately, due to the ease of dissemination available via the Internet this original full length ending can at least be viewed now, though in a degraded quality reproduction.

In 2015 Phase IV was reissued on DVD and Blu-ray by Olive films in the USA, in a Region Code A locked version which means that in order to be able to watch it in the UK or Europe you would need an American player or one that has been modified to be multi-region. Unfortunately, this version still did not include the original ending due to it not being available to license.

Phase IV is a beautiful and beautifully shot film. A strange beauty but beauty nonetheless. It is not all 1970s grit and grime as was sometimes the case with cinema from this period, and there is some kind of utopian undercurrent to what occurs and how it is portrayed.

This is enhanced by the insect sequences shot by wildlife photographer Ken Middleham and their vivid, rich colours.

These sequences, although they record the actions of real ants, create a fantastical sense of them evolving into another, higher state beyond that of humans. It is also a film that though not all that well known (and the semi-lost ending hardly at all), seems to have somehow or other reverberated through and influenced culture since its inception.

In particular, lines of connection can be drawn from Phase IV to Beyond the Black Rainbow which was written and directed by Panos Cosmatos.

The plot of that film centres around the Aboria Institute, a new age research facility founded in the 1960s by Dr Arboria which is set in "award winning gardens" and dedicated to finding a reconciliation between science and spirituality, allowing humans to move into a new age of perpetual happiness.

In the 1980s his work was taken over by his protégé Dr Barry Nyle who despite outward appearances of charm and normality is actually mentally unstable and has thoroughly corrupted the Institute and its aims.

He spends his time trying to understand the preternatural psychic abilities of a young woman under his care, nominally as part of a therapeutic process but in fact he has imprisoned her in a state of heavy sedation in a hidden quasi-futuristic facility underneath the Institute.

Panos Cosmatos has spoken about how Phase IV was one of the major influences on his film, saying that:

> "There is a sub-genre of what I call 'trance film' and I really wanted this film to fall into the trance or dream genre without it being specifically a dream. I wanted it to feel like a lucid dream state. The whole time you are probing forward, deeper and deeper into an unknown world."

He includes Phase IV within this sub-genre of trance film, with which Beyond the Black Rainbow shares a deliberate, still or slow almost hypnotic pace.

It also uses a rich, sensuous colour scheme and accompanying geometric design, structures and architecture in the creation of its hidden world, which links with the underground insect sequences and the mirrored research facility and reflective structures that the ants build in Phase IV.

The lines of connection and inspiration between Phase IV and Beyond the Black Rainbow are not a direct transference and replication, rather, as also said by the director it is in an "abstracted, vaguely recognisable way".

This sense of non-replication can be linked to the representations of the 1980s when Beyond the Black Rainbow is set, which do not create a detail-perfect simulacra but rather a reflection of that time which in text that accompanies the film's DVD/Blu-ray release has somewhat aptly and evocatively been described as "a Reagan-era fever dream".

Although referring to a different time period than the late 1960s to 1970s, which much of hauntological-leaning work tends to, Beyond the Black Rainbow shares with that area of culture a sense of the reimagining or fragmented recall of cultural memories which are explored and used in order to create a parallel world view of previous eras.

Accompanying which, as with some of hauntological work, Beyond the Black Rainbow also shares a sense of Cold War dread, although here it again is moved to the 1980s and is expressed through the film being deeply imbued with an underlying sense of the paranoia that the fears and worries of that time caused and enabled the flourishing and proliferation of.

Also, in a similar manner to sections of hauntologically-labelled work, Beyond the Black Rainbow has a strong sense of being a rediscovered lost artifact; this is a film which could have tumbled from the further reaches of an early 1980s video shop's shelves but one from that "fever dream" rather than being passed down directly via historical reality.

Watching it can instill the sense that you are viewing an overlooked David Cronenberg film from that time.

As with Cronenberg's films Beyond the Black Rainbow is often a far from easy and often a particularly unsettling watch, one which while less concerned with overtly transgressive body horror than some of Cronenberg's films, shares with them an almost dreamlike sense of a convincing parallel and corrupted or distorted reality.

Somewhat appropriately considering the above and despite such things being more or less obsolete and no longer widely manufactured, alongside the DVD and Blu-ray editions it was also released on limited edition VHS videocassette by Mondo, who alongside such things specialise in limited edition posters featuring commissioned artwork reinterpretations of films.

If the film could be a rediscovered and refracted Cronenberg project from a parallel world, then its soundtrack could well be a Tangerine Dream-esque soundtrack from that world.

The soundtrack is by Jeremy Schmidt (working as Sinoia Caves), and utilises mellotron choirs, analogue synthesizers and arpeggiators to create a period aesthetic and atmosphere.

It puts me in mind of the further reaches and undercurrents of what has been loosely labelled new age music, including some of the work that can be found on the compilation *I Am the Center: Private Issue New Age in America – 1950-1990* (released in 2013 by Light in the Attic) such as Wilburn Burchette's "Witch's Will" which, as with the soundtrack to Beyond the Black Rainbow, creates an atmosphere that is restful, draws you in and yet is also portentous and unsettling.

Connected to this, one of the themes of the film seems to be the corrupting of new age principles (as referred to earlier when mentioning the activities of Dr Barry Nyle at the Arboria Institute); it presents a world where there has been a curdling or perverting of philosophies of empowerment and enlightenment from when the Institute was founded in the 1960s.

There is a drawing from psychedelic thoughts and practices of that time, which is given explicit expression in a psychedelic trip sequence.

However, this is far removed from any flower child, peace and love lysergic vision of the world, with this sequence being more a nightmarish bad trip with violent results.

The atmosphere the film creates in the day-to-day operation of the hidden facility also shows or implies altered states of mind but one produced through paranoia, sedation, control and the institutional intrusions of Dr Nyles' corrupt techniques and procedures.

As previously mentioned, Beyond the Black Rainbow is not always an easy and often an unsettling film, so if you should seek it out then tread gently but it has a visual beauty, entrancing atmosphere and sense of cinematic and cultural exploration that makes it a somewhat unique film experience.

52

Winstanley, A Field in England and *The English Civil War Part II*: Reflections on Turning Points and Moments When Anything Could Happen

Winstanley is the 1975 Kevin Brownlow and Andrew Mollo film biography and tribute to Gerrard Winstanley, who was a religious reformer and political activist in the 17th century.

Gerrard Winstanley was one of the founders of an English group known as the True Levellers or Diggers, who occupied previously public common lands which had been privatised, living in what could be considered some of the first examples of or experiments in socialist communal living.

The community he helped to create was quickly suppressed but left a legacy of ideas which inspired later generations.

Winstanley is a curiosity which lingers in the mind, one which ploughed its own furrow and created its own very particular corner of British filmmaking.

Previous to this film Brownlow and Mollo made *It Happened Here* (1965), which was an alternative history imagining of what would have happened if Britain had been occupied by the Nazis; both films were made largely independently and on very small budgets.

Despite that low budget there is a great attention to detail and authentic recreation in Winstanley; one particularly memorable detail is that soldiers are shown as wearing political tracts and publications strapped to their hats as a way of showing their allegiances and beliefs, as they did at the time.

In many ways Winstanley could be seen as a companion piece to Ben Wheatley's also low budget fictional historic fantasy film *A Field in England* (2013), possibly the more erudite, learned, historical brother to its rambunctious more recently released sibling.

There are a number of similarities to the films; both are set around a similar time period of the English Civil War, have similar costumes, are set in the rural landscape, shot in crisp black and white and show a flipside and/or the undercurrents of English history.

Bearing this in mind Winstanley was an odd film to watch after watching A Field in England.

At times the viewer may almost become confused about which film they are watching; some of the characters and their faces in Winstanley seem as though they have tumbled from A Field in England (or vice versa).

In some ways that is because the physiognomy of those who appear in both films feels right; many of the characters look as though they could have come from these fields, rather than the sometimes too well fed look that can trip up modern visual re-enactments of times gone by.

Accompanying the BFI DVD/Blu-ray release of Winstanley is the "making of" documentary, *It Happened Here Again* in which there is a curious mixture of centuries and styles.

In the documentary the costumed cast are pictured in amongst contemporary families, the rickety cars and vans of the 1970s and folk who aesthetically could have tumbled from 1970s Open University broadcasts.

Alongside these are pictured a number of countercultural or hippie-styled people who helped on the film, both behind and in front of the camera and who could be seen to be some kind of link between the ideals of Winstanley and compatriots then and possibly similar travellers in alternative ways of living during the 1970s.

This is particularly the case with Sid Rawle, one of the actors in the film, who in real life was a campaigner for peace and land rights, a free festival organiser and leader of the London squatters' movement.

In many ways the then-contemporary world seen in the documentary feels as or more exotic than the 17th century imagery and characters do.

There is a sense of it capturing a very specific time and place in English history during the mid 1970s; possibly the last days of the utopian sixties dream and aesthetics before punk and the Thatcherite 1980s arrived and made much which immediately preceded them seem almost to belong to a separate parallel world: one far distant from our own.

In this sense, the images in the documentary seem as though they are from a long-lost land and time that appears separate and apart from today.

The period during which Winstanley was made could also be seen as a link to the time when it and A Field in England were set as there are similarities to both points in history; periods of unrest and historical points of battle and change in society.

In the 17th century it was the battle between magic, religion, science, the old ruling order/economic models and the new; in the 1970s during Winstanley's production Britain was wracked by internal unrest, economic strife and the battle which would lead to the turning of elements of society towards the right and the adoption or possibly ascendancy of a related new economic/political model.

That particular change also led to another battle, sometimes fought amongst the fields of England and its neighbours; the bitterly fought Miners Strike of 1984-1985 where the government of the day clashed with miners over pit closures.

This was a defining conflict at the time between those who believed in more collectively-organised labour and a post-war progressive consensus (with regards to the state intervening in the welfare of the nation) and a political, economic and philosophical grouping which wished to move towards a more monetarist, consumer and individual-orientated society.

With regards to A Field in England, Ben Wheatley has talked about being interested in making a film about a period when Britain was in "free fall and chaos… a moment when anything could happen", which could apply equally to Britain at either of the above times in the 17th or 20th centuries.

These were times when history could have gone various ways and which could be seen as the start of turning points in the world and society.

Connecting back to the period in which Winstanley is set, the Miners Strike of 1984-1985 has been called the *The English Civil War Part II* by artist Jeremy Deller, who used the phrase as the title of a book released in 2002, which documented and reflected on the strike and a re-enactment of a defining conflict during it which has come to be known as "The Battle of Orgreave".

That re-enactment, also called *The Battle of Orgreave,* was initiated by Jeremy Deller and was a partial re-enactment of what has come to be thought of as one the turning point conflicts of the strike that originally took place on 18 June 1984 and involved violent clashes between striking miners and the police.

The events or "battle" took place at a British Steel Corporation coking plant in Orgreave, Yorkshire, which processed fuel made from coal, that the miners wished to stop the collection of supplies from and a large number of striking miners converged on this one point on that date.

Some observers have since commented that the events of the day may have been a "set up" by the authorities intended to divert the energies and attention of the striking miners from other more strategically important targets, alongside enabling a public defeat of the miners in a situation those who opposed them had specifically chosen and organised for this purpose.

The resulting violent clashes also served as a way of discrediting those on strike, with media reports at the time generally depicting the violence being due to the police defending themselves from attack. This view has since been subject to considerable dispute and debate, with some considering that the violence was largely instigated by the police and historical reports showing that the order of events in some television news footage of the time was allegedly accidentally reversed in order to show that the miners attacked the police first.

The re-enactment featured both miners and policemen who had been involved in the strike alongside members of re-enactment societies and a documentary of the event filmed by Mike Figgis was televised by mainstream broadcaster Channel 4.

The English Civil War Part II book is a companion piece to the re-enactment and contains personal accounts by those who were involved in the strike and the re-enactment, alongside memorabilia from the strike including pamphlets, news clippings, photographs from personal scrapbooks, song texts, a CD containing interviews with former miners and some of their wives and also photographs of the re-enactment.

While being to a degree documentary or archival in nature, the book combines these elements to create a moving and evocative tribute to the conflict and those whose lives it affected.

Thanks to:

The performers who have contributed music to the *A Year In The Country* releases: including Grey Frequency, Hand of Stabs, Michael Tanner, David Colohan, The Straw Bear Band, Polypores, The Rowan Amber Mill, Time Attendant, Sproatly Smith, Cosmic Neighbourhood, Circle/Temple, Keith Seatman, Listening Center, Alaska, Michael Begg, Panabrite, Unknown Heretic, Magpahi, Lutine, Vic Mars, Bare Bones, Endurance, Pulselovers, Depatterning, Sharron Kraus, Field Lines Cartographer, Howlround, United Bible Studies, The Hare And The Moon, Twalif X, The British Space Group, Unit One, Sophie Cooper, The Soulless Party, She Rocola, Assembled Minds and The Séance.

The people who have sold the A Year In The Country releases: Jim Jupp of Ghost Box Records, The state51 Conspiracy and all at Norman records, in particular Ant and Phil.

Those who have bought and supported the A Year In The Country releases and artifacts.

Everybody who was written about A Year In The Country and reviewed the music releases, including John Coulthart, Simon Reynolds, Matthew-Sedition and Dave Thompson and all at *Terrascope, Avant Music News, Music Won't Save You, Rockerilla, Bliss Aquamarine, Was Ist Das?, Shindig!, The Wire, The Active Listener, Include Me Out, Wyrd Daze, Folk Words, Landscapism, fRoots, The Sunday Experience, The Golden Apples of the Sun, Electronic Sound, Both Bars On, Rue Morgue, Mojo, Folk Radio, Goldmine, Heathen Harvest, Saint Etienne Disco, Diabolique, The England Project, Quiet World & Wonderful Wooden Reasons, Bandcamp Daily, Incendiary, Violet Apple, 33-45, We Are Cult, Whisperin' & Hollerin', Folk Horror*

Revival, *Forestpunk*, *A Closer Listen* and *Psychogeographic Review*.

All those who have included A Year In The Country released tracks in their radio broadcasts, podcasts etc including Stuart Maconie and Gideon Coe and all at *Evening of Light*, *More Than Human*, *The OST Show*, *Syndae*, *Sunrise Ocean Bender*, *Flatland Frequencies*, *The Unquiet Meadow*, *Gated Canal Community Radio*, *Late Junction*, *Phantom Circuit*, *Free Form Freakout*, *The Crooked Button*, *Project Moonbase*, *Awkward Moments and You, the Night & the Music*.

To William "Billy" Harron for accidentally pointing me in the direction of the undercurrents of folk. Suzanne Prince for the editing and Ian Lowey for the dab-hand design work.

My family for the ongoing support.

And to everybody whose work has inspired me on the wanderings through the pathways of A Year In The Country.

Tip of the hat to you all!

Made in the USA
Las Vegas, NV
23 August 2022